LIABILITY EXP

by

Dan Cassidy, B.A., F.C.I.I.
Glasgow College

OTHER BOOKS IN THE SERIES

Risk Analysis

Corporate Risk Management

Risk and the Business Environment

Business Finance for Risk Management

LIABILITY EXPOSURES

by
Dan Cassidy, B.A., F.C.I.I.
Glasgow College

LONDON

WITHERBY & Co. Ltd.
32-36 Aylesbury Street
London EC1R 0ET

Published for:
The Institute of Risk Management

First Edition 1989

©

Institute of Risk Management
and
Dan Cassidy, B.A., F.C.I.I.
1989

ISBN 0 948691 75 1

Printed and Published by

Witherby & Co. Ltd.
32-36 Aylesbury Street
London EC1R 0ET

Tel: 01-251 5341
Fax: 01-251 1296

INTRODUCTION

The business enterprise must identify and endeavour to control the liability risks to which it is exposed and therein lie difficulties for the risk manager or risk management adviser. The sources of legal liabilities are numerous and the complexity and the insidious nature of the risks present a special challenge. Therefore a basic knowledge of the law of civil responsibility is essential together with some familiarity with common exposures to risk in commerce and industry.

There is potential legal liability wherever a company's activities reach, from the action or inaction of the company's servants, from the ownership of property of all kinds and from the use of the company's products and services.

This Book attempts to deal with some of these liabilities and to give the Reader a grounding in this engrossing subject which is increasingly important to modern business in the climate of escalating consumer protection measures and growing awareness of individuals' rights.

The description of legal liability given here is according to the "state of the art" at the time of publication but the law, especially Statute law, is subject to change and the Reader is advised to be aware of media reports of developments affecting civil liabilities.

I greatly appreciate the help I received from a number of persons in preparing this book. In particular I want to thank Professor G. C. A. Dickson for encouraging me to undertake the project and to Mr. Kenneth Davidson for the laborious task of checking the script and for his constructive criticism. I am indebted also to my Wife, Margaret who patiently checked the final draft.

CONTENTS

Index to Cases

Index to Statutes

Chapter 1

LEGAL LIABILITIES — SOURCES — PARTIES TO AN ACTION

1.0

The law fulfills several functions in that it controls the behaviour of members of society, it provides a means of settling disputes and it secures freedom of the individual, provided certain rules are complied with.

In the United Kingdom, England and Wales, Scotland and Northern Ireland each have their own legal system and court structure. There are differences in the laws of each but substantial similarity on many points. In Northern Ireland legal procedure closely resembles that of England and Wales but there are differences in enacted law. However a large volume of modern legislation applies throughout the United Kingdom. This text is based on the law of England and Wales.

The main sources of law are legislation, common law and European Community law. Legislation consists of Acts of Parliament, orders and byelaws made by local government exercising powers conferred by Parliament. Common law, the ancient law of the land deduced from custom and interpreted in court cases by the judges, has never been precisely defined or codified but it forms the basis of the law unless it is superceded by legislation. European Community law deals mainly with economic and social matters. In certain circumstances it takes precedence over United Kingdom law. English law makes a fundamental distinction between civil and criminal law and in this Course we are concerned mainly with those aspects of civil law which govern the making of reparation to others for injury done to them and for damage to their property. Liability to make reparation may be imposed by the law or may be incurred by voluntary entering into contracts with others.

1.1 Contract

A contract is an agreement which the law will recognise and contracts are an integral part of business transactions, for example, contracts for the supply of goods, the granting of credit, transportation of goods, leasing of premises and contracts of employment. When two or more parties enter into a contract they acquire not only rights but also obligations to others. If one party is in breach of his contractual terms resulting in loss to the other, he is normally liable in damages for that loss.

1.2 Tort.

Liability in tort is not voluntary; it is imposed on us by law. According to Professor Winfield "tortious liability arises from a duty primarily fixed by law: this duty is towards persons generally and its breach is redressible by an action for unliquidated damages".

The law upholds certain rights both personal and those in respect of property and in the event of infringement compels the wrongdoer (tortfeasor) to pay damages to the victim. Tort, or civil wrong, is distinguished from crime because in this case the remedy is usually compensation and not punishment of the wrongdoer by a criminal court.

For liability to attach it is necessary that the tortfeasor is at fault, usually meaning that he is in breach of some duty owed to the wronged party. A tort may arise even in the absence of fault, where there is strict liability. In these instances the defendant acts at his peril and will be obliged to compensate his victim irrespective of whether or not the injured party can prove that he was to blame.

1.3   Damage and Liability

In the matter of the rights of persons to compensation there are two distinct concepts, (a) DAMNUM and (b) INJURIA. Damnum refers to actual physical damage suffered whereas Injuria is an injury having legal consequences, i.e., where there occurs a breach of a duty owed. The two need not always go together. For example, if a pedestrian negligently crosses a busy street and causes an accident resulting in injury to a motorcyclist, the cyclist suffers Damnum (the physical injury) and Injuria because he has a right in law to recover compensation. Let us suppose that the same physical hurt occurs to the cyclist at a pedestrian crossing and the pedestrian is in no respect at fault there is Damnum without violation of the cyclist's rights (DAMNUM SINE INJURIA). There can occur the violation of a legal right without actual physical damage resulting (INJURIA SINE DAMNUM). An example would be the negligent pedestrian in the first case causing the cyclist to fall off his machine without resultant injury or damage.

The law of tort generally does not lay emphasis on the mental element or the question of malicious intent. The effect of the act is more important, although in the tort of Defamation mental intent can be relevant.

1.4   The Parties to an Action in Tort

There are two types of legal person or 'legal persona' : human beings and corporate beings. The latter referred to as corporations, have a legal existence and a legal status as artificial persons. The corporation, although comprised of human persons has a legal existence quite separate from them. The status of some legal personae, human or otherwise, will be considered, in relation to their involvement in actions in tort.

1.4.1   The Crown and it's Servants

Before the passing of the Crown Proceedings Act, 1947 there was no remedy against the Crown in tort. The common law rule was that "the Crown can do no wrong". It could not be charged with negligence or other torts nor was it responsible in tort for the acts of it's servants and agents in the course of their duties. In practice, however, the Crown usually accepted responsibility. By section 2 (1) of the Act "... the Crown shall be subject to all those liabilities in tort to which, if it were a private person of full age and capacity, it would be subject in respect of torts committed by its servants or agents". The Act does not apply to the many public bodies which are not deemed to be agents of the Crown, e.g., nationalised industries. The scope of the Act is confined to servants directly and indirectly appointed by the Crown and paid out of the Consolidated Fund. Nothing in the Act authorises proceedings to be brought against the Sovereign in her private capacity.

1.4.2   Foreign Sovereigns and Ambassadors

These enjoy immunity from actions in tort. The only remedy for injuries done by this category of person is by way of diplomatic and executive action by the British Government. The right of action exists in fact but it is suspended during the term of office and can be pursued when the term ends.

1.4.3   Minors or Infants

These terms relate to persons under eighteen years of age. A minor is, in general, liable for his torts in the same manner and to the same extent as an adult. There are no rules of exemption as in the case of contracts which are not for the benefit of minors. The age of the defendant will, or course, have a bearing in an action for negligence. A six-year old who pushes another into a swimming pool could not be sued for negligence, but if he were a sixteen-year old there can be liability. The degree of care expected of a minor would be determined by his age. A parent is, as such, not liable for the torts of his children even while they are under age and living in his house, but he may be liable where the child, in committing a tort, is acting as his employee or agent. Moreover a parent may be liable for his own personal negligence in affording or allowing his child an opportunity of doing mischief.

With regard to injury to an unborn child the Congenital Disabilities (Civil Liability) Act, 1976, provides that a person responsible for an occurrence affecting the parent of a child resulting in the child being born disabled, will be liable to the child if he would have been liable in tort to the parent affected. There are various qualifications, including no liability for a pre-conceptual event if the parents accepted the particular risk. The Act also places liability on a pregnant woman for injury to her unborn child arising out of the driving of a car whilst she is pregnant. The duty of care owed to the child in these circumstances is the same as the driver owes to others.

1.4.4   Husband and Wife

The common law rule that one spouse could not sue the other in tort has been superseded by the Law Reform (Husband and Wife) Act, 1962 which grants the right to each party to a marriage to sue the other in tort as if they were not married. In the majority of cases of actions one spouse is a nominal defendant and the real defendant is often a motor insurer. In the absence of insurance, cases are rare. In fact Section 1 (2) of the Act permits the court to stay an action if it appears that "no substantial benefit would accrue to either party from the continuance of the proceedings". An action could simply mean the transference of money from one pocket to another. Moreover, this discourages actions for trivial grievances between spouses. A spouse is not responsible for the torts of his/her partner unless the wrongdoer is acting as agent.

1.4.5   Corporations

A corporation can sue in respect of torts committed against it resulting in injury to its business but certain torts such as assault cannot be committed against a corporation. It can be sued and is liable under the principles of master and servant or principal and agent for the torts of its servants or agents committed whilst acting within the scope of their authority. This liability is governed by the same rules as those which determine the liability of any principal or employer. The individual members of a corporation are not, as such, liable personally for the torts of the corporation.

1.4.6   Partners

Partners are jointly and severally liable for each other's torts committed in the ordinary course of the business of the partnership (Partnership Act 1890). In addition, each partner may have a primary duty in tort.

1.4.7   Joint Tortfeasors

If the same damage is caused to a person by two or more wrongdoers those wrong-doers may be either joint tortfeasors or independent tortfeasors. Persons are deemed to be joint tortfeasors where they jointly commit a wrongful act, wither acting together in furtherance of a common design or where one is aiding or directing the other. Joint tortfeasors are liable for the same tort and this may happen in at least three classes of cases:

(a) where one person employs, authorises or procures another to commit a wrongful act, it is imputed to both principal and agent (he who acts through another acts through himself).

(b) where the law imputes to one person a wrongful act committed by another even though he had no part in it. Thus a principal may be responsible for the wrongful acts of an independent contractor.

(c) where two or more persons join together in some form of common action in the course of which some tort is committed. There must be unity of action, e.g. a landlord and his lodger were looking for a gas leak when the lodger struck a match causing an explosion. It was held that they were engaged in a joint enterprise and the act was done in pursuance of a concerted purpose. It was common action.

Persons independently committing wrongful acts are, however, not joint tort-feasors, even though their independent acts may be the cause of the same wrongful damage, for example where two vehicles travelling in opposite directions are both negligently driven and as a result collide, causing injury to a passer-by.

Joint tortfeasors are jointly and severally responsible for the whole damage sustained. Thus each is himself responsible in full. The injured party may either:

(i) sue any one of the joint tortfeasors separately for the full amount of the loss or

(ii) sue them all jointly in the same action, and if successful execute the judgement against them in any proportion he chooses or against any one of them in full.

At common law a judgement against one tortfeasor would release all others, even though it was not satisfied, and there could be no further action against the remainder, but now by virtue of s.3 of the Civil Liability (Contribution) Act, 1978

4

a judgement against any person liable in respect of any debt or damage shall not be a bar to an action against any other person jointly liable with him in respect of the same debt or damage. Thus, where an injured person who has taken successful action against one joint tortfeasor and is unable to recover damages because of that tortfeasors lack of resources, he may proceed against the other, subject to the provision that the sums received must not exceed in aggregate the damages awarded in the first action. Ordinarily the plaintiff will not be entitled to costs in the later action unless he can show good reason for having brought those actions. The Act also provides that a joint tortfeasor has a right of contribution from other joint tortfeasors, the amount being decided by the court and it may "direct that the contribution from any person may amount to a complete indemnity. The joint tortfeasor being sued in isolation, and seeking contribution has to serve on the other joint tortfeasors a Third Party Notice. This constitutes a separate cause of action. The considerations applicable to joint tortfeasors must not be considered to apply where there is no unity of action, the injury being caused by the independent action of two or more parties. In such cases, the wrongdoers are not jointly liable for the same tort but severally liable for the same damage.

Illustration

A ship, the *Kourst*, negligently changed course and as a result found itself on a collision course with another vessel, the *Clan Chisholm*. The latter was careless in failing to reverse its engines to avoid a collision. After impact, the *Clan Chisholm* collided with a third ship, the *Itria*. The *Itria* sued the *Clan Chisholm* and recovered damages albeit limited because of a statutory provision. Pursuing the balance of the cost of damage, the *Itria* sued the *Kourst*. It was held that the *Kourst* and the *Clan Chisholm* were not joint tortfeasors but only several tortfeasors causing the same damage. (The *Kourst*, 1924.)

1.5   VICARIOUS LIABILITY

In addition to the person who actually commits a tort there may be on occasions another person or corporation liable although he has not acted directly. In such cases both are liable as joint tortfeasors. The most common instance of vicarious liability is that of the master and servant.

1.5.1   Master and Servant

A master is vicariously liable for the torts of his servant committed in the course of his employment. The principle is: "he who acts through another, acts for himself" (Latin : Qui facit per alium, facit per se). This encourages the employer to maintain a safe system of operation and as a general rule the employer is in a better financial position to compensate the plaintiff and moreover he is usually insured. It can also be argued that the employer benefits from the activities of his employee and in equity, should bear the burden of risk attaching.

The law defines a "servant" as "any person employed by another to do work for him in the terms that he, the servant, is to be subject to the control and direction of his employer in respect of the manner in which his work is to be done" (Salmond on Torts). In other words a servant is employed under a contract of service as an integral part of a business and he is under the control of his employer as to (i) what he must do, and (ii) HOW, WHEN and WHERE he must do it. By this criteria the servant is distinguished from an independent contractor. The right of CONTROL is the most important test in deciding the relationship of master and servant. In Performing Rights Society Ltd. v Mitchel and Booker (Palais de Dance) Ltd, 1924 the judge said "The nature of the task undertaken, the freedom of action given, the magnitude of the contract amount, the manner in which it is paid, the powers of dismissal, and the circumstances under which payment of the reward may be withheld, all these bear on the solution of the question. It seems . . . reasonably clear that . . . the final test to be generally applied, lies in the nature and degree of detailed control over the person alleged to be a servant. This circumstance is, of course, one only of several to be considered, but it is usually of vital importance". Other matters considered would be the stamping of insurance cards, powers of appointment and dismissal and whether income tax is deducted by P.A.Y.E. (Short v Henderson Ltd. 1946).

A chauffeur would therefore be a servant whereas a taxi driver is an independent contractor. A servant works under a contract of service and his role is integral to the master's business. An independent contractor undertakes to carry out certain tasks, under a contract for services and he is not part of the business but merely an accessory to it.

Although the control test is the most vital factor in determining the status of 'servant' the courts tend to extend the definition to include persons of whom it cannot realistically be said employers control how they do their work. For example, a hospital board which employs a surgeon has not the expertise to direct the surgeon in his professional capacity, nevertheless several cases have established vicarious liability on hospital authorities (Cassidy v Ministry of Health, 1951).

1.5.2 In the Course of his Employment

In order to establish the vicarious liability of a master it is necessary to show that the servant was acting in the course of his employment at the material time. In the majority of cases this will be self-evident but in some instances it may be difficult to determine whether a particular act was done "in the course of his employment". What acts are within the course of employment is a question of fact in each case and case law provides guidelines. Acts personal to the servant would not normally be regarded as being within the scope of employment such as the use of violence against third parties. In Warren v Henlys Ltd., 1948 a petrol pump attendant was considered to have acted outwith the scope of his employment when he assaulted a customer following an argument over payment of petrol. On the other hand a door-keeper at a dance hall who had by implication, authority to use physical force if necessary to eject trouble makers was held to be acting within the scope of his authority when he physically restrained a would-be undesirable customer (Daniel v Whetstone Entertainments, 1962).

The master will not be liable for his servant's torts where the servant acted outside the scope of his employment and was on a "frolic of his own". In Hilton v Thomas Burton (Rhodes) Ltd., 1961, workmen left a demolition site during working hours in their employer's van and drove it to a cafe. On the way back the van overturned because of the negligent driving by one of the men, and another, a fellow employee, was killed. His widow raised an action against the driver and also against the employer. The employer allowed the man to drive the van for any reasonable purpose, including getting refreshments. It was held that the men were on a frolic of their own and therefore the employer was not vicariously liable. The vehicle was being used entirely for the servant's own purpose.

A wrongful way of doing an authorised act will render the master liable. The test is whether the servant was doing what he was employed to do, even though he has done it negligently or dishonestly. The master cannot avoid liability by merely prohibiting a particular way of working. In Limpus v London General Omnibus Co., 1862, the bus driver had written instructions not to race with or obstruct the buses of a rival company. The driver did obstruct a rival bus resulting in his bus colliding with that of the rival company. His employer was held vicariously liable for the resultant damage. The driver was doing what he was employed to do, namely driving the bus. He was simply doing it disobediently, a wrongful mode of doing an authorised act.

In cases where a servant combines his master's business activity with some deviation on his own behalf the mere fact of the deviation will not exhonerate the master. For example where a lorry driver is instructed to travel from A to destination B and in the course of the journey he takes a deviation, a route through C which is indirect, any accident occurring during the deviation would be considered as being in the course of employment (Storey v Ashton, 1869).

1.5.3   Indemnity to Master

With the doctrine of vicarious liability well established, actions are seldom taken against employees personally. However, having paid a claim because of the negligence of an employee the employer has a right to obtain an indemnity from the servant. In Lister v Romford Ice and Cold Storage Ltd., 1957, a lorry driver, driving his firm's lorry, negligently injured his father who was, at the time, acting as mate on the lorry. The firm, having paid damages to the passenger attempted to recover from the lorry driver. The counter claim was upheld by the court on the ground that the driver had been in breach of an implied condition in his contract of employment, that he carry out his duties with reasonable care and skill. This decision created considerable unrest especially amongst trade unions who considered that the employee should not be made to pay. Rather than endanger good industrial relations, members of the British Insurance Association entered into a gentleman's agreement that employers liability insurers would not institute a claim against the employee, unless the weight of evidence indicated collusion or wilful misconduct on the part of the employee.

In a later case, Morris v Ford Motor Co., 1973, Lord Denning expressed the view that the employee would feel very much aggrieved, if called upon to pay. His argument was likely to be that the liability was covered by insurance and the insurance company should, therefore, pay. Since the employer took the benefit of the employee's actions, he should bear the burden.

1.5.4   Servants loaned to other firms

When a workman is loaned to another firm and commits a tort in the course of his work the question of which 'master' is vicariously liable arises. The matter is dertermined by reference to the question of who has the power or the right to

7

control the servant. There is a presumption that control remains with the original employer (Mersey Docks and Harbour Board v Coggins and Griffiths (Liverpool) Ltd., 1947). The onus of proof is on the original employer to establish that the borrowing master had sufficient control over the servant at the material time. Mersey Docks and Harbour Board hired out a crane and a skilled workman to operate it to a stevedoring company. The contract stipulated that the workman was to be the servant of the hirers, Coggins and Griffiths but the power to dismiss him remained with the Board. While working, the crane driver was under the immediate control of the hirers in that they could direct him on where to work and what cargo to unload, but they could not direct him in working the controls of the machine or his method of operating it. Due to negligent handling of the crane by the driver, a third party was injured. The House of Lords decided that the Board remained the employers of the crane driver and were vicariously liable. The test is "who has the authority to control the manner in which the work is done". That is the general rule but the hirer may intervene to give a specific order and if this is obeyed by the workman and damage results the hirer will be vicariously liable with the workmen.

A crane can be regarded as a complicated piece of machinery and the training in it's operation would ordinarily be the responsibility of the owning master. There may be a distinction where a servant is lent with no tools or, say, simple hand tools. In this case it is easier to assume that the lending employer intended to allow the hiring employer to direct the manner or method of working (Garrard v South & Co., 1952).

1.5.5   Liability for the Torts of Independent Contractors

When an independent contractor is carrying out work for an employer, control over the method of doing work is ordinarily vested in the contractor. He is usually expert in a particular field and is his own master in regard to method, therefore the employer is not normally liable for his torts. There are exceptions, however, and in the following instances, the employer or principal can be responsible:

(a) Where the principal is negligent himself as when he selects an independent contractor without due care to see that the contractor is competent or where he gives the contractor incorrect instructions or information.

(b) Where the contractor is engaged to do work on or adjoining the highway the principal is liable for torts causing danger on the highway.

(c) Where the principal authorises or subsequently ratifies what the contractor has done.

(d) Where the liability is strict and therefore cannot be delegated. For example failure to fence dangerous machinery in a workplace in breach of a statutory duty under the Factories Act, 1961 or the escape of dangerous things under the Rule in Rylands v Fletcher, 1868.

(e) Where a contractor is engaged to do something ultra-hazardous. In Honeywell and Stein Ltd. v Larkin Bros., 1934, the plaintiffs employed the defendants to take flashlight photographs in a cinema. A fire occurred as a result of the work and the plaintiffs were liable to the owners of the cinema. It is common practice for the principal to demand from the contractor some form of indemnity for such liability, supported by insurance cover.

1.6 Principal and Agent

An agent is defined in Towle and Co. v White, 1873, as "a person invested with a legal power to alter the principal's legal relations with third parties". The principal is ordinarily bound by what the agent does on his behalf. Usually an agent, as distinct from a servant, is engaged to perform a specific task, and has authority to carry out whatever is required in that undertaking but has no general authority.

A principal is jointly and severally liable with his agent for torts committed by the agent whilst he is acting within the scope of his authority. Authority may be express or implied. If the principal subsequently ratifies an act by the agent which was unauthorised, he will be liable.

Whilst it is clear that a servant is the agent of his master when acting in the course of his employment, there are many instances of agents who are not servants, e.g. an estate agent who negotiates the purchase of a house on behalf of a client or a representative given powers to act for a principal whilst the principal is abroad.

In Ormrod v Crosville Motor Services Ltd., 1953, an arrangement was made by the owner of a motor car and his friend whereby the friend was to drive the car from Birkenhead to Monte Carlo so that both the owner and his friend might use the car during a holiday in the South of France. The owner of the car travelled in another car as a competitor in the Monte Carlo Rally. The car was involved in a collision due to the friend's negligent driving and damage to a third party resulted. In court the question of the vicarious liability of the car owner was at issue. Held: the friend was acting as the owner's agent at the material time because the owner had an interest in the arrival of the car in Monte Carlo and the journey was for his benefit. The friend was the owner's agent and rendered him vicariously liable to the third party. This does not imply that someone driving another's car is necessarily the agent of the owner. In Morgans v Launchbury, 1973, the defendant wife, a car owner, gave her husband permission to take her car on a pub crawl. He eventually became too drunk to drive and asked his drinking companion to drive him home in the vehicle. An accident occurred and the wife was held not liable for the companion's negligent driving.

1.7 Parent and Child

A child can both sue and be sued in tort, but cannot conduct litigation in person. The standard of care required of a child when deciding negligence is considerably lower than that required of an adult. Ordinarily, a parent, as such, is not vicariously liable for the torts of his child although he may be held liable if the child acted at the material time with the parent's knowledge and consent, or where the parent is negligent in supervising the child. Where the child acts as the parent's servant or agent liability attaches. Most case law in this area involves liability arising out of dangerous toys. In Bebee v Sales, 1916, a father permitted his fifteen-year-old son to have an air gun with which he knew the boy had already broken a window. Later the child shot another boy in the eye. The father was held liable for the injury as he knew that the gun was dangerous in the boy's hands but continued to allow him to use it.

On the other hand the case of Donaldson v McNiven, 1952, demonstrates the limit of the parent's liability. The defendant parent who lived in a populous district of

Liverpool, allowed his son, aged 13, to have an air gun on condition that it was never used outside the house. The boy was provided with a large cellar within the parental home in which to use the air gun. Without the defendant's knowledge, the son fired the gun in an alley-way and injured the plaintiff, a child of five years. Held: there was no negligence on the parent's part in supervising the child. The child acted in express defiance of the orders of his father. In Newton v Edgerley, 1959, a father was held vicariously liable when he gave his twelve-year-old son a .401 rifle without giving him adequate instructions for handling it safely and injury to a third party resulted.

1.8   Husband and Wife

The rule used to be that a married woman was liable for her torts only to the extent of her separate property and beyond this the husband was vicariously liable. By virtue of the Law Reform (Married Women and Tortfeasors) Act, 1935, a wife is fully liable for her torts and the husband, as such, is no longer held responsible for any tort committed by her whether before or after the marriage, unless, there is a relationship also of master and servant or principal and agent. The liability in tort of a married woman is the same as that of other persons.

1.9   Partners

A partnership is "the relationship which subsists between persons carrying on a business in common with a view of profit." A partnership firm is not a legal persona like a corporation; it is an aggregate of its members but it can sue and be sued in its own name. Individual partners are agents for the firm in furthering the partnership business. The firm is therefore liable for torts committed by a partner on its behalf, and partners are jointly and severally liable for the firm's torts. Any tort committed in the course of the business or on specific authority is presumed to be done on the firm's account and each of the partners is equally responsible. In Hamlyn v Houston & Co., 1903, one partner of a firm induced, by means of a bribe, the servant of the plaintiff to act in breach of his contract of service. The firm was held liable.

Chapter 2

GENERAL DEFENCES IN TORT:
TRESPASS: NUISANCE: NEGLIGENCE

2.1   General Defences

The civil liabilities imposed by the law of tort are not absolute and a plaintiff will not always succeed with his case. There are defences which can be raised by the defendant in any action in tort, if appropriate, and other defences which apply to particular torts, e.g. privilege as a defence to Defamation. The general defences are outlined below.

2.1.1   Volenti Non Fit Injuria

This means "to the willing is not done injury" and the principle is referred to as the doctrine of "assumption of risk". Basically it comes to this; if a person agrees to run the risk of harm, he cannot maintain a successful action against the person who causes harm to him. It may be applicable, for instance, to persons who attend sporting events as spectators, where they place themselves in a position which they know exposes them to the risk of injury. In Murray v Harringay Arena Ltd., 1951, a little boy taken by his parents to see an ice-hockey match was injured by the puck. The Court held that the parents accepted the risk of injury by occupying the front seats. If a person participates in, say, a game of Rugby football, he is presumed as accepting the physically rough aspect of the game which is the norm and any injury to him as a result would not give rise to an action. In Hall v Brooklands Auto Racing Club (1933) the plaintiff was deemed to have accepted the risk of a competing car in a race colliding with another car and crashing through the railings, injuring him. The principle is not confined to sporting events. In Dann v Hamilton, 1939, the plaintiff, a passenger in a motor car, was injured due to the driver's negligence. The plaintiff voluntarily accompanied the defendant driver knowing that he was under the influence of drink to the extent that the chances of an accident from negligent driving were considerably increased. Held: Volenti Non Fit Injuria applied and her action was barred.

Suits by workmen against employers must now be considered. In the last century this defence was important to employers who merely had to show that the employee knew of the danger, to escape liability for injury. This position could not be tolerated today. From several cases involving injured workmen there developed the principle that a distinction must be drawn between mere knowledge of a risk ("scienti") and actual consent to run the risk ("volenti"). Merely because a workman knows of a risk, does not mean that he consents to run it, and where knowledge does not amount to consent, the defence will fail. Often workmen are not in a position to complain and in any case, as stated in the last Chapter, the onus should be on the master to carry the risk. In Smith v Baker & Sons, 1891, a workman was engaged in cutting rock. He was aware that his job was dangerous, because a crane swung constantly overhead with loads of stones. His employers permitted the crane to be used carelessly and he was injured by a falling stone. The House of Lords held in favour of the employee, for while he was aware of the risk, his knowledge did not amount to consent to run it, in the circumstances.

Absence of employee's consent is the feature of the decision in Bowater v Rowley Regis Corporation, 1944. The plaintiff, a carter, was ordered by his employers, despite his protests, to take out a horse known by them to be unsafe. He took out the animal and was thrown off the cart when the horse bolted. He sued in negligence and the Court of Appeal rejected the employer's defence of Volenti.

As a general rule, Volenti cannot be pleaded by an employer in the case of an action for breach of a statutory duty. It would seem to be contrary to public policy to permit anyone, including employers to escape the consequences of a breach of a duty imposed by Act of Parliament. However if the employee himself is in breach of a statutory duty resulting in his injury the defence may be valid (Shatwell v I.C.I. Ltd., 1964). The principle of Volenti Non Fit Injuria has given rise to an interesting problem in the sphere of the "RESCUE CASES". The "rescue cases" are so called because they involve litigation brought by persons who sustain injury in intervening to avert danger created by others. If the intervention is regarded as a reasonable thing to do to effect the saving of life or property, the law will not regard it as assumption of risk. In Haynes v Harwood, 1935, the Court of Appeal established that, "the plaintiff has, under the exigency caused by the defendant's wrongful misconduct, consciously and deliberately faced a risk, even of death, to rescue another from imminent danger of personal injury or death, whether the person endangered is one to whom he owed a duty of protection, as a member of his family, or is a stranger to whom he owes no such special duty". The defendant's servant carelessly left a horse-drawn van unattended in a busy street. A boy threw a stone at the horses and they bolted. The plaintiff, a policeman, realising the danger they created to a considerable number of people took action, at great personal risk to bring the horses to a halt. In so doing he suffered serious personal injuries and in the litigation which ensued the defendants pleaded Volenti. In finding in favour of the policeman the Court took the view that he had acted under the compulsion of moral duty and in a serious emergency. A doctor descended a gas-filled well to attempt to rescue two workmen overcome by fumes and died in the attempt. The widow proved negligence against the employers of the workmen, who raised the defence of Volenti. The Court rejected the defence on the grounds that it was foreseeable that such an attempt at medical treatment would be made.

2.1.2   Inevitable Accident

Circumstances sometimes arise in which it is possible for the defendant to assert that the damage which occurred was completley outwith his control; or in other words, that although he may be said to have "caused" it, he did not intend it and he was in no respect careless. "Inevitable accident" is in effect saying that the plaintiff has not failed to observe the standard of care required of him. This defence does not often apply since most accidents have a cause. A good illustration of this defence is the case of Stanley v Powell, 1891. The defendant whilst firing a gun at game accidentally and without negligence shot the plaintiff with a pellet which richocheted from a tree at a considerable angle. The defendant was a member of a shooting party and the plaintiff was a beater. Although Powell was the initial cause of the injury, he did not intend to cause it and was in no way careless; in fact it was a most unusual accident and not one which a reasonable man would be expected to foresee.

2.1.3   Act of God (or Vis Major)

In this defence the plea is that it is something which occurs in the course of nature over which the defendant has no control and no human care or forethought could have avoided the accident. It is too remote to form the basis of liability. A good example is the case of Nichols v Marsland, 1876. The defendant maintained on her land some artificial lakes by way of ornament. As a result of a sudden and violent rainfall the lakes overflowed and considerable damage was done to nearby premises. The defendant successfully pleaded the defence "Act of God". The rainfall had been of extraordinary intensity, and while she could be expected to make provision for normal weather conditions, she could not be expected to guard against such isolated phenomena. An act need not be violent or exceptional to be an act of God. The test is; could the harm have been prevented by human care? For example, if an accident is caused by the sudden death of a motor vehicle driver from a disease he did not know he had or against the effects of which he could not have taken precautions, it will be an Act of God. But this defence would not stand the test if, for instance, the driver was a diabetic who had neglected to take corrective measures.

2.1.4   Emergency

In certain circumstances the defendant may plead that he was placed in a dilemma and "in the agony of the moment" he chose the wrong alternative. This principle of alternative danger is known as the Rule in Bywell Castle. In Bywell Castle, 1879, a ship which was endangered by improper navigation of another vessel, at the last moment took a wrong course and collided with a third party. The owners were held not liable. Where a person is placed in danger by the act of another, that person is not negligent if he exercises such care as may be reasonably expected of him in the difficult position in which he is so placed. He is not to blame if he does not do quite the right thing in the circumstances.

2.1.5   Necessity

In some instances even damage done intentionally may be excused where the defendant was acting under the compulsion of necessity to act to prevent a greater evil. The defence is rare indeed. An example: Fire was spreading across A's land and B's property. B entered A's land and destroyed heather to deprive the fire of fuel so as to prevent its spread to his own land. A sued B for trespass. Held: B acted under necessity and his action was justified (Cope v Sharpe, 1912).

2.1.6   Private Defence

A tort committed by a person in defence of himself or his property or members of his family will not ordinarily result in liability. A person may defend himself or another person for whom he is responsible. In Cresswell v Sirl, 1948, the defendant shot the plaintiff's dog which was trespassing and attacking his sheep. The Court of Appeal set out the following rules in respect of this defence: (a) the burden of proof is on the defendant to justify the shooting; (b) the defendant must prove, first, that the dog was either actually attacking the sheep, or that, if it were left at large, it would renew the attack; secondly, that shooting was the only practical mode of stopping the dog's attack.

The degree of force applied must be reasonable. Force is "reasonable" if it is appropriate to the degree of force which has to be resisted. If innocent bystanders are harmed by the action taken in defending oneself or one's property, it is not actionable by them (Scott v Shepherd, 1773).

2.1.7   Other Defences

The defence that the action has run out of time and is therefore barred will be dealt with under the heading of Limitation of Action later in the text. Other defences which are specific to certain torts will be outlined with their subject in the text.

2.2   Trespass

The principles of the various torts will now be considered beginning with Trespass. Generally, Trespass relates to intentional acts. If the act is intentional it is trespass, and if the act is negligent, it is negligence and not trespass.

There are three forms of trespass:

1. Trespass to the person,
2. Trespass to chattels (goods), and
3. Trespass to land.

In all instances trespass is actionable "per se" (by itself) in that the plaintiff does not have to prove actual damage, the invasion, etc. is in itself enough to constitute an actionable wrong.

2.2.1   Trespass to the Person

This has three aspects.

(a) Assault. The basis of this wrong is that a person is put in fear of violence. There need not be actual intention or power to use violence; it is enough that the victim reasonably believes that he is in danger of it. Words are not sufficient by themselves, they must be accompanied by action. Pointing a gun at a person in a threatening manner, even though it is unloaded and provided the plaintiff does not know this, would constitute actionable assault. An assault is a crime in addition to being a tort.

(b) Battery. This is the actual carrying out of the threat of assault and it also is a crime as well as a tort. It is touching a person in a hostile manner or against his will and the slightest contact will suffice. Contact with the wronged person need not be direct, e.g. pulling a chair from under a person causing him to fall to the floor is battery, or throwing a missile and striking him at a distance.

(c) False Imprisonment. This is the unlawful restraining of the liberty of a person. The imprisonment must be total, therefore if the person has any reasonable means of leaving the area of restrictment, it will not be a tort. An unlawful arrest or any act which prevents a person from leaving, say, his house or car is imprisonment. A police constable is protected in respect of arrests made by the authority of a warrant and in certain circumstances he may arrest without a warrant, by reason of statutory powers. The remedies against false imprisonment are breaking away, the writ of habeas corpus and an action for damages.

14

2.2.2   Trespass to Chattels (Goods)

This is a wrong against the possession of goods, thus it is a trespass to take away a chattel or to do wilful damage to it, but the tort is wider than this. It applies where a person intentionally interferes with goods in the possession of another, or carries out an unjustifiable act which denies the person of the legal right to possess the goods. The merest touch of the goods is sufficient, even if no damage results. In Kirk v Gregory, 1876, the plaintiff was the executor of a person who died in his own house. The defendant, worried about the risk to the deceased's jewellery arising from the presence of various persons in the house moved certain rings from one room to another, in the genuine belief that this was necessary. The defendant was held liable in trespass for the loss of the rings.

Nearly all actions under this tort are brought under the head of Conversion which is any intentional interference with goods which denies the plaintiff's right of possession or use. A common example is a person buying a car under a hire-purchase agreement and subsequently selling it to a third party without disclosing the outstanding hire-purchase debt. The purchaser will obtain a good title to the car, thus there is infringement of the title of the finance company.

2.2.3   Trespass to Land

This is unjustifiable interference with the possession of land. It is an invasion of property, however minute. It is actionable "per se", i.e. without proof of negligence, even if it is done in ignorance. Trespass occurs not only where there is entry without lawful permission but also where a person on land with the permission of the owner, remains on the land after the permission of the owner has been withdrawn.

The interference with the land must be direct but it need not necessarily involve personal entry; it is trespass where objects are placed on the land, e.g. dumping of rubbish or allowing a creeper to grow upon it.

Any entry beneath the surface of the land or above the surface can be trespass therefore tunnelling or mining and a direct infringement of the air-space over another's land by, say, an advertising sign, can constitute trespass. As regards trespass by aircraft, the Civil Aviation Act, 1949 gives immunity in trespass and nuisance in respect of flying at a reasonable height. However the owners of aircraft are strictly liable (i.e. without proof of negligence) for any actual damage caused to land.

The remedies available to a plaintiff are:

(i) Damages, if actual damage has occured, but otherwise the amount awarded may be nominal, i.e. 1p,

(ii) Forcible ejection. Where this remedy is applied the owner cannot use more force than is reasonable and after he has requested the trespasser to leave and having given him reasonable time to do so.

2.3   Nuisance

The law of Nuisance aims to safeguard the citizen's rights to his enjoyment of his property, his comfort, and his safety. Nuisance is defined as a "wrong done to a man by unlawfully disturbing him in the enjoyment of his property, or, in some cases, in the exercise of a common right". Nuisance is of three types: Public Nuisance, Private Nuisance and Statutory Nuisance.

2.3.1 Public Nuisance

A public nuisance is a criminal offence because it interferes with common rights and not solely an individual's private rights. It is an act or omission endangering or interfering with the lives, comfort, property or common rights of the public. Examples are obstruction of a public highway, smoke from chimneys causing damage to property generally or a pop music festival which causes widespread noise. Normally a public nuisance is not actionable for damages unless a particular individual suffers special damage, for example, where the demolition of a building results in the neighbourhood being covered in dust, but one private car is damaged by falling masonry. In Fisher v Ruislip-Northwood U.D.C., 1945, a motor car came into collision with an unlit air-raid shelter. The public nuisance caused by the unlit obstruction was actionable at the suit only of the individual who suffered damage. Public nuisance falls within the category of a tort only when particular damage has been suffered by an individual. To constitute public nuisance there has to be a continuous state of affairs or some element of repetition. In Castle v St. Augustine's Links, 1922, damges were awarded against a golf club to a taxi-driver injured by a golf ball driven from the course on to the highway. The teeing-off position was sufficiently close to the highway and the frequency of stray balls landing on the road was such that it constituted a public nuisance. However, in Bolton v Stone, 1951, it was held that there was no nuisance when it was shown that cricket balls landed on the highway from an adjacent cricket ground on only about six occasions in thirty years. The plaintiff was injured by a cricket ball knocked from the ground.

2.3.2 Private Nuisance

Private nuisance is a civil wrong and can be defined as "Interference for a substantial length of time by an owner or occupier of property with the use or enjoyment of neighbouring property". Examples of private nuisance are vibrations, unreasonable noise, the escape of noxious things such as gas, smoke, smells and damp. The duration of the offence is also a factor in private nuisance and in general, it is necessary for the offence to be a lengthy one. The courts will not often grant an injunction against a temporary nuisance because damages are an adequate remedy. Occasional escapes of gas and water have been held to constitute nuisance, however. Interference must be unreasonable and substantial.

Other points which have a bearing on determining private nuisance are:

(i) a person cannot take advantage of his peculiar sensitivity or that of his property to harmful influences;

(ii) the standard of comfort must be expected to vary with the district, where claims for inconvenience are concerned. "What would be a nuisance in Belgrave Square would not necessarily be so in Bermondsey" (Sturgess v Bridgeman, 1879).

(iii) a person can be liable for nuisance by taking over property where there is an existing nuisance, even where it was unknown to him, if within reason, he could have been aware of it.

(iv) he can still be liable after he vacates property if he caused the nuisance.

(v) malice or evil motive may underly the offence as in the case of Hollywood Silver Fox Farm Ltd. v Emmett, 1936. The defendant deliberately fired off a shotgun at intervals in order to prevent the breeding of animals.

Nuisances on the public highway depend upon duration of the state of affairs. Leaving an unlit vehicle on the highway does not in itself constitute the tort, it depends upon whether the person responsible acted reasonably, especially if the vehicle was a danger.

To sue in private nuisance the plaintiff must have some title to the property affected, either as owner of it or as a tenant, therefore this does not include members of the occupier's family, servants or guests. The plaintiff must show that the interference or discomfort goes beyond that which the reasonable occupier would be expected to endure. Liability for nuisance is vested in the person who creates it as a general rule but a landlord will be liable jointly with his tenant, (a) where he knew or ought to have known of the nuisance at the start of the tenancy, (b) where he has reserved the right to enter and repair, (c) where he has covenanted to repair, (d) where he has authorised the nuisance. An occupier is responsible for nuisance created by his servants and by anyone under his control, lawfully on the premises including members of his family and independent contractors engaged by him.

2.3.3   Independent Contractors creating a Nuisance

The employer or principal who employs a contractor for work which is likely to cause nuisance will be liable unless he takes reasonable steps to prevent the nuisance, whereas, ordinarily, as we saw in Chapter 1 (1.5.5) a principal is not vicariously liable. Liability certainly lies with the employer in nuisances involving creating dangers on the highway and removal or weakening of support to land. An occupier of land has an absolute right to the lateral support of his neighbour's building, consequently the neighbour who "causes" removal of support through the work of his contractor will be liable.

2.3.4   Defences to Nuisance

The following defences are applicable to the tort of nuisance:

(a) Statutory Authority. The nuisance was covered by statutory authority but the defence will be of no avail if the defendant has been negligent.

(b) Prescription. When a nuisance has been continuous for not less than twenty years, the right to carry on the activity may be acquired. In Sturges v Bridgman, 1879, the defendant, a confectioner, had used pestles and mortars for more than twenty years. The plaintiff, a physician built a consulting room in his garden next to the confectioner's premises, and found that the

17

noise from the activity interfered with his practice. Held: That it was possible to acquire a prescriptive right to commit a nuisance but in this instance the defendant had not acquired that right because the nuisance only arose when the physician's premises were built.

(c) Consent (of the Plaintiff). A possible defence but consent will not be implied solely on the grounds that the plaintiff came to the nuisance (Sturges v Bridgman, 1879).

(d) Damage was minimal. Where the damage is trivial. The law does not concern itself with trifles (De minimis non curat lex).

(e) Character of the neighbourhood. The defendant could plead that whilst the act complained of might be a nuisance elsewhere, it cannot be regarded as such in the particular locus.

2.3.5 Ineffectual Defences to Nuisance

The following pleas may not succeed in defence of nuisance:

(i) That the defendant used all possible skill and care. Absence of negligence is not a defence to nuisance.

(ii) Public benefit. If the plaintiff is injured it is no defence that the activity benefits the public generally, however substantial the public benefit and relatively slight the plaintiff's injury.

(iii) Suitable place for carrying on the activity. With the exceptions of statutory authority or the consent of the person affected a nuisance cannot be continued on the basis that the locus is a suitable place.

(iv) Contributory acts of others. It is of no avail to plead that the act in itself was too negligible to amount to a nuisance, unless taken with the aggregate effect of the activities of a number of others. In such a case, each contributor is liable in nuisance and for his own proportion of the damage.

(v) Reasonable use of property. Reasonable use of his own property will not exempt a defendant from nuisance because the creation of a nuisance is unreasonable by definition. If he creates a nuisance, he cannot say that he is acting reasonably.

(vi) Volenti non fit injuria. The defendant cannot escape liability by showing that, the plaintiff came to a nuisance alreading existing.

2.3.6 Remedies

The remedies available for nuisance are:

(a) The plaintiff may sue for damages.

(b) He may ask the court for an injunction if damages would not be a sufficient remedy or where the nuisance is a continuing one.

(c) He may abate the nuisance. Abatement is action taken by the victim to terminate the nuisance without entering another person's land, or if entry is effected, after notice requesting removal of the nuisance has first been given.

Thus the occupier of land may without notice cut off the overhanging branches of his neighbour's tree, or cut the roots of a neighbour's tree which encroach on his own ground.

2.4.1 Negligence

The tort of negligence is committed when damage is caused to another by someone whose behaviour falls below a standard of care fixed by law. The standard of care may vary with the circumstances and it is usually measured by the concept of the reasonable man. Negligence is the absence of care according to the circumstances or alternatively it may be defined as "The omission to do something which a reasonable man, guided by those considerations which ordinarily regulate the conduct of human affairs would do, or doing something which a prudent and reasonable man would not do" (Blyth v Birmingham Waterworks Co., 1856). In litigation for damages in tort negligence is the most frequent cause of action.

The tort of negligence has three ingredients and to succeed in an action the plaintiff must show:

(i) the existance of a duty to take care which was owed to him by the defendant,

(ii) a breach of such duty by the defendant,

(iii) resulting damage to the plaintiff. The damage must not be too remote.

2.4.2 The Duty of Care Owed to the Plaintiff

We proceed now to look at the first of the component parts. It is a question of law whether in any given circumstances a duty of care exists. There was no general principle before 1932, the law had been developed under the influence of privity of contract. In Donoghue v Stevenson, 1932, the plaintiff drank ginger beer from an opaque bottle in which, it was alleged, there was a decomposed snail which caused the plaintiff to be ill. The House of Lords, by a bare majority, held that a manufacturer of goods is liable if the goods are used by a consumer without an intermediate examination, because the manufacturer owes the consumer a duty of care. This case had enormous influence on the development of the concept of the duty of care. Lord Atkin, in his key speech in the case formulated the "neighbour" principle when he said "The rule that you are to love your neighbour becomes in law, you must not injure your neighbour; and the lawyer's question, Who is my neighbour? receives a restricted reply. You must take reasonable care to avoid acts or omissions which you can reasonably foresee would be likely to injure your neighbour. Who, then, in law is my neighbour? The answer seems to be — persons who are so closely and directly affected by my act that I ought reasonably to have them in contemplation as being so affected when I am directing my mind to the acts or omissions which are called in question". There has been a tendency to extend and strengthen the neighbour principle and it has been used to show that a duty was owed, for example, to persons living in the neighbourhood of a Borstal Institution, where damage was caused by escaping inmates (Home Office v Dorset Yacht Co., 1970) and by a local authority to a lady locked in a public lavatory due to a faulty door lock (Dutton v Bognor Regis U.D.C., 1972). The limits of the neighbour principle are not well defined and remain flexible. In Bourhill v Young, 1943, a motor cyclist was fatally injured in a road crash through his own fault. The plaintiff, a pregnant lady who was alighting from a tramcar some yards distant from the accident heard but did not actually witness the event. She later looked at the scene and the sight of blood caused her shock and, subsequently, a miscarriage. The House of Lords held that a duty of care was not owed to her because it could not easily be foreseen that the deceased's act would cause her to suffer injuries.

The common law obligation on persons in certain circumstances is to act with reasonable care so as not to injure others likely to be affected. It will not always follow that a duty of care is owed to an injured party (DAMNUM SINE INJURIA). For example there is no duty to prevent the subsidence of one's neighbour's property by the abstraction of water in undefined channels or the effects of competitive trading on a neighbour's business. A university, or for that matter an organisation such as the Institute of Risk Management owes no legal duty to its students in respect of examinations. Generally there is no duty owed in regard to pure economic loss and this will now be considered.

2.4.3 Liability for Economic Loss

The law does not protect a man's financial or economic loss to the same extent as his direct physical injury. Liability for economic loss may be dealt with under two headings — (i) resulting from negligent acts, and (ii) resulting from negligent misstatements.

2.4.4 Negligent Acts Causing Financial Loss

Generally there is no liability for financial loss unless there is also loss to the person or property. In Electrochrome Ltd. v Welsh Plastics Ltd., 1968, the defendant's employee negligently drove a lorry so as to damage a fire hydrant on an industrial estate where the plaintiffs had a factory. As a result of the damage it was necessary to cut off the supply of water for some hours and the plaintiffs' factory was therefore unable to operate. The plaintiffs sued for the amount of their loss. It was held that the claim must fail as the duty of care owed by the defendant was owed to the owners of the hydrant and not to the plaintiff. In Spartan Steel and Alloys Ltd. v Martin & Co. (Contractors) Ltd., 1973, the defendants negligently severed an electric power cable supplying power to the plaintiffs' factory causing interruption of work for several hours. The plaintiffs were compensated for physical damage to the metal in their furnace (£368) and loss of profit for the sale of that melt (£400) but were not allowed a claim for loss of profit on four further melts (£1,767) which represented the anticipated profit which could have been realised but for the power cut. The last item was considered as too remote. There may not appear to be much logic in this outcome but it is a matter of public policy. It safeguards a business (and its insurers) against a potential catastrophic risk where, say, a mains cable is cut and perhaps thousands of purely financial loss claims could result. In both British Celanese Ltd. v A. H. Hunt (Capacitors) Ltd., 1969, and S.C.M. (United Kingdom) Ltd. v W. J. Whittal & Son, Ltd., 1971, the cutting of electricity supplies damaged the plaintiffs' machines and materials, so that production ceased temporarily. In both cases the economic loss, in addition to the material loss was recoverable in negligence because the economic loss in both cases flowed directly from the foreseeable damage to the plaintiffs' property. So far then, liability for economic loss depends upon actual physical damage occurring and the economic loss must follow directly from the damage. A more recent case has to some extent amended the Spartan Steel decision. In Junior Books Ltd. v Veitchi Co. Ltd., 1982, the defendants laid composition flooring in the plaintiffs' new factory, but two years after the floor was laid it developed cracks. Held: there was no contractual remedy because the flooring specialists were engaged by the main contractors and not the plaintiffs but the proximity between the parties was sufficiently close for the defendants to owe a duty of care to the plaintiffs not to lay a defective floor which would cause the plaintiffs a financial loss. It is considered that the Junior Books decision will not have the effect of "opening the floodgates" to claims for pure economic loss, in the absence of physical damage because in that particular case the House of Lords was at pains to qualify the decision on the grounds that "the relationship between the parties was as close as it could be short of actual privity of contract" and this close proximity was the necessary factor in holding the defendants liable for financial loss.

2.4.5   Negligent Mis-statements Causing Financial Loss

Liability for physical loss caused by mis-statements has long been recognised but until 1963 the principle did not apply outside of a contractual or fiduciary relationship. In Hedley Byrne & Co. Ltd. v Heller & Partners Ltd., 1963, the appellants, being doubtful about the financial position of Easipower Ltd., asked their bank to contact Easipower's bankers, the respondents, to ascertain whether Easipower would be good for a contract to the extent of £100,000 per annum. The respondents replied: "Respectably constituted company, considered good for its ordinary business engagements". The appellants, relying upon the advice, placed an order and as a result lost £17,000 when Easipower went into liquidation. They sued the respondents alleging they had been careless in failing to make a proper check as to Easipower's creditworthiness. The action failed only on the grounds that the information had been given "without responsibility". However, despite the decision in the case a principle was established that:

"If in the ordinary course of business or professional affairs a person seeks information or advice from another who is not under a contractual or fiduciary obligation to give the information or advice in circumstances in which a reasonable person so asked would know that he was being trusted or that his skill or judgement was being relied on and the person asked chooses to give the advice or information without clearly so qualifying his answer as to show that he does not accept responsibility then the person replying accepts a legal duty to exercise such care as the circumstances require in making his reply."

In Esso Petroleum Co. Ltd. v Mardon, 1976, the petroleum company mis-informed the new tenant of a filling station as to the expected turnover because in reality it was much less than the figure advised. Held: the statement was a negligent representation made by a party holding himself out as having special expertise, in circumstances which gave rise to a duty to take reasonable care to see that the representation was correct. Legal liability for negligent mis-statements in situations other than where there is a contractual relationship will exist only if there is a special relationship. A special relationship will exist where the enquirer is trusting the other to exercise a reasonable degree of care and where the other knew or ought to have known that the enquirer was relying upon him. Also where the person asked for an opinion was an expert on whose statement it would be reasonable to rely. However liability will not attach if the defendant has disclaimed responsibility, as in the case of Hedley Byrne.

21

2.4.6   The Standard of Care Expected

The standard of conduct required is that of the reasonable man, variously described as "the man on the Clapham omnibus" or "the man in the street". "The reasonable man is presumed to be free both from over-apprehension and over-confidence," said Lord MacMillan in Glasgow Corporation v Muir, 1943. In determining whether the defendant's conduct constitutes negligence in the circumstances, the standard of the reasonable man is considered and not that of the defendant. It is an objective standard. It is no defence that a person acted "to the best of his judgement" if his "best" falls short of that of the reasonable man.

The law requires a reasonable standard of care and this expected standard may vary, dependent upon the following criteria:

(i) the possibility of harm occurring. The degree of care expected increases with the greater likelihood of the defendant's conduct causing harm. "People must guard against reasonable probabilities, not fantastic possibilities."

(ii) the risk of serious injury. The more serious the possible outcome, the greater the degree of care. In Paris v Stepney Borough Council, 1950, a one-eyed workman lost the sight of his remaining eye due to the negligence of his employer in failing to provide him with protective goggles. The House of Lords held that the gravity of the consequences (total blindness) if an accident did occur had to be taken into account in determining the measure of care.

(iii) the cost of avoiding the harm. Here is an economic balance between the cost of avoiding the risk and the activity creating the risk. "In every case of fore-seeable risk, it is a matter of balancing the risk against the measures necessary to eliminate it" — Lord Denning in Latimer v A.E.C. Ltd. (1953.)

The test of the man in the street is discarded when measuring the standard of care of a professional man, i.e. someone exercising some special skill or expertise such as an accountant or a brain surgeon. It is expected of a professional person that he should show a fair, reasonable and competent degree of skill. It is not required that he should show the highest possible degree of skill, for there may be persons in his profession who have higher education and greater advantages than he has. A doctor does not have to guarantee a cure nor does a barrister undertake to win his case. It is enough that they exercise the reasonable degree of care and skill expected of a member of that profession.

2.4.7   Proof of Negligence and "Res Ipsa Loquitur"

The onus of proving negligence is on the plaintiff who alleges it and who must produce reasonable evidence that the damage or injury was caused by the defendant's negligence. In cases, however, where the act or omission prima facie indicates negligence, the burden of proof is transferred to the defendant who must show that he was not negligent. This doctrine is known as "Res Ipsa Loquitur" (the thing speaks for itself) and it comes to the rescue of the plaintiff also where the true cause of the accident lies solely within the knowledge of the defendant. In Scott v London and St. Katherine Docks Co., 1865, the plaintiff, a customs officer, proved that when he was passing the defendant's warehouse six bags of sugar fell upon him. Held: "where the thing is shown to be under the management of the defendant or his servants, and the accident is such as in the ordinary course of things does not happen if those who have the management use proper care, it affords reasonable evidence, in the absence of explanation by the defendant, that the accident arose from want of care". Note that there has to be an element of control by the defendant therefore if a vehicle has an unexplained skid the principle will apply; the driver being considered as having sufficient control over the vehicle.

The application of the principle does not always mean that the defendant has been negligent. In Pearson v N.W. Gas Board, 1968, the plaintiff's husband was killed and her house destroyed by an explosion of gas. The defendants were able to establish that severe frost caused the gas leak and there was no reasonable way in which the explosion could have been prevented.

"Res Ipsa Loquitur" applies in cases where the facts indicate negligence but where there is no apparent explanation and the plaintiff is unable to show the cause of the accident. It will not apply where there is an explanation. The defendant may rebut the presumption of negligence by showing that he was not negligent or by showing that the accident could reasonably have occurred without his negligence.

2.4.8 Damage to the Plaintiff

It is necessary for the plaintiff to show that he has suffered some damage since negligence is not actionable per se (in itself). Not all damage is actionable because some damage may be considered too remote, i.e. not sufficiently closely connected with the harm suffered by the plaintiff. It is possible for a wrongful act to give rise to a succession of events ultimately terminating in injury to another, but the tortfeasor will only be liable if that injury is not too remote. The general rule is that the plaintiff will be liable only for that damage which is the reasonably foreseeable consequence of his action or omission.

In the Wagon Mound case (Overseas Tankship (UK) Ltd. v Morts Dock and Engineering Co. Ltd., 1961), a ship negligently discharged oil while bunkering, and the oil was carried on the surface of the water under a wharf. A piece of fibre waste floating on the oil was set alight by sparks from welding operations. The oil caught fire and the surrounding wharves were severely damaged. The action failed because the fire was not reasonably foreseeable, because oil would not normally ignite under these conditions. Before this decision the rule was that a defendant in negligence was liable for all the direct consequences of his act, notwithstanding that he could not reasonably foresee them. In Doughty v Turner Manufacturing Co. Ltd., 1946, the defendants had on their premises a large bath containing sulphuric acid heated to a temperature of 800 degrees centigrade. The lid was knocked into the bath by the plaintiff's fellow workman. A chemical reaction caused an eruption of the acid injuring the plaintiff. The Court of Appeal held the defendants not liable in negligence because the cause was not merely a splash (foreseeable) but an explosion which in the light of the state of knowledge at the time was not foreseeable. Reasonable foreseeability is therefore the test of remoteness of damage in negligence cases and not whether the damage is the direct consequence of the act. Foreseeability applies to the type of damage and not to its amount. Provided the type of damage was reasonably foreseeable it does not matter if the amount or cost of the damage was greater than could have been reasonably anticipated.

Another instance where the foreseeability principle is set aside are cases where the damage is aggravated by physical peculiarities of the victim; the so called "physical weakness" cases. The "egg-shell skull" rule is that you take your victim as you find him. In Smith v Leech, Brain & Co., 1961, the Court of Appeal allowed Smith's estate to recover damages from the defendants following his death from cancer of the lip. Owing to the negligence of the defendants molten metal splashed him and activated a pre-malignant cancer. The rule is that if the consequences of a slight injury are aggravated by the condition of the person injured, the wrongdoer is nonetheless liable to the full extent despite the fact that he may have no knowledge of that condition and no reason to suspect it.

2.4.9 Liability for Nervous Shock

The term "Nervous Shock" means physical symptoms of illness brought on by shock or psychiatric illness and not merely the victim "getting a fright" or even distress or grief. An accident may occur due to negligence, for example, and as a result an onlooker, although not injured physically, suffers illness due to shock brought on by what was witnessed. Historically the law resisted claims under this head, presumably on the grounds of difficulty of proof and the possibility of fraudulent claims. Moreover, if there was no limit to the right to claim many possible claims could come from relatives not present at the accident and numbers of strangers indirectly affected. There has been a gradual development of the principle of a duty to avoid causing nervous shock and damages for illness caused by nervous shock are not necessarily too remote and are recoverable in certain circumstances.

2.4.10 Contributory Negligence

At common law it was a complete defence if the defendant could prove that the plaintiff had contributed to the damage by his, the plaintiff's, fault. In Butterfield v Forrester, 1809, A wrongfully obstructed the highway by placing a pole across it. B, who was on horseback, rode into the pole. Although it was dusk, the pole could be seen at a distance of 100 yards, but B had been riding carelessly. It was held that A was not liable to B because B had not used sufficient care himself.

The position is now different as a consequence of the Law Reform (Contributory Negligence) Act, 1945, of which Section 1(i) provides "where any person suffers damage as a result partly of his own fault and partly of the fault of any other person or persons, a claim in respect of that damage shall not be defeated by reason of the person suffering the damage, but the damage recoverable in respect thereof shall be reduced to such extent as the court thinks just and equitable having regard to the claimant's share in the responsibility for the damage".

For contribution to apply the plaintiff's negligence must contribute to his injury. Both parties must have been negligent and the negligence of each must have contributed to the injury or damage. The 1945 Act applies not only to negligence of the plaintiff but also to "breach of a statutory duty or other act or omission which gives rise to a liability in tort".

Contributory negligence may be pleaded as being partly or even wholly responsible for the plaintiff's loss or damage and in assessing the amount of contribution the court has firstly to find and record the total damage which would have been recoverable had the plaintiff not been at fault. If it is a jury case the jury has to determine the amount by which those damages are to be reduced. For example, if the damages are calculated to be £10,000 and the plaintiff is found to be 25% to blame, the award will be reduced to £7,500. In Sayers v Harlow U.D.C., 1858, a deduction for contributory negligence was made where the plaintiff injured herself through her own negligent performance in attempting to extricate herself from a difficult situation. She entered the defendants' public convenience and found that she was locked in a cubicle, due to a faulty door lock. While attempting to climb over the top of the door by placing one foot on a toilet roll holder she fell and was injured. A number of cases before the courts have established contributory negligence in the matter of failure to wear car seat belts. In one case, Froom v Butcher, 1976, for example it was held that failure to wear a seat belt was contributory negligence and indicated that the appropriate deduction was 25% if wearing the belt would have prevented the injury altogether, and 15% if it would have reduced its extent.

2.4.11   Nuisance and Negligence Distinguished

Nuisance can be distinguished from negligence in that it is essentially a wrong resulting from interference with the enjoyment of land whereas negligence relates to duties owed in much wider aspects of human affairs. Nuisance is generally continuous and the wrongdoer has an absolute duty to prevent it, whereas in negligence the duty is not an absolute one, it is a matter of degree, depending upon the circumstances. The wrongdoer in nuisance cannot plead that he has taken all reasonable care, the absence of negligence is not a defence to nuisance. Nuisance and negligence may overlap and an act or omission may constitute both negligence and nuisance e.g. where a person allows premises adjacent to a highway to fall into a state of disrepair.

Chapter 3

STRICT LIABILITY: BREACH OF STATUTORY DUTY: RYLANDS v FLETCHER: LIABILITY FOR FIRE: LIABILITY FOR ANIMALS: DEFAMATION

3.0 Strict Liability

Strict liability is liability which arises without negligence i.e. the defendant can be liable for the damage even though he may have acted neither intentionally nor negligently. It arises in situations which present special danger or where special interests are being safeguarded such as the risk to the employee in the workplace. The source of strict liability is found in common law but statute law increasingly imposes strict liabilities, for example the Health and Safety at Work Act, 1974, the Animals Act, 1971, the Civil Aviation Act, 1949, and the Consumer Protection Act, 1987. Strict liability does not imply absolute liability, however, because the defendant may have some defence available.

3.1 Breach of Statutory Duty

Many statutes impose duties the breach of which may give a right of action to persons injured and often the liability is a strict one. Breach of a statutory duty is prima facie actionable but the plaintiff's case depends upon interpretation of the relevant statute in the light of the facts and circumstances.

The onus is on the plaintiff to prove:

(i) that the provision of the statute was broken,

(ii) that the breach caused the injury,

(iii) that the injury is one which the statute was intended to prevent, and

(iv) that he was a person or one of a class of persons the statute intended to protect.

It must be shown that the statutory duty was imposed on the defendant. In Harrison v N.C.B., 1951, it was held that the duty imposed by the Coal Mines Act, 1911, in relation to safety precautions for shot-firing was imposed upon shot-firers rather than upon the defendant employer. In Galashiels Gas Co. Ltd. v O'Donnel (or Millar), 1949, a workman was killed because of the unexplained failure of the brake mechanism of a hoist in his employer's works although every practical step had been taken by the employers to ensure that the mechanism worked properly and that the hoist was safe to use. It was held that the obligation created by the Factories Act, 1937, i.e. that "Every hoist or lift shall be of good mechanical construction, sound material and adequate strength, and be properly maintained . . . in an efficient state, in efficient working order, and in good repair", was of an absolute and continuing nature. The deceased workman's widow succeeded in her action for damages because there was a breach of the employers' statutory duty making them liable. In John Summers & Sons Ltd. v Frost, 1955, it was held that the duty to fence dangerous parts of machinery was a strict one so that the employers were in breach of this statutory duty in failing to fence a grindstone, even though such fencing would make the machine unusable.

3.2 The Nature of Statutory Duty

The duty imposed by statute may either be a strict one independent of negligence or the breach may be actionable only on proof of negligence or wrongful intent. It is a matter of construction of the wording of the particular statute. If the statutory duty is construed as absolute, a non-negligent failure to comply with it, as in the case of the Galashiels Gas described above, will be a breach. On the other hand the statutory wording may require that all "practical" or "reasonably practicable" measures be taken in which case the duty is less strict and can be equated with negligence. What is "reasonably practicable" may be determined by the resources available to cope with the risk, the state of knowledge and the time scale and trouble required to effect remedial measures balanced against the risk. Now we have a concept "statutory negligence" but this is distinguished from the common law tort of negligence because in the latter the standard of care is decided by the courts whereas in breach of statutory duty it is laid down in the statute. Moreover the defence of "volenti non fit injuria" cannot be pleaded in a case of alleged breach of a statutory duty.

3.3 The Rule in Rylands v Fletcher

This is a rule of strict liability which is restricted to the risk to one's neighbour arising out of the escape of certain "things" from the defendant's land. The doctrine takes its name from the case of Rylands v Fletcher, 1868, and the facts were as follows: The defendant employed independent contractors to build a reservoir on his land for the purpose of supplying water for his mill. In the course of excavating on the defendant's land, the contractors came upon a disused mineshaft which, unknown to them, connected with working mines underneath adjoining land. The contractors negligently failed to seal off the shaft properly and when the reservoir was filled with water, the mines were flooded.

The defendant was not negligent nor was he vicariously liable for the negligence of his independent contractor, yet he was held liable. Blackburn, J. delivering his judgement in the Court of Exchquer Chamber, said:

> "We think that the true rule of law is, that the person who for his own purposes brings on his lands and collects and keeps there anything likely to do mischief if it escapes, must keep it in at his peril, and, if he does not do so, is prima facie answerable for all the damage which is the natural consequence of its escape."

This liability is something more than negligence; the defendant will be answerable where his acts are neither intentional nor negligent interferences with the interests of the wronged person. This tort is akin to nuisance but, as stated, its application is confined to the escape of things. It is confined also to what Lord Cairns in the House of Lords referred to as "a non-natural use" of land.

3.3.1 Bringing on to Land and Non-natural Use of Land

The defendant must bring the thing on his land; he must do this for his own purposes. It therefore does not apply to things naturally upon the land such as weeds and destructive wild animals, or, say water naturally accumulating on the land. If the latter flows from X's land into Y's mine by force of gravitation or by percolation, X is not liable under the Rule in Rylands v Fletcher for that escape provided he did nothing to accumulate it there. Non-natural use of land was described in Rickards v Lothian, 1913: "it must be some special use bringing with it increased danger to others, and must not merely be the ordinary use of the land or such a use as is proper for the general benefit of the community". Non-natural use of land includes the storing of gas, electricity, sewage, rainwater in a reservoir and the use of a blow-lamp to thaw frozen pipes (where the "thing" was fire). Even human beings have constituted "non-natural" use where a landowner permitted caravan dwellers to camp on his land. They committed insanitary acts in the neighbourhood which amounted to a menace to health and the landowner was held liable (Attorney-General v Corke, 1933). On the other hand, it has been held that the lighting of a fire in a fireplace of a house did not come under the Rule. Likewise the wiring of a building for the supply of electric light and installation of water pipes for water supply is considered natural use. The planting of trees is natural use, but planting poisonous trees would come under the Rule.

3.3.2 The Thing must Escape

There must be an escape from a place where the defendant has occupation of or control over land to a place which is outside his occupation or control. In Read v J. Lyons & Co. Ltd., 1946, the appellant was employed by the Ministry of Supply to inspect the filling of shell cases in the respondents' factory. When the appellant was in the shell filling shop a shell exploded and she was injured. There was no evidence of negligence on the part of the factory owners. It was held that the appellant could not recover damages as the element of "escape" required by the doctrine of Rylands v Fletcher was lacking. Likewise "escape" did not occur in Ponting v Noakes, 1894, where the plaintiff's colt reached over the defendant's land and ate some branches of a poisonous tree, the tree never having extended beyond the defendant's boundary.

The actual damage caused by the escape need not be immediately caused by the thing accumulated. If, for example, dynamite accumulated for quarrying purposes explodes and causes rocks to splinter on to adjoining land the damage caused by the rocks would be recoverable under the Rule.

3.3.3 Who May Sue

The Rule is not confined to damage to interests in adjoining land; it appears that every type of damage is recoverable provided it is not too remote. Successful actions have been brought both for property damage and personal injury where plaintiffs have not had an interest in adjoining land. Rylands v Fletcher is therefore an action arising from the escape of noxious things from the defendant's land but is wider than merely the protection of adjoining land. There must be proof of actual damage and this damage is limited to damage to the person or property; there is no case for mere interference with enjoyment of land. Pecuniary loss on its own is not recoverable.

3.4 Defences to Rylands v Fletcher

Although liability is strict in that absence of due care on the part of the defendant is not relevant, the following defences are possible:

(i) Statutory authority
(ii) Consent of the plaintiff

(iii) Act of a stranger
(iv) Default of the plaintiff
(v) Act of God.

The defences are summarised below.

3.4.1 Statutory Authority

The construction of the wording of the particular statute determines whether the defendant can succeed. Public authorities storing water, gas or electricity may be exempt from liability provided they exercise reasonable care. In Green v Chelsea Waterworks Co., 1894, a water main belonging to the defendants burst, flooding the plaintiff's premises. It was held that the company, being authorised by statute to lay the main, and having a statutory duty to maintain a supply of water and having been guilty of no negligence, was not liable for the damage. By way of contrast the defendants were held liable in Charing Cross Electricity Supply Co. v Hydraulic Power Co., 1914, although the facts were the same as the Green case. The difference was that although the defendants had statutory authority to lay the mains they were under no statutory obligation to do so. The principle appears to be that if the activity is carried out under a statutory duty as distinct from a statutory power, Rylands v Fletcher is excluded.

3.4.2 Consent of the Plaintiff

Express or implied consent of the plaintiff to the defendant bringing things on to his (the defendant's) land may defeat the action. In such a case the defendant is not liable except for negligence. The chief example of this is where there are several tenants occupying the same building. If water from the common water supply escapes from, say, an upper storey and provided there was no negligence, the tenants in the lower levels who suffer damage are deemed to have consented to the accumulation of water in the building. The defence would not apply however to excessive accumulation of water for, say, a special industrial process. An important element in deciding consent is whether the plaintiff benefits from the storage of the substance.

3.4.3 Act of a Stranger

The occupier of land is in general not liable for escape caused by a stranger. If a trespasser starts a fire on the defendant's land and it spreads to a neighbour's property the defendant will not be liable unless he had knowledge of the fire's existence and failed to extinguish within a reasonable time. The onus is on the defendant to show that the escape was due to the deliberate act of a stranger over whom he had no control and against whose acts he could not reasonably be expected to have taken preventative steps. It follows that if a trespasser breaks the locking mechanism of a well secured sluice valve allowing water to escape and cause damage the owner will not be liable but if the landowner has left the valve unsecured and the presence of trespassers is foreseeable the defence is unlikely to relieve him of responsibility under the Rule. In the latter instance there is negligence also. A "stranger" within the meaning of the rule includes, in addition to a trespasser, any person who, without entering on the premises of the defendant, wrongfully and without the defendant's authority causes the escape. Any person employed or authorised by the defendant to deal with things on his land likely to do mischief is not a stranger. This includes an independent contractor, whose actions will render the employer or principal liable, even if he is acting outwith the scope of his authority. The student will recognise this as an exception to the general rule that a principal is not vicariously liable for the torts of an independent contractor.

3.4.4   Default of the Plaintiff

In certain instances the action of the plaintiff will be regarded as "courting the danger" thus causing this own injury. In Dunn v Birmingham Canal Navigation Co. 1872, the plaintiff worked his mines under the canal knowing full well that there was a danger of water leaking into them. The plaintiff's mines were flooded by water from the canal and he brought an action but it failed. The student will recall the principle of extra sensitivity in actions in nuisance and here again a defendant may escape liability on the grounds of special sensitivity of the plaintiff's property. In Eastern and Southern African Telegraph Co. v Cape Town Tramways Co., 1902, the plaintiffs complained that the electrical current used to operate the defendant's tramway system caused interference with the receipt of messages through their submarine cable. There was no physical damage to the actual cable; the trouble was due to the sensitivity of the system. The action failed.

As in the tort of negligence, the provisions of the Law Reform (Contributory Negligence) Act, 1945, can apply to Rylands v Fletcher and damages will be apportioned according to the degree of fault of the parties.

3.4.5   Act of God

This defence, already referred to in Chapter 1, is a possible defence to Rylands v Fletcher and the case quoted i.e. Nichols v Marsland, 1876, involves the escape of water from artificial lakes following a violent thunderstorm. The defence was successful but it is of little practical importance because the instances of natural phenomena of the type appropriate are rare.

3.4.6   Comparison of Rylands v Fletcher and Nuisance

The Rule in Rylands v Fletcher has a closer affinity with nuisance than it has with negligence, although it can overlap. The Rule has an obvious similarity with private nuisance but they are not the same. In many instances of nuisance there is no element of bringing things on to the defendant's land. No accumulation or escape is necessary in nuisance and the use may be natural yet constitute nuisance. The Rule refers to the escape of physical "things" whereas nuisance includes also intangibles such as noise and smells. The occupier's liability for the acts of independent contractors differs in that he is not normally liable for the contractor's nuisance.

3.5   Liability for the Escape of Fire

This liability has to be considered separately from Rylands v Fletcher because the law is somewhat different. The old common law rule was that the occupier was liable for damage done by the mere spread of fire from his premises and from fire resulting from his negligence and that of his servants, agents and guests. Liability for fire may arise under:

(i) the law of negligence and nuisance,
(ii) the Rule of Rylands v Fletcher, and
(iii) statute.

3.5.1 Negligence and the Effect of the Fires Prevention (Metropolis) Act, (1774)

In order to ease the burden of responsibility of an occupier of premises, which amounted to a form of strict liability for the mere happening of a fire the common law rule was modified by the Fires Prevention (Metropolis) Act, 1774, which provides that a person on whose land a fire "shall accidentally begin" has a defence. An accidental fire is defined as "a fire produced by mere chance or incapable of being traced to any cause" (Filliter v Phippard, 1847). The result is that unless there is intention or negligence the occupier is not liable. If the fire begins accidentally, as defined above, but then is allowed to spread through negligence the "Act" defence is not available. It is important to note also that the defence does not apply if there is escape of fire under the constituent requirements of the Rule in Rylands v Fletcher.

3.5.2 Liability for Fire Caused by Independent Contractors

Another special aspect of liability for fire is that a person is vicariously liable for the negligence of his independent contractors resulting in fire. The facts of Balfour v Barty-King, 1957, are that part of a large country house had been converted into separate dwelling-houses. The plaintiff and the defendant each owned one of these dwellings and their properties were adjoining. Owing to a severe frost the pipes in the defendant's loft became frozen and he called in a firm of builders whose workmen proceeded to apply a blow-lamp to the pipes. Some felt lagging on the pipes caught fire and the flames spread to the plaintiff's property causing considerable damage. The defendant was held liable because the fire was caused by the negligence of his independent contractors who were invited by him to do the work and it was not therefore the act of a stranger. Moreover, the use of the blow-lamp was in the circumstances a dangerous and non-natural use of the premises. Both of these principles are analogous with Rylands v Fletcher.

3.5.3 Strict Liability for Fire Under Rylands v Fletcher

It is evident that "fire" may constitute the thing being kept on premises and where the Rule applies and the 1774 Act does not provide a defence, there will be strict liability. In Musgrove v Pandelis, 1919, the defendant's servant started the engine of the defendant's car while it was in a garage and the petrol in the carburettor caught fire. The servant was negligent in not turning off the petrol tap and in consequence the fire spread and burnt the car, the garage and property over the garage which was occupied by the plaintiff. The defendant was held liable under the Rule in Rylands v Fletcher. The 1774 Act afforded no defence because the fire did not begin "accidentally" but as a result of the servant's negligent omission to turn off the petrol. The car with its tank full of petrol was a thing likely to cause mischief within the Rule.

In H. and N. Emanuel Ltd. v Greater London Council, 1917, a firm of independent contractors were engaged to remove two bungalows and all materials and rubbish from a site owned by the defendant Council. The contractors started a fire to burn unwanted materials and sparks blew on to the plaintiff's property causing a fire. Held, the Council as the occupier of the site was liable for the escape of fire caused by the negligence of anyone other than a stranger. The contractors were on the site with the Council's permission and although the Council, by the terms of the contract forbade the Contractors to start fires on the site, the Council could reasonably have anticipated that they might start a fire.

3.5.4   Statutory Liability for Fire Damage

Strict liability for fires caused by the escape of sparks or cinders from railway locomotives is governed by the Railway Fires Acts, 1905, and 1923, which provide that railway companies shall be liable notwithstanding their statutory authority, to the extent of £200 for damage done to agricultural land or crops. However, if negligence can br proved the aforementioned limit is inapplicable. In view of the very small number of steam-driven railway locomotives in use the provision of these statutes is of little practical importance.

3.6   Liability for Animals

The development of the law of liability for animals is a reflection of social changes and it ranges from the centuries old rules on cattle trespass to recent legislation dealing with the use of guard dogs and keeping of exotic pets.

A person may be liable for injury or damage done by his animals (i) at common law in trespass, nuisance, negligence, the Rule in Rylands v Fletcher and (ii) under the Animals Act, 1971. The duty varies from the ordinary duty of care to that of strict liability, depending upon the circumstances and the kind of animal. A person may commit nuisance by keeping a noisy dog or negligence by allowing a restless dog off the lead in a busy thoroughfare, resulting in injury to road users. It is clear therefore that a person may commit a tort by means of an animal but because animals sometimes present special hazards the common law had developed with strict liability imposed for:

(a) animals with known dangerous propensities,
(b) cattle trespass, and
(c) injury done by dogs to livestock.

3.6.1   Liability for Animals of a Dangerous Species

The Animals Act, 1971, retains the common law principle of strict liability for dangerous animals. Section 6 of the Act defines animals of a dangerous species as:

(a) one which is not commonly domesticated in the British Islands;

(b) whose fully grown animals normally have such characteristics that they are likely, unless restrained, to cause severe damage or that any damage they may cause is likely to be severe.

This latter definition presents some difficulty of interpretation because no example is given. In one decided case an Alsatian guard dog was regarded as within this description.

33

Where any damage is caused by an animal belonging to a dangerous species the person who is a keeper of the animal is strictly liable for the damage. The keeper is the person who has ownership or possession of the animal and if that person is under sixteen years old the head of the household is responsible. Damage includes damage to property, personal injury and possibly disease and nervous shock.

3.6.2   Animals Not Belonging to a Dangerous Species

Section 2(2) of the Act imposes liability, subject to certain provisions, on keepers of animals which do not belong to a dangerous species. A keeper is liable if:

(a) the damage is of a kind which the animal, unless restrained, was likely to cause or which, if caused by the animal, was likely to be severe. This would include the dangerous Alsatian which bites a person and, say, an animal with Foot and Mouth disease which spreads infection to other animals, and

(b) the likelihood of the damage or of its being severe was due to characteristics of the animal which are not normally found in animals of the same species or are not normally so found except at particular times or in particular circumstances. An example is a bitch with a litter which at such times only is likely to attack strangers.

(c) those characteristics were known to that keeper or were at any time known to a person who at that time had charge of the animal as that keeper's servant or, where that keeper is the head of the household, were known to another keeper of the animal who is a member of that household and under the age of sixteen. "Knowledge" of the keeper is the important factor and the plaintiff has to prove this.

3.6.3   Defences to Actions Against Keepers of Dangerous Animals

Liability is strict in the sense that it does not depend upon proof of negligence but there is provision in the Act for defences. They are:

(i) Contributory negligence and fault of the plaintiff. There is no liability for damage which is due wholly to the fault of the person suffering it. If the damage is due partly to the fault of the plaintiff then apportionment in accordance with the Law Reform (Contributory Negligence) Act, 1945 applies.

(ii) Volenti non fit injuria, e.g. where the plaintiff interferes voluntarily in a dog fight. It should be noted that when a person is employed by a keeper of an animal and incurs the risk incidental to his employment he shall not be regarded as accepting it voluntarily.

(iii) It is a defence that the damage occurred on property where the plaintiff was a trespasser if it is proved either that the animal was not kept there for the protection of persons or property or if the animal was kept there for the protection of persons or property, that keeping it there for that purpose was not unreasonable.

3.6.4   Liability For Straying Livestock

Section 4 of the Animals Act imposes strict liability on a person in possession of livestock which stray on to another's land but it is not actionable per se, i.e. damage must be proved consequent upon the entry. Liability is for:

(i) damage done to the land or any property on it, or

(ii) any expenses reasonably incurred by the other person in keeping the livestock whilst it cannot be restored to the person to whom it belongs or while it is detained in pursuance of Section 7 of the Act, or in ascertaining to whom it belongs. Section 7 gives the occupier of land a right to retain livestock straying on to the land, subject to time limits and the provisions as to settlement of claims under Section 4.

The defences available for actions for straying livestock are (i) plaintiff's own fault, (ii) contributory negligence, and (iii) where the livestock strayed from a highway and its presence there was a lawful use of the highway.

The Act supports a well established common law rule that the occupier of premises adjoining a highway is presumed to accept the risks incidental to the passage of ordinary traffic along that highway.

3.6.5   Animals Straying on to the Highway

At common law, the occupier of land was under no obligation to fence his land so as to keep his domestic animals off the highway, therefore he was not liable, except in exceptional circumstances, for damage resulting (Searle v Wallbank, 1947). Section 8 of the Act abolished this rule and now an ordinary duty of care is owed to prevent damage from animals straying on to the highway. It is not a strict liability but the duty is to take reasonable care and all the circumstances must be considered. However there are situations where the duty imposed by Section 8 is inapplicable. No breach of duty is committed by a person by reason only of the fact that he has placed animals on land if: (a) the land is common land, or is land situated in an area where fencing is not customary or is a town or village green: and (b) he had a right to place animals on that land.

There are certain grazing rights in common land and also the legislation recognises the impracticability of fencing in areas such as moorland sheep farms and the more remote areas of the country. In these situations the onus is on the road user to exercise due care for the safety of animals straying on to the highway.

3.6.6   Liability for Dogs

Section 3 imposes strict liability for damage to livestock thus: "Where a dog causes damage by killing or injuring livestock, any person who is a keeper of the dog is liable for the damage, except as otherwise provided by this Act". This is a necessary remedy for the farming community to combat the menace of stray dogs. There are two defences: first, the keeper is not liable if the damage was wholly the plaintiff's own fault. Secondly, there is no strict liability if the livestock was killed or injured on land to which it had strayed and either the dog belonged to the occupier or its presence on the land was authorised by the occupier. A person may be entitled to shoot a dog which is endangering his livestock provided he can show there was no other means of stopping it.

35

Regulations for the keeping and use of guard dogs are contained in the Guard Dogs Act, 1975. Section 1 provides that a person shall not use, or permit the use of, a guard dog on any premises unless a competent handler is present and a warning notice is exhibited at the entrance. A guard dog must be under the control of the handler at all times whilst it is being used except while secured so that it is not at liberty to go freely about the premises.

3.7 Defamation

The tort of Defamation protects an individual's private interest in his good name or reputation. Defamation is the publication of a false statement which injures the reputation of another, as it appears to other people. It has been defined as a statement which tends to lower a person in the estimation of right-thinking members of society generally, or to cause them to shun or avoid him. The statement may be made orally or in writing, or even by paintings or gestures. For a statement to be actionable, proof of the following is necessary:

(i) The statement must be published by the defendant to other persons; publication to the plaintiff himself is not enough. Communication to the spouse of the person making the statement is not publication. A person may say what he/she wishes to a spouse so long as the spouse does not communicate it to others.

(ii) The statement must have been defamatory. The statement is judged by the standard of an ordinary, right-thinking member of society who would ordinarily regard the defamed with feelings of ridicule, hatred, fear, dislike, disesteem or contempt. Innocent intention is no defence; the test is the meaning which would be imputed by reasonable persons.

"Right-thinking members of society" is, hopefully, self-explanatory. A member of the criminal fraternity would not be liable for defamation if he informed other criminals that one of their member had served a prison sentence because it would not be disapproved by them. In Byrne v Dean, 1937, the police removed an illegal gaming machine from the premises of a golf club. A verse was placed on the notice board, which inferred that a member, Byrne, had told the police about the machine. The phrase "May he Byrne in Hell and rue the day" was the substance of Byrne's action for defamation. It was held that he had not been defamed, because right-thinking members of society would approve of a person notifying the police of illegality.

(iii) The statement must have referred to the plaintiff. It is for the judge to decide if the statement is likely to be understood as referring to the plaintiff. The statement need not refer directly to the plaintiff but may be latent. The test is: Would a person to whom the statement was published reasonably think it referred to the plaintiff? In Hulton v Jones, 1910, a series of newspaper articles was based upon the dissolute life of a fictitious person called Atemus Jones, who was described as being on holiday in Dieppe with a woman who was not his wife, and frequenting a casino, etc. The publishers did not know it, but there was a real Atemus Jones whose friends gave evidence that they thought the article referred to him. He was awarded damages.

3.7.1   Libel and Slander

The tort of defamation is of two kinds, namely Libel and Slander. Libel is defamation in a permanent form, such as writing, but also including sculpture, painting, films and radio and television broadcasts transmitted for general reception.

Slander is the temporary or transient form of defamation, usually the spoken word but including gestures and mimes. There are important differences between Libel and Slander. Libel may be a criminal offence as well as a tort but Slander is not a crime. Libel is actionable per se, i.e. without proof of actual damage. Slander is actionable only on proof of special damage, that is monetary loss but there are four instances where slander is actionable without proof of special damage. These are imputations:

(i)   that a person has committed a crime punishable by imprisonment;

(ii) that a person has an existing infectious disease. Diseases include venereal disease, leprosy, plague and probably any contagious skin disease such as scabies;

(iii) against a person in any office, trade or profession that he is unfit to hold that office or practice his profession;

(iv) that a woman is unchaste.

3.7.2   Defences to Defamation

(a) Denial:
    (i) that the matter is defamatory and
    (ii) that it was published.

(b) Justification. The defendant may be able to prove that the allegations are true. Substantial truth of the statement is sufficient, it need not be absolutely true in every detail. As regards rumour, proof of the existence of a rumour is not sufficient; its substance must be true.

(c) Fair Comment on a Matter of Public Interest. In the interests of free speech and criticism, opinions passed on matters of public concern may be defended on the grounds that the statement was fair comment made in good faith on a matter of pubic interest. Any element of malice or spite would defeat the defence. The defence could be applied to matters of public affairs, politics, publication of books, plays and films. So long as the comment reflects the person's views honestly held, even though they may be biased, the defence is relevant.

(d) Privilege. In some instances the public interest overrides the individual's right to an untarnished reputation and statements made are protected. The protection given depends upon whether the situation is one of Absolute Privilege or Qualified Privilege. Absolute Privilege gives complete protection from actions for defamation and it applies to the following:
    (i) Proceedings in either House of Parliament including not only speeches but official reports of proceedings.
    (ii) Judicial proceedings, including all statements in court by judges, jury and witnesses.

    (iii) Communications between husband and wife.

    (iv) Communications between a solicitor and his client on professional matters, but not as a personal friend.

    (v) Communications between high-ranking officers of state.

If the occasion is one of qualified privilege the defence protects only in the absence of malice. This covers statements honestly if mistakenly made. This defence applies when there is a reciprocal interest between the publisher and the recipient, one having a duty to make the statement and the other having an interest in receiving it.

In Watt v Longsdon, 1930, the foreign manager of a company wrote to a director, the defendant, and said that the plaintiff was "a blackguard, a thief and a liar . . . who lived and lives exclusively to satisfy his own passions and lust". The defendant showed this letter to the plaintiff's wife and to the chairman of the board of directors. It was held that the second publication was privileged in the absence of malice, for the person had a duty to warn the chairman, who in turn had an interest in receiving it. Showing the letter to the wife, however, was not privileged because the defendant did not have a sufficient interest or duty, legal, moral or social, to make the communication.

Qualified privilege applies also to reports on parliamentary and judicial proceedings provided they are fair and accurate and to derogatory statements in testimonials and references.

(e) Apology. This defence comes to the rescue of an editor of a newspaper or periodical if defamation has occurred in the absence of malice or gross negligence. For unintentional defamation the defendant may make an offer of amends, i.e. to publish or join in the publication of a suitable correction of the words complained of and a sufficient apology to the aggrieved party. This is provided for in the Defamation Act, 1952.

Chapter 4

STATUTES REGULATING LIABILITIES

4.0 Modification of Common Law

So far, this Text has dealt mainly with liability at comon law, but in this Chapter the effect of various statutes on the law of liability for injury and damage will be summarised. More statutory modifications are dealt with later in conjunction with the particular area of liability, for example in Chapter 6 on liability for defective products the Consumer Protection Act, 1987 and other consumer protection legislation are described.

A statute is superior to all sources of law and judges must enforce this law even though it is contrary to an existing binding precedent at common law. Thus there is the supremacy of Parliament in matters pertaining to the law of the land. From time to time Parliament has seen fit to change or modify the common law in the light of social changes, and this process is a continuing one.

4.1 Death of a Party and Survival of Causes of Action

The death of one (or both) parties to an action in tort can give rise to two main issues. One is the survival of the action after the death and the other concerns the rights of the dependants of, say, a bread winner who was killed as a result of the breach of a duty of care owed to him. The question of whether a cause of action survives the death of the person injured must be distinguished from the issue of any right of action for damages given to his relatives. The former question will be addressed firstly in the following section.

4.2 The Law Reform (Miscellaneous Provisions) Act, 1934

Until 1934 there prevailed the common law maxim "actio personalis moritur cum persona" (a personal action dies with the parties to the cause of action) therefore ordinarily, no executor or administrator of a deceased person's estate could sue or be sued for any tort committed by the deceased or against him, in his lifetime. Thus it was said to be cheaper to kill than to injure or cripple and this anomaly had to be removed. The Law Reform (Miscellaneous Provisions) Act, 1934 (Section 1) provides that ". . . on the death of any person after the commencement of this Act all causes of action subsisting against or vested in him shall survive against, or, as the case may be, for the benefit of, his estate. Provided that this subsection shall not apply to causes of action for defamation. Any cause of action against, for example, a negligent motorist who was himself killed as a result of his own negligence now survives and would have to be satisfied by the motorist's legal personal representatives. Bear in mind also that if the victim dies the action "lives on" for the benefit of the deceased's estate.

"The rights conferred by this Act for the benefit of the estate of deceased persons shall be in addition to and not in derogation of any rights conferred on the dependants of deceased persons by the Fatal Accidents Acts, 1846 to 1908" (Section 5). More will be said about the Fatal Accidents Act (now dated 1976) later. In addition to actions for damages the estate may also bring actions for pain and suffering of the deceased in the interval between incurring the injury and death and for loss of earnings in respect of the same period. However damages recoverable in an action by the legal personal representatives of the deceased shall not include exemplary damages, and the damages are to be calculated without reference to any loss or gain to the estate caused by the death. An example of gain to the estate would be the proceeds of a life assurance policy. It is interesting to note that funeral expenses can be claimed by the estate.

4.3   The Fatal Accidents Act, 1976

This Act which consolidated previous statutes, the earliest of which was dated 1846, gives certain dependants of a deceased person a right of action for a wrongful act causing death. There is a right of action where a person is killed by another and would have had a right of action against the other if he had been merely injured and not killed. This legislation is strictly for dependency and this can be established only by certain relatives defined by the Act. They are: husband, wife, children, grandchildren, step-children, father, mother, step-parents, and grand-parents. It also includes any person who is or who is the issue of, a brother, sister, uncle, or aunt of the deceased. Illegitimate and adopted children are deemed to be children and any relationship of affinity is to be regarded as a relationship of con-sanguinity. Relationship by affinity means by marriage and consanguinity means by blood. Only pecuniary loss is considered and any of the designated relatives claiming must show some pecuniary loss as a result of the death. There is a sufficient pecuniary loss if the relative can show some reasonable expectation of pecuniary benefit and in all events dependency begins to run from the date of death.

Damages are assessed according to the pecuniary loss suffered by each dependant and no action lies for the relatives' mental suffering as a result of the death but there is provision for awards for Bereavement to a much restricted range of relatives, discussed later. In assessing damages the court ascertains the net average weekly earnings of the deceased and deducts from that the cost of keeping the deceased himself. In assessing damages payable to a widow there shall not be taken into account the re-marriage of the widow or her prospects of re-marriage. The Act prohibits deductions from damages in respect of money paid to relatives under insurance policies, pension, gratuities or social security benefits. If the dependants have incurred funeral expenses in respect of the deceased, costs can be awarded. Where any person dies as the result of his own fault and partly the fault of any other person or person, and an action is raised on behalf of his estate under the Law Reform (Miscellaneous Provisions) Act, 1934 and the damages are reduced for contributory negligence, any damages recoverable under the Fatal Accidents Act will be reduced to a proportionate extent.

Bereavement now constitutes a cause of action. An action under this Act may consist of or include such a claim. A claim for bereavement can be brought for the benefit of the wife or husband of the deceased and where the deceased was a minor who was never married, for the benefit of his parents if he was legitimate and for his mother if he was illegitimate. The sum awarded as damages for bereavement is £3,500 and where the award is for the parents of the deceased the sum shall be divided equally between them. The Lord Chancellor has the power to vary the sum of £3,500.

4.4 Possible Overlapping of Claims under Law Reform Act and Fatal Accidents Act

Where the persons claiming as dependant relatives and those claiming as being entitled to the deceased's estate are not the same the actions under the respective Acts are quite separate and there is no overlap in awarding damages. However it is often the case that dependant relatives are also entitled as beneficiaries to the proceeds of the deceased's estate and here the law has to reckon with the possibility of double compensation. Normally in such instances both cases will be dealt with at the same time and in the same court. To avoid double compensation the court will in assessing damages for loss of dependancy under the Fatal Accidents Act, take into account damages received by the estate where this mitigates the loss of dependancy. Note that this allowance does not operate in reverse because damages awarded to the estate under the Law Reform Act are by way of compensation to the deceased for a wrong done to him and it would not be equitable to reduce the award by sums received by dependants under the Fatal Accidents Act.

4.5 Administration of Justice Act, 1982

The provisions of this Act described here relate not only to rights in the event of death but also to liability for damages to injured persons surviving.

Section 1 of the Act implements the recommendations of the Pearson Commission that damages for loss of expectation of life as a separate head of damages should be abolished. The purpose of this award was to compensate the injured party for loss of happiness and moreover right to such damages (of a nominal amount) was vested in his estate in the event of his death. In place of "loss of expectation of life" the Act provides as follows: "If the injured person's expectation of life has been reduced by the injuries, the court, in assessing damages in respect of pain and suffering caused by the injuries, shall take account of any suffering caused or likely to be caused by awareness that his expectation of life has been so reduced". Damages can also take account of distress by a plaintiff who realises that his dependants will be denied the benefits of his care for them. The estate therefore no longer has a claim for loss of expectation of life on behalf of a deceased person but the living plaintiff is entitled to claim damages for "awareness that his expectation of life has been reduced".

Section 2 abolishes actions by a husband for loss of the services or society of his wife and actions by a parent on the ground of his having been deprived of the services of a child.

Section 3 amends the Fatal Accidents Act by enlarging the list of dependant relatives. A former spouse of the deceased can claim and also a person not married to the deceased but living in the same house with him (her) as spouse at the death and for at least two years prior to that date. This amendment reflects trends in our society. Remember that any claimant in this category would have to show pecuniary loss or reasonable expectation thereof.

Section 4 amends the Law Reform Act by providing that the claim for bereavement under the Fatal Accidents Act shall not survive for the benefit of the person claiming, in the event of his/her death.

Section 5. When assessing damages the value of maintenance of an injured person, which is provided by a public authority, should be taken into account.

Section 6. This section makes it possible for the court to award provisional damages for personal injuries, where there is the possibility of further deterioration in the plaintiff's condition in the future. The court can award damages for what is known of the plaintiff's condition and it permits him to claim for damages again later if deterioration takes place. This is a "wait and see" approach to the problem of serious deterioration and whilst it will no doubt benefit the plaintiff it could cause problems for an insurer in the matter of setting aside a reserve for a possible future claim. The implementation of this section was delayed until 1986.

4.6 Limitation of Actions to Prevent Unreasonable Delay

Control over the time available to a plaintiff to bring an action in tort or contract is the subject of legislation because it could be unfair on a defendant to have to bear the prospect of lengthy delay in a potential action bringing uncertainty and difficulty in future planning. The law is intended to ensure that a person may with confidence feel that after a given time he may regard as finally closed an incident which might have led to a claim against him. There is a history of Limitation Acts, described by Lord Kenyond as "statutes of repose", reviewing limitation of time, culminating in the Limitation Act, 1980, a consolidating measure. The principle is that by lapse of time a right of action becomes no longer enforceable.

4.7 The Limitation Act, 1980

This Act provides that an action founded on tort or simple contract shall not be brought after the expiration of six years from the date on which the cause of action accrued. This is the general rule but there are important exceptions. There is a special time limit of three years for actions in respect of personal injury, or which include personal injury and which arise out of negligence, nuisance or breach of duty (whether the duty exists by virtue of a contract or of provision made by or under a statute or independently of any contract or any such provision.)

4.7.1 When the Cause of Action Accrues

Time begins to run against the plaintiff on the date the cause of action accrues, that, in effect, being the earliest time at which an action could be brought. The rules are:

(i) in the case of a tort actionable per se that is without proof of actual damage, e.g. libel, time runs from the date on which the act was committed.

(ii) in torts which are actionable only on proof of damage time runs from the commencement of the damage.

(iii) in the case of Conversion and Detinue time runs from the date of the wrong and not from the date of possession of the goods.

(iv) in a continuing tort such as nuisance time recommences at every fresh instance of the tort occurring from day to day.

(v) in actions for fraud, concealment or mistake time runs from the date that the fraud, concealment or mistake is discovered or could have been discovered with reasonable diligence.

4.7.2   Absence of Knowledge

In respect of actions in respect of personal injury the three year period begins to run from the date the cause of action accrued or the date of knowledge (if later) of the person injured. The "date of knowledge" provision removed a weakness in previous legislation that could cause hardship to plaintiffs suffering from slowly progressive diseases who found their cases statute-barred because they had run out of time before becoming aware of latent disease. This injustice is illustrated in the case of Cartledge v E. Jopling & Sons Ltd., 1963, where the defendant employer who failed to provide efficient ventilation in his factory escaped liability to the plaintiff, his employee, who had contracted pneumoconiosis. The plaintiff was unaware of his condition, through no fault of his own, until more than six years after it developed in him. (At that time the limitation period for personal injury was six years.) "Knowledge" is defined as knowledge:

(a) that the injury is significant,

(b) that it is attributable in whole or in part to an act or omission constituting negligence, nuisance or breach of a statutory duty,

(c) of the identity of the defendant or if it is alleged that the act or omission was that of some person other than the defendant, of the identity of that person.

Actions under the Fatal Accidents Act, 1976 cannot be brought after the expiration of three years from:

(a) the date of death,

(b) the date of knowledge of the person for whose benefit the action is brought, whichever is the later.

Likewise, actions for the benefit of a deceased person's estate under the Law Reform Act are subject to the same "date of knowledge proviso".

4.7.3   Actions Based Upon the Fraud of the Defendant

When the action is based upon the fraud of the defendant, or any fact relevant to the plaintiff's cause of action has been deliberately concealed from him by the defendant, or the action is for relief from the consequences of a mistake, time does not run until the plaintiff has discovered the fraud, concealment or mistake, or could with reasonable diligence have discovered it. However a person who purchases property in good faith and for valuable consideration is not to be prejudiced by this provision.

4.7.4   Legal Disability

Where a potential plaintiff is legally "disabled" from bringing an action, say in the case of a minor or a person of unsound mind at the time the cause of action accrues, the limitation period does not commence until his legal disability ceases, or his death, whichever occurs first. The disability must exist at the time when the cause of action first arises. If time starts to run and then the disability, say insanity, occurs this will not affect or delay the running out of the time. It is possible therefore, for the limitation period to span a considerable number of years in exceptional circumstances. For example if a right of action accrues to a two-year-

43

old infant but no action is taken on his/her behalf at the time, the plaintiff, on reaching legal maturity some sixteen years on has a further three years from that date to raise an action.

4.7.5   Court's Discretion to Set Aside Time Limit

The Act allows the court to exercise its discretion to set aside the time limits to permit actions for personal injuries or death to proceed. The judge, in the exercise of his discretion, is directed to take account of all the circumstances of the case, but especially a number of specific points. These include the extent and causes of the plaintiff's delay and its probable effect upon the evidence in the case, the length of the plaintiff's disability and his conduct once he becomes aware of his possible right to damages. On this latter factor the steps the plaintiff takes to obtain legal advice and any other expert advice and its nature, would have a bearing on the decision. With regard to the defendant, the judge should consider his behaviour after the cause of action arises, including the extent to which he co-operates with the plaintiff in making information available to him.

4.8   The Latent Damages Act 1986

Prior to the Latent Damages Act becoming law in September 1986 the law on latent damage was in a very unsatisfactory state and this was recognised by the House of Lords in Pirelli General Cable Works Ltd. v Oscar Faber and Partners, 1983, 1 ALL ER 65 HL (E). Claims for latent damage that is, damage which remains hidden for some time such as defects in the structure of buildings, could become time barred after six years from the date when cracks occurred. The owner of the building may not discover the defect until many years after time has run out under the Limitation Act. In the Pirelli case the defendants were consultant engineers responsible for designing a tall chimney for the plaintiffs. The inner walls of the chimney were lined with refractory concrete which proved inadequate and it cracked allowing heat to damage the outer skin of the chimney. The chimney was constructed in 1970 and although the cracks appeared only a short time after construction the plaintiffs were not aware of the damage until 1977. They issued a writ in 1978. The House of Lords ruled that the date of discovery was not the correct test to apply to determine, but the date the damage occurred which was some time in 1970 and therefore the case was statute barred. Lord Scarman recognised that the law as it stood operated unfairly against a property owner and recommended amending legislation as the solution. The Latent Damage Act extends the time limit of six years for bringing actions for negligence causing latent damage not involving bodily injury to three years from the time the plaintiff knew or ought to have known facts about the damage (if this is later than six years). The Act bars claims made after fifteen years from the defendant's breach of duty. This long stop period is inapplicable where there is deliberate concealment of the defect. The fifteen year limitation period and the drafting of the "deliberate concealment" clause worries architects and consulting engineers who justifiably fear that claims against them personally could follow them into their retirement and also add to the cost of professional indemnity insurance. The Act extends the right of action to subsequent purchasers of property where they did not or could not know about the damage at the time of purchase.

It remains to be seen how the courts will interpret the terms of this Act, which is considered complex and difficult. Certainly the liabilities of those involved in building construction and the professional liabilities of architects and consulting engineers have been extended.

4.9   The Law Reform (Personal Injuries) Act, 1948

A basic principle of the law of reparation is that a person should not make a profit out of compensation for pecuniary loss. The fact that a plaintiff may have a right to compensation for injury through tort and at the same time be entitled to one or more forms of social security benefits has resulted in a legislative measure to limit to an extent an injured person's opportunity to obtain double payment.

The above Act (as amended by the Social Security Act, 1975) in Section 2 reads: "In an action for damages for personal injury . . . there shall be taken into account, against any loss of earnings or profits which has accrued or probably will accrue to the injured person from the injuries, one half of the value of any right, which has accrued or probably will accrue to therefrom in respect of any of the following benefits under the Social Security Act 1975 . . . namely —
sickness benefit,
invalidity benefit,
non-contributory invalidity pension,
injury benefit
disablement benefit,
for the five years beginning with the time when the cause of action accrued . . .".

In addition to sickness and injury benefit, supplementary benefits and unemployment benefit can be taken into account to reduce the defendant's liability for damages. Note the five-year period only; there is no provision for offsetting benefits after the first five year period of disability. The case of Denman v Essex Area Health Authority, 1984, demonstrates the application of this principle. The court deducted from the damages awarded one half of the total social security benefits paid to the plaintiff amounting to £24,353 for the five year period following the injury. After five years the plaintiff was still drawing social security benefits totalling £4,750 per annum but this was ignored and not used to offset the damages awarded.

Section 3 of the 1948 Act defines "personal injury" as including any disease and any impairment of a person's physical or mental condition.

Section 1 abolished the defence of "common employment" a common law defence which an employer could plead in an action against him by an employee injured by the negligence of a fellow employee. The principle was that the injured employee had no remedy against the employer because he was deemed to accept the risk inherent in working with other employees, a risk common to all of them. This form of defence implying voluntary acceptance of the risks of the workplace could not survive, of course.

4.10   Civil Evidence Act, 1968

At common law a criminal offence could not be used as evidence in civil proceedings to assist a plaintiff to discharge the onus of proof where he was alleging negligence. The effect of Section 11 of the above Act was that if a person is proved to have committed an offence, he shall be deemed to have committed that offence until the contrary is proved. If, therefore, the conviction relates to the incident from which negligence is alleged the burden of disproving negligence rests with the defendant.

4.11 Administration of Justice Act, 1969

This Statute obliges judges hearing personal injury claims to award interest on damages payable to the plaintiff. This is of some significance because actions in tort may take several years to resolve. The principle is that interest is only awarded on money that the plaintiff has been kept out of by the defendant's wrongful act, consequently there is no interest awarded on damages for loss of future earnings. Until this Act took effect interest awards were discretionary only, by virtue of the provisions of the Law Reform (Miscellaneous Provisions) Act, 1934. The following guidelines are the result of the case of Jefford and Another v Gee, 1970:

(i) the interest was payable because the plaintiff had been entitled to the money all along,

(ii) the plaintiff had been kept out of the money to which he was entitled,

(iii) no interest to be allowed on damages for future loss of earnings. This is equitable because the plaintiff has not been kept out of money under this head,

(iv) interest on Special Damages to be allowed from the date of accident until the date of trial at half the appropriate rate.

(v) interest on damages for pain and suffering and loss of amenities to run, at the full rate, from the date of service of the writ to the date of trial. The object here is to encourage the plaintiff's advisers to serve the writ without undue delay.

(vi) in Fatal Accident Act cases interest for pecuniary loss is at half the rate and is awarded from the date of death to the date of trial. No interest is payable on awards for future loss from the date of trial.

(vii) the rate of interest should be that rate which was payable on money in court, which was placed on short-term investment account. The average rate is taken for the period for which it was awarded.

It is only compulsory to award interest on court judgements. It is different with settlements out of court and in fact the parties may agree expressly that no interest be included.

Chapter 5

LIABILITY AT LAW FOR DAMAGES

5.0 Damages or Compensation

Damages is the recompense given by process of law to a person for the wrong done to him by another. The ideology is "to make the defendant pay" and this usually means making up for the loss caused by means of cash payment, this being the most common remedy in the law of tort. Whilst the law of tort is primarily concerned with providing indemnity to the wronged party and not punishment of the wrongdoer, nevertheless in some instances an award of damages fulfils not only the function of compensation but imposes a measure of punishment as well, i.e. in the case of punitive or exemplary damages. It follows that by awarding damages the court deters the defendant and others from injurious conduct in the future.

In the law of contract the most common remedy for breach of contract is also damages.

In this chapter the classification of damages in Tort and the principles relating thereto will be examined and also the factors governing the asssessment of damages.

5.1 Classifications of Damages

The various types of damages may be placed into two categories: (i) general damages and special damages; (ii) nominal, real (or substantial), contemptuous, exemplary and aggravated damages.

5.1.1 Special Damages Distinguished From General Damages

Special damage is that damage in respect of which the plaintiff can give a precise pecuniary estimate, or which can be quantified at the time of trial. Special damage must be strictly pleaded and proved to the court whereas general damages do not require strict pleading, being at the discretion of the judge. The defendants must have due notice of the claim for special damages otherwise the plaintiff will not be allowed to pursue it. Damages capable of being precisely quantified as special damages would include such items as loss of earnings and hospital expenses. Likewise items such as the cost of repairing a car following an accident would constitute special damages. The feature of special damages is that they relate to things that are past whereas general damages ordinarily compensate for future losses, i.e. those which cannot be quantified before the trial. Examples of claims under the head of general damages include pain and suffering, loss of future earnings, loss of amenity, a trader's loss of future profit and, returning to the motor accident example, loss of use of the car in the future. Note that loss of earnings up to the date of the trial is special damages whereas loss of future earnings constitutes general damages. In British Transport Commission v Gourley, 1956, Lord Goddard made the following distinction:

> "In an action for personal injuries the damages are always divided into two main parts. Firstly there is what is referred to as special damage, which has to be specially pleaded and proved. This consists of out-of-pocket expenses and loss of

earnings incurred down to the date of trial, and is generally capable of sub-
stantially exact calculation. Secondly there is general damage which the law
implies and is not specially pleaded. This includes compensation for pain and
suffering and the like, and, if the injuries suffered are such as to lead to continuing or permanent disability, compensation for loss of earning power in the
future. The basic principle so far as loss of earnings and out-of-pocket expenses
are concerned is that the injured person should be in the same financial position,
so far as can be done by an award of money, as he would have been had the
accident not happened."

The student will recall that the Administration of Justice Act, 1969, provides for
interest to be awarded in personal injury cases where the plaintiff has been kept
out of money (Chapter 4: 4.10).

5.1.2   Nominal Damages

An infringement of a legal right may occur but no damage may be sustained by
the plaintiff. In such circumstances the court may award a small sum, for example
£1.00, to mark the vindication of that right. Nominal damages are recoverable only
in torts which are actionable per se, for example in libel and in certain cases of
slander. Another example is trespass to land where no actual physical damage or
other loss is suffered by the plaintiff. In Ashby v White, 1703, nominal damages
were awarded against the defendant, a returning officer at an election, who wrongfully and maliciously refused the plaintiff's vote even though the candidate he
intended to vote for won the election. In Constantine v Imperial London Hotels,
1944, the plaintiff, a famous West Indian cricketer, was awarded nominal damages
of £5.00 because the defendants refused him admission to one of their hotels. The
defendants in fact provided him with accommodation at another of their hotels.

5.1.3   Real or Substantial Damages

In awarding real damages the objective is to put the person whose right has been
invaded in the same position as if it had not been — restitution in tegrum. Exact
indemnity is not always possible and there are some types of damage where it is
not possible to give true compensation by awarding money, for example in the case
of pain and suffering. In such cases the court can only award a monetary sum that
it considers fair and reasonable. In actions in negligence, damage must be proved
and it is the court's task to determine the measure of compensation in each case.

5.1.4   Contemptuous Damages

Where the court considers the plaintiff, in bringing the action, is being frivolous
or vindictive it may award derisory or contemptuous damages, usually amounting
to the smallest coin of the Realm (1p). In effect the court, whilst recognising the
plaintiff's right to succeed, wishes to show its disapproval of his conduct in
bringing the action. Moreover, the plaintiff is unlikely to be awarded costs.

In Newstead v London Express Newspapers, 1940, described as a "gold-digging'
action for defamation the plaintiff was awarded one farthing.

5.1.5   Exemplary Damages

Damages awarded over and above real damages with the purpose of punishing the defendant or making an example of him are termed exemplary damages or variously, punitive damages and vindictive damages. These may be awarded where the defendant's conduct was outrageous, for example fraud, cruelty, malice or the like. There has been some uneasiness in the past regarding this function of the civil courts in meting out punishment, without the in-built safeguards of criminal law procedure. Moreover there is the anomaly that money taken from a defendant by way of punishing him becomes a windfall to the plaintiff and awards may be excessive. As a result of Rookes v Barnard, 1946, a House of Lords decision, the courts in awarding exemplary damages are restricted to the following exceptional cases:

   (i) express authorisation by statute,
  (ii) oppressive, arbitrary or unconstitutional conduct by government servants,
 (iii) conduct calculated to result in profit for the defendant.

In the Rooks v Barnard case Lord Devlin in approving the award of exemplary damages said: " the defendant's conduct has been calculated by him to make a profit for himself which may exceed the compensation payable to the plaintiff".

In Cassel v Broome, 1972, the House of Lords upheld an award of £25,000 as exemplary damages against the defendant who published a book knowing that it contained defamatory statements, in order to make a profit for themselves.

5.1.6   Aggravated Damages

Aggravated damages may be awarded where the defendant's conduct was such that the plaintiff deserves more than ordinary damages to compensate him for the unpleasant manner in which the tort was committed. The plaintiff may be compensated for injured feelings or, for instance if trespass to land occurs and the trespasser creates an inordinate noise or disturbance. In Bisney v Swanston, 1972, the defendant parked his trailer in the car park of a transport cafe spitefully in order to cause the maximum possible interference to the cafe business. In addition to ordinary damages for loss of business the court awarded £250.00 aggravated damages. Aggravated damages are always compensatory and not punitive and in that aspect they can be distinguished from exemplary damages.

5.2   Measure of Damages

Now we shall look at the factors determining the measurement of damages or the means of trying to place the wronged party in the same position as he was in before his right was invaded (restitutio in tegrum). Bear in mind that for certain types of loss a perfect compensation is not possible, e.g. where the plaintiff has lost an eye. In such instances restitution becomes merely compensation in terms of money. Some personal injuries are so severe that no amount of monetary payment can be an adequate compensation and the courts merely attempt to be fair and reasonable, given that it is impossible to standardise damages. The courts are guided by reference to the general run of assessments for similar cases in the past with due allowance for inflation. Assessment of damages is a matter for the judges and only rarely and in very exceptional cases will a jury be called upon to undertake this task.

Measurement of damages may be classified under (a) injury to the person and (b) damages to property.

5.2.1 Damages for Personal Injuries

In assessing damages for personal injuries, two main factors have to be considered, namely, the actual physical loss suffered, like loss of a limb, and financial loss. In Fair v London and North Western Railway Co., 1869, Cockburn, C. J. said: "In assessing damages the jury should take into account two things; first, the pecuniary loss the plaintiff sustains; secondly the injury he sustains in his person, or in his physical capacity for enjoying life. When they come to the consideration of the pecuniary loss they have to take into account not only his present loss, but his incapacity to earn a future improved income".

5.2.1A Damages for Actual Physical Injury

Included in the assessment of damages under this head are pain and suffering endured, past, present and future, loss of amenity sustained, past, present and future and the effect on the health of the sufferer.

The plaintiff is entitled to compensation both for pain and suffering up to the date of the trial and for such as he will experience in the future. The duration of the suffering is important and also the state of consciousness of the victim. No award for pain and suffering is made where the plaintiff is rendered unconscious and remains so (Wise v Kaye, 1962). Damages can include an award for the mental anguish the plaintiff suffers in knowing that his expectation of life has been reduced or that his ability to enjoy life has been reduced.

Where nervous shock accompanies physical injury damages can be allowed as part of pain and suffering. Included also under this head is post traumatic neurosis which indicates effect on the central nervous system. The symptoms of a post accident neurosis include a change of personality, loss of confidence, listlessness, nightmares, loss of sleep, a fear of heights and loss of confidence while driving a motor vehicle.

Damages for pain and suffering are not capable of precise calculation and must necessarily be a matter of degree. In Philips v London and South Western Railway, 1879, Bramwell L. J. stated: ". . . you must give him (the plaintiff) compensation for his pain and bodily suffering; of course it is almost impossible for you (the jury) to give an injured man what can be strictly called a compensation; but you must take a reasonable view of the case, and must consider, under all the circumstances, what is a fair amount to be awarded to him".

Damages for loss of the amenities of life are quite distinct from awards for pain and suffering and may represent permanent loss of amenity (a limb, for example) or temporary loss such as a term in hospital. Dependence on the help of others or inability to take part in games are other examples of loss of amenity. The age of the person has to be taken into account because an elderly person will not suffer the same loss as a young man. In Heaps v Perrite Ltd., 1937, Greer, L. J. said of the plaintiff who had lost both hands". . . the joy of life will have gone from him. He cannot ride a bicycle, cannot kick a football. At any rate, if he can kick a football he cannot catch one. He cannot have any of the usual forms of recreation which appeal to the ordinary healthy man".

Disfigurement may feature in awards for loss of amenity, especially where a young woman is disfigured. The court will take a more serious view where the disfigurement impairs career or marriage prospects or where it causes the victim to avoid social occasions. Once a plaintiff has been deprived of the amenities of life the fact that he cannot appreciate the extent of his deprivation is no ground for reducing the damages to be awarded. The plaintiff's unconsciousness is not relevant in these instances but you will recollect that it has a bearing in claims for pain and suffering.

In recent years the courts have grappled with the problems of impairment to health resulting from the victim's exposure to industrial dusts including asbestos and to excessive noise. The main elements of damages in these cases are usually pain and suffering and loss of active life resulting from permanent damage to lungs or from hearing deficiency.

5.2.1B   Damages For Financial Loss

Financial or pecuniary loss following injury comprises two different types, one negative e.g. deprivation of earnings and the other positive, being the extra expenses incurred as a result of the injury. Loss of earnings and expenses incurred up to the date of the trial can be calculated easily and will be awarded as special damages but future loss of earnings and prospective expenses in the future are not so easily assessed. The latter constitute part of the general damages award.

In assessing loss of earnings the plaintiff's tax liability is taken account of and net earnings only used in the calculation. Net earnings means that national insurance contributions are deducted. In Cooper v Firth Brown Ltd., 1963, Lord Goddard directed the jury thus: ". . . It seems to me that the object of damages is to compensate the plaintiff for what he has lost, and what he has lost is what would have been in his pay packet when he took it home". Calculations of damages for the period up to the trial becomes a matter of multiplying the net weekly wage or salary by the number of weeks on incapacity. The sum realised may have to be reduced if there is any possibility that the plaintiff may have been unable to earn the same wages for reasons other than the injury, e.g. a recession in the particular employment.

On the other hand, assessing pecuniary loss in the future is a more complicated matter. The main item will usually be loss of future income or, in fatal cases, loss of dependency. In assessing loss of future earnings it is the practice to firstly estimate the number of years of working life that would have been left to the plaintiff had there been no injury. The annual sum of lost earnings (termed the multiplicand) is multiplied by the estimated number of years of working life (the multiplier) and a lump sum arrived at. In practice the maximum multiplier is eighteen years even in cases where the subject has, in actuarial terms, a much longer life expectancy. The multiplier applied is also usually less than the full period of the expected loss because the plaintiff receives the damages in a lump sum with the consequent advantages of investment income. Some examples of courts' application of the multiplier are:

(i) Life expectancy 10 years: multiplier 7;

(ii) Life expectancy 39 years: multiplier 14 but reduced to 9 because of favourable chance of recovering earning capacity;

(iii) Life expectancy 36 years: working life expectancy 30 years: multiplier 14.

The problem with a once-and-for-all lump sum is the effect on the capital of future inflation. There is no doubt that any award given in the period since the second world war to cover future loss of earnings would inevitably be reduced in value by the fall in the purchasing power of money over the longer term and thus result in under-compensation. The courts have not been prepared to take inflation into account and to suggest that the plaintiff can invest the capital sum at the prevailing rate of interest is not a complete answer to the problem. Where the injury is such that the victim's life expectancy has been curtailed there is the question of allowing for loss of earnings for the "additional" years he would normally have lived but for his injury i.e. "the lost years". The principle is that loss of earnings can be recovered for the lost years with an appropriate deduction for the expenses of maintaining the plaintiff.

A plaintiff is entitled to recover all medical expenses reasonably incurred in the treatment of his injuries, including medical fees, the cost of surgical appliances, drugs etc. Even the cost of a holiday if considered part of the treatment and as convalescence is admissible. The cost of nursing (apart from the foregoing) and constant attendance in the case of serious and permanent injuries is admissible and this future expense will be capitalised in the same way as loss of future earnings.

5.2.1C   Offset to Damages

The plaintiff's tax liability and his national insurance payments have already been referred to as deductible when calculating loss of earnings (see 5.2.1B above). What of other payments or benefits which accrue to the plaintiff as a result of his injury and which are independent of any damages awarded? The courts, in endeavouring to provide indemnity in awarding damages do not deduct as offsets all benefits and therefore to some extent the principle of exact compensation is compromised. Possible benefits are:

(i) Payment by an employer as occupational sick pay: this is deducted when calculating the measure of damages;

(ii) Social security benefits. Under the Law Reform (Personal Injuries) Act, 1948 (see Chapter 4) one half of certain benefits for the first five years is offset. Unemployment benefit is deducted. On the other hand supplementary benefit is not deducted on the doubtful ground that the payment is discretionary.

(iii) Insurance policy benefits: These are not offset, the rationale being that the plaintiff has paid for this himself and his prudence in arranging cover should not be of benefit to the wrongdoer.

5.2.1D   Assessment of Damages on Death

The method of assessment of damages for dependants under the Fatal Accidents Act (Chapter 4) is much the same as that adopted for loss of prospective earnings for living plaintiffs, with the difference that the multiplicand is not the net annual earnings but the net contribution to the support of the plaintiff. The court has to estimate how long the plaintiff would have continued to benefit out of the deceased's future income and decide upon a multiplier which will produce a total sum which effectively reduces the total loss to its present value. Other possibilities such as illness or accident, or possible promotion at work resulting in increased support, have to be taken into account. One factor, the possibility of a widow remarrying, must not be used to reduce damages, by virtue of the Law Reform (Miscellaneous Provisions) Act, 1971. Where the contribution by the deceased takes the form of services e.g. in the case of a deceased housewife, the court will convert this into money and allow accordingly. Any damages given under the Law Reform (Miscellaneous Provisions) Act 1934 will be deducted from a defendant's claim under the Fatal Accidents Act. Section 4 of the Fatal Accidents Act, 1976 provides that in assessing damages in respect of a person's death in any action under the Fatal Accidents Act there shall not be taken into account any insurance money, pension or gratuity which has been or will be paid as a result of the death. No deduction is made for a dwelling house or furniture if the dependant had the use of such before the death and continues to enjoy that use afterwards.

5.2.1E   Administration of Justice Act, 1982
Provision for Periodic Review

The once-and-for-all lump sum award is subject to a number of criticisms. It may be to the disadvantage of the plaintiff whose faculties deteriorate unexpectedly after the award is made. Either side of the dispute may wish to delay the action in order to benefit from a change in the victim's condition for the better or worse. The system may disadvantage the defendant because the judges, aware that the case will not be reviewed again may come down on the side of generosity to the plaintiff and should the plaintiff effect a rapid recovery after the award the defendant cannot ask the court later for repayment.

The Pearson Commission, in 1978, recommended that provision for periodic payments of damages for claims of "serious and lasting" injury affecting earning capacity or causing substantial pecuniary loss, be implemented. It was suggested that the once-and-for-all assessment be made only in cases where a court was satisfied upon the application of the plaintiff that a lump sum would be more appropriate. As a result of the Commission recommendations, Section 6 of the Administration of Justice Act 1982 will empower the Court to issue a declatory judgement in favour of the plaintiff permitting a review of the award, in the event of serious deterioration in his physical or mental condition. The case can thus be reopened and a further award of damages made, as appropriate. Section 6 will take effect on such day as the Lord Chancellor may by order appoint and it will have effect retrospectively. It will apply to "actions whenever commenced, including actions commenced before the passing of this Act" (S.73.2). Outstanding cases where the chance of deterioration exists will therefore be subject to this provision.

5.2.2 Damage to Chattels

The term "chattels" means all forms of tangible property including money, cheques and other negotiable instruments but not including land. In general the measure of compensation is the difference between the value of the chattel as damaged and the value before the damage occurred. In cases of partial damage this will be the cost of repair plus any depreciation in value, or where there is better-ment, less the amount of increase in value as a result of new parts replacing old ones. In addition, any reasonable expenditure in hiring a substitute chattel will be allowed. In the event of the chattel being completely destroyed or damaged beyond repair the measure of damages is its market value or the cost of replacement plus any consequential loss. The latter could include the expense of obtaining a substitute and the business interruption cost due to loss of the chattel. For temporary deprivation of a chattel a plaintiff can recover for the loss of use and for other expenses arising from the deprivation including the cost of hiring a replacement.

5.2.2A Damages for Conversion

Conversion is defined as an intentional dealing with a chattel which is seriously inconsistent with the possession or right to immediate possession of another person. It is concerned with a person's title to personal property and the tort requires an intentional dealing with a chattel which constitutes a sufficiently serious infringement on the plaintiff's right to possess that chattel as to amount to a denial of it. An example is a person hiring a car under a self-drive hire agree-ment and then selling it and keeping the proceeds of the sale.

Section 3 of the Torts (Interference with Goods) Act, 1977 provides for three possible remedies for conversion:

 (i) an order for delivery of the goods and for payment of consequential damages.

 (ii) an order for delivery of the goods or the defendant may pay damages representing the value of the goods plus payment of consequential damages in either case.

 (iii) damages.

Assessment of damages is based on market value, or if the chattel has no market value, its replacement value. A person with less than full legal ownership, for example a bailee, who had actual possession of the chattel is entitled to recover the whole value of the chattel and not merely to the extent of his interest. The balance recovered is deemed to be held in trust for the person entitled to it.

5.2.2B Damage to Land and Buildings

The plaintiff is entitled to full restitution for his loss as in the case of chattels. The measure of damages is the depreciation in selling value and where applicable special damages such as loss of profits.

Where a building is damaged, the plaintiff is entitled to the cost of repair and any depreciation in the market value i.e. the drop in the market value of the building as repaired. In addition the cost of obtaining alternative accommodation and any consequential loss can be recovered. The measure of damages for wrongful occu-pation of land is the depreciation in the market value of the land and the rental value of the land during the time of the occupation.

Chapter 6

LIABILITY FOR DEFECTIVE PRODUCTS: UNITED KINGDOM AND OVERSEAS

6.0 Liability Arising out of Goods and Services Supplied at Home and Abroad

Potential legal liabilities arising out of the sale or supply of goods and services both in the United Kingdom and in a selected number of overseas countries will be examined in this Chapter. The laws on liability for defects in products is subject to development and change and the Student is advised to keep abreast of this by reference to the national press and to legal and insurance journals. So far as the United Kingdom is concerned, the enactment of the E.E.C. Directive on strict liability is imminent and this will have important consequences for producers of products. The legal liability in the United Kingdom arising out of the sale or supply of goods will be dealt with here by considering firstly the common law and the modifications by statute and then the implications for producers with the coming in of the strict liability as required by the Directive. The legal liability of exporters of goods to the USA and to Europe is important and will be looked at also.

6.1 Manufacturers' and Vendors' Liability in the United Kingdom

At common law, it was assumed in general terms that the parties to a sale of goods or services had full freedom to agree or to decide between themselves the terms of any contract. The rule relating to the sale of goods is "caveat emptor" (let the buyer beware). This principle, which is based upon the premise that the buyer had the opportunity of satisfying himself as to the quality of the goods he proposed to buy, often operated harshly against the buyer who commonly was in no position to obtain satisfaction from the seller. The Infants Relief Act, 1873 protected people under 21 (now people under 18) from the consequences of contracts with unscrupulous traders and from their own folly but the first general recognition that frequently suppliers and potential customers of goods could not be said to meet on level terms was evidenced by the passing of the Sale of Goods Act, 1893. This Act was amended by the Supply of Goods (Implied Terms) Act, 1973. In turn, the law as amended by both statutes was consolidated into a single statute, the Sale of Goods Act, 1979.

6.1.1 The Liability in Negligence

Consumer protection has been a growth industry in the 1970's and '80's and this trend does not look like diminishing. It is important to note that the remedies available to the consumer or user given by the Sale of Goods Act, 1979 are for the benefit of the buyer, a party to the contract, and not for any person who is not a party to the contract of sale. Should the latter suffer loss his remedy lies in a common law action in negligence. The position of the person who is not a contractual party is improved with the advent of strict liability. The new legislation on strict liability is not in place of the existing liability in contract and tort but is in addition.

At this point we are considering the product liability situation at common law before strict liability came via the Statute Book. The common law liability takes its direction mainly from the dictum of Lord Atkin in Donoghue v Stevenson, 1932, vis:

"A manufacturer of products, which he sells in such a form as to show that he intends them to reach the ultimate consumer in the form in which they left him with no reasonable possibility of intermediate examination and with the knowledge that the absence of reasonable care in the preparation or putting up of the products will result in an injury to the consumer's life or property, owes a duty to the consumer to take that reasonable care."

The defendant was a manufacturer of aerated waters (see also Chapter 2, 2.4.2.) and was sued by the plaintiff for injuries she suffered as a result of drinking part of the contents of a bottle of ginger beer, which, it was alleged, contained the decomposed remains of a snail. The bottle of ginger beer had been purchased for the plaintiff by her friend whilst visiting a cafe owned by one V. Mincella. The bottle was of dark opaque glass and the plaintiff had no reason to suspect that it contained anything but pure ginger beer. As a result of the nauseating sight of the snail floating out of the bottle after she had consumed some of the contents and in consequence of the impurities in the ginger beer Mrs. Donoghue suffered from shock and severe gastroenteritis. She alleged that Stevenson, the defendant, had failed in his duty to provide an efficient system of inspection of the bottles before being filled and a system of working which would not allow snails to get into bottles. The case was brought in negligence against the manufacturer and not in contract against Mincella because the injured party had not in fact purchased the product herself, consequently there was no privity of contract between her and the cafe owner. Although the case never went to proof, the House of Lords established the "neighbour" principle (see 2.4.2) and Mrs. Donoghue was paid damages out of court. The word "manufacturer" in this context has since been enlarged to include assemblers, repairers, suppliers, erectors, installers and inspectors and certifiers of buildings. The manufacturers' duty at common law is not restricted to defective food and drinks but also to a wide range of products, for example, buildings, chemicals, tombstones, motor vehicles, hair dyes, underwear etc. It also covers cases where the offending element is not a foreign body in the product but something intrinsically part of it, e.g. a bone in a chicken sandwich.

The manufacturer will be liable to the consumer or user in the event of his failure to take reasonable care in the manufacture of his product provided the product causing the injury has the same defect as it contained when it left the manufacturer and the manufacturer should have contemplated that the product would be consumed or used in the same condition as it was when it left him. Where there is privity of contract the plaintiff may then choose whether to bring the action in contract or in tort or perhaps even both.

6.1.2   The Sale of Goods Act, 1979

The Sale of Goods Act, 1979 introduced no new law whatsoever but consolidated previous statutes dealing with the protection of the buyer.

Section 12: Warranties of Title. There is an implied condition on the part of the seller of goods that in the case of a sale, he has a right to sell the goods and in the case of an agreement to sell, he will have a right to sell at the time when the property is to pass. Moreover there is an implied warranty that the goods are free, and will remain free from any charge or encumbrance not disclosed or known to the buyer before the contract is made and that the buyer will enjoy quiet possession of the goods. The buyer should therefore buy with more confidence as to his rights to possession after the purchase. The term "quiet possession" is not defined. The obligation under Section 12 cannot be excluded or restricted by agreement (Unfair Contract Terms Act, 1977).

Section 13: Warranty of Description. In a sale by description there is an implied condition that the goods shall correspond with the description. A typical example of a sale by description would be a sale of a quantity of fertiliser described as having added to it a certain proportion of magnesium sulphate intended to correct a deficiency of magnesium in the soil. If the fertiliser supplied contained the weed-killer sodium chlorate instead, the seller would be in breach of Section 13. In Roberts & Co. v Yule, 1896, machinery merchants sold a second-hand four horse power gas engine described as "in excellent order" to the purchaser for £47.10s. The buyer found that the engine required an expenditure of £8.10s. on it to make it function properly. It was held that the buyer was entitled to reject the engine because it did not conform to the description.

Section 14: Warranties as to Quality. As a general rule, it is the responsibility of the buyer to satisfy himself that the goods which he is buying are of the quality which he requires and are fit for the purpose for which he needs them (caveat emptor). However there are three exceptions to this rule provided under the headings: (i) Merchantable Quality, (ii) Fitness for a particular purpose, and (iii) Usage. Contracting out of these implied undertakings is strictly limited.

(i) Merchantable Quality. Where the seller sells goods in the course of a business, there is an implied condition that the goods supplied are of merchantable quality, except that there is no such condition —
   (a) as regards defects specifically drawn to the buyer's attention before the contract is made; or
   (b) if the buyer examines the goods before the contract is made, as regards defects which examination ought to reveal.

"Merchantable Quality" is defined in the Act as "If they are as fit for the purpose or purposes for which goods of that kind are commonly bought as it is reasonable to expect having regard to any description applied to them, the price (if relevant) and any other relevant circumstances". In Brown & Son v Craiks Ltd., 1970, the plaintiffs purchased a quantity of rayon cloth from Craiks, intending to resell it for dress material and Brown sued Craiks on the grounds of failure of merchantable quality and also that the cloth was not fit for the particular purpose. The claim failed on the merchantable quality issue because the cloth was reasonably capable of being used and was saleable for a number of industrial purposes. The claim in respect of unfitness for a particular purpose also failed because Brown could not prove that they had informed Craiks of the particular purpose for which they required the cloth. Goods may be of "merchantable quality" therefore without being fit for the purpose for which the buyer requires them. The words "relevant circumstances" in the definition mean that different standards of merchantable quality can be applied, for example to new and second-hand goods. An antique clock, for example, may be sold for a con-

57

siderable price, but if the buyer complains that it is not a very good time-keeper, the seller can rely upon the age of the clock as a relevant circumstance. Likewise a new watch can be purchased for as little as £5.00 and its price would be relevant to its standard of time-keeping and therefore its merchantable quality. The seller is liable if goods are not of merchantable quality even if he is not negligent. Freedom from fault is no defence under the Sale of Goods Act.

(ii) Fitness for a particular purpose. The provisions differ according to whether the sale is an ordinary sale or a sale on credit terms. In the case of an ordinary sale, where the seller sells goods in the course of business and the buyer, expressly or by implication, makes known to the seller any particular purpose for which the goods are being bought, there is an implied condition that the goods supplied under the contract are reasonably fit for that purpose, whether or not that is a purpose for which such goods are commonly supplied, except where the circumstances show that the buyer does not rely, or that it is unreasonable for him to rely, on the skill and judgement of the seller.

The provision relating to a sale on credit terms covers the situation where a "credit broker" (e.g. a retailer) sells goods to a finance company which then sells them to the retailer's customer (the buyer) on credit terms. The buyer has the benefit of the same implied condition as to fitness for a particular purpose, provided he makes that purpose known to the credit broker with the same exceptions as above. A case illustrating undertaking of fitness is Buchanan and Carswell v Eugene Ltd., 1936. The plaintiffs who were hair-dressers bought an electric hair drying machine from Eugene Ltd., manufacturers and suppliers of hairdressing appliances. Mrs. P, a customer of the plaintiffs, was injured by the machine when it was in use and in an action against Buchanan and Carswell recovered damages. Buchanan and Carswell sued Eugene to reccover these damages on the ground that Eugene had supplied a machine that was not reasonably fit for the purpoose for which it was required. It was held that an action based on unfitness for a particular purpose was relevant and that the plaintiffs would therefore, if they succeeded in proving that there had been a breach of the implied condition, be entitled to an award of damages.

The onus of proof is on the seller because the courts presume reliance on the seller's skill and judgement where the goods are purchased for their normal and obvious purpose and only when the intended use is out of the ordinary is the case that the buyer is required to expressly intimate the intended use in order to get the protection of this implied condition.

(iii) Usage. An implied condition or warranty as to quality or fitness for a particular purpose may be annexed to a contract of sale by usage.

Section 15: Sale by Sample. A sale is a sale by sample where there is an express or implied term to that effect in the contract (not merely because a sample has been exhibited and has induced the sale). In a sale by sample there are three implied conditions thus:

(i) That the bulk will correspond with the sample in quality;

(ii) That the buyer will have a reasonable opportunity of comparing the bulk with the sample and

(iii) That the goods will be free from any defect, making them unmerchantable, which would not be apparent on reasonable examination of the sample.

In Godley v Perry, 1960, the plaintiff, G, a boy of six was injured when firing a stone from a toy plastic catapult which he had purchased in P's shop and he lost an eye. The catapult, manufactured in Hong Kong was one of a quantity bought by P's wife from a wholesaler, who had, in turn, bought from an importer. Both P's wife and the wholesaler had tested one of the catapults at the time they made their respective purchases. G brought an action against P and P in turn sued the wholesaler who then sued the importer. All succeeded and the cases against the wholesaler and the importer were based on the implied term in Section 15 that the goods should be free from any defect, making them unmerchantable, which would not be apparent on reasonable examination of the sample.

6.1.3 Restrictions on Contracting Out of Liability

The Sale of Goods Act restricts people's rights to contract out of the Act provisions. Any "consumer contract" clause is void if it purports to exclude the buyer's right to goods which are both "merchantable" and "reasonably fit for the purpose supplied". This restriction also applies to warranty of title. Section 3 of the Unfair Contract Terms Act 1977 states: "This section applies as between contracting parties where one of them deals as a consumer or on the other's written standard terms of business". "As against that party, the other cannot by reference to any contract term — (a) when himself in breach of contract, exclude or restrict any liability of his in respect of the breach" — Section 3.

Contracting out of liability for selling substandard products and unsafe products is not possible in the case of consumer sales. For a person dealing other than as a consumer liability can be restricted or excluded only where the contract terms satisfy the requirement of reasonableness. The law is not so protective of the business buyer, therefore. In the terms governing a "business sale" the seller cannot contract out of the warranty of title but can do so in the case of merchantable quality, description, fitness for purpose and sample, provided the terms meet the test of reasonableness. The seller must prove that the contractual term was reasonable at the time the contract was made, otherwise it will have no legal effect. In general the only people who can rely upon the contracts are the parties to them and no one can obtain rights to a contract to which he is a stranger. There is never any reason why a party involved in a business sale should not insert a clause restricting liability: it may be effective. The courts are more likely to uphold a limitation clause than an exclusion clause.

6.1.4 The Supply of Goods and Services Act, 1982

This Act implies the same terms relating to safety, quality and reliability into contracts for work and materials (e.g. house repairs, vehicle repairs, building) and contracts of hire. In the past bailees of hired property often had to assume onerous responsibility for damage to the property, howsoever caused. Henceforth, hirers out of products and services including after sales services are under the same obligations to their customers as sellers of products. The customer no longer needs to persuade the garage which repairs his car or the television service engineer that they are obliged to carry out the work carefully and safely.

6.1.5 The Consumer Credit Act, 1974

The phrase "consumer credit" has several definitions in the Act but in effect "consumer" denotes the ordinary citizen who requires goods for his own use while "credit" indicates that he has insufficient resources to purchase and obtains finance by way of a loan or some other similar transaction from another party who is in business for that purpose. The consumer may be an individual or partnership but the Act does not apply to a registered company however small. Most of the provisions of the Act do not apply if the amount of credit exceeds £15,000 (cases above this amount must be determined by common law).

Section 75 of the Act provides that if the debtor or consumer has a claim against the supplier of the goods or services in respect of a misrepresentation or breach of contract he has also a claim against the creditor, for example a hire purchase company. This means that finance companies can be responsible for repair or replacement of faulty goods and also for claims in respect of bodily injury or damage to property arising out of faulty goods in respect of which they are providing finance. Any organisation providing finance for consumer credit business must be alive to the potential product liabilities falling on it as a result of this legislation.

6.1.6 Consumer Safety Act, 1978

This Act vests in the Secretary of State powers to make safety regulations relating to composition, design, construction, finishing and packaging, testing and inspection. The object is to exercise control over the safety of goods before they go on the market for consumption. The Act excludes food, feeding stuffs and fertilisers, medicinal products and controlled drugs because these are the subject of other regulations. A breach of the regulations is a criminal offence and of course it also creates a civil liability.

Despite the operation of the regulations the consumer associations were far from satisfied, maintaining that services often fall short of what is desired. The Act did not provide the necessary "teeth" they said and consumer goods especially toys frequently brought misery. Even stricter measures were necessary and consequently the Consumer Safety (Amendment) Act 1986 was implemented giving new and sweeping powers to deal with unsafe goods before they reach the public. For example Customs can retain for forty eight hours goods suspected of being in breach of safety provisions.

Both of the above Statutes have now been repealed by the Consumer Protection Act, 1987 (see 6.1.7I).

6.1.7 Background to Strict Liability

The inadequacies of compensation law in the United Kingdom were highlighted by the findings of the Winn Committee in the mid sixties and by the Pearson Commission in 1978. Justice was not always seen to be done and the UK law was at variance with the majority of Western nation systems in expecting product risks to be borne in the main by the victim. The Loach case (described in the *Sunday Times* 8-2-76) is an illustration of the distressing state of the law, post Donoghue v Stevenson. A car crash on the M1 motorway in May 1971 killed Ken Loach's five-year-old son, seriously injured his wife, killed her 84-year-old grandmother, broke Loach's jaw and emotionally injured his other small son. It was established beyond dispute that the accident was caused by a wheel falling off another car and that the Loaches were totally blameless. The wheel collapsed as a result of a crack, causing the car to crash into the Loaches' car. Examination revealed that the wheel had been cracked behind the hubcap to the extent of about five inches for some time previously and the crack suddenly extended itself to some twenty-two inches, around the disc resulting in collapse as it approached the Loaches' car. The owner had bought the nine-year-old car just one month previously and received an M.O.T. certificate with it. He could not be held to be negligent for failing to know about a concealed flaw in his car. There was no evidence of a breach of duty on the part of the seller, the garage, nor by the M.O.T. tester. The police did not think that the tester could be expected to remove all hubcaps and examine the wheel discs when doing an M.O.T. test. An action against the manufacturer would fail as being too remote. To argue that the wheel disintegrated because of some inherent deficiency which the manufacturers should have foreseen would be very difficult since the product had been in use for nine years. After five years of litigation the Loaches were not only without compensation but had to pay legal costs.

It was time to extend the strict liability for products applicable to contracting parties under the Sale of Goods Act to the wider field of users generally and in any case membership of the European Community meant that there was no longer an option.

6.1.7A The EEC Directive on Strict Liability and Its Implementation in the United Kingdom: The Consumer Protection Act 1987

The EEC Directive No. 85/374/EEC dated 25th July 1985 on the approximation of the laws, regulations and administration provisions of the Member States concerning liability for defective products has been enacted in the UK by means of the Consumer Protection Act 1987. The drafters of the Act did not follow exactly the wording of the Directive but the intention is to comply with the Directive and the Act must be construed accordingly. The Directive provisions are identified in the following summary of the relevant sections of the Statute. This Act not only provides for strict liability for defective products (Part I) but also consumer safety (Part III) and misleading price indications in Part III. It should be appreciated that strict liability is in addition to existing rights in contract and in tortious liability. Part I became effective on 1st March, 1988, and the main Sections are described below.

6.1.7B   Parties Who Are Liable

The principle of strict liability for defective products enshrined in Article 1 of the Directive is expressed in Section 2 of the Act. Article 3 defines who shall be liable and the parties are described in Section 2 as:

(i) A producer of the product. "Producer" is defined in Section 1 as
    (a) the person who manufactures it. (This will include a component manufacturer.)
    (b) in the case of a substance which has not been manufactured but has been won or abstracted, the person who won or abstracted it;
    (c) in the case of a product which has not been manufactured, won or abstracted but essential characteristics of which are attributable to an industrial or other process having been carried out (for example, in relation to agricultural produce), the person who carried out that process. A pea-canner would be liable, for example, but a person does not become a producer simply by virtue of packaging goods unless that packaging alters essential characteristics of the product. However he may be caught as a supplier (see below).

(ii) Any person who, by putting his name on the product or using a trade mark or other distinguishing mark in relation to the product, has held himself out to be the producer of the product. Thus the "own brander" is liable because he gives the impression that he is the producer of the product.

(iii) Any person who has imported the product into a member State from a place outside the member State in order, in the course of any business of his, to supply it to another. This refers to importers into the EEC Community and not to importers into the UK. Thus if a Hi-Fi unit is imported from Japan into France and subsequently sold in the UK, liability falls on the French importer, not a subsequent importer into the UK (although he is of course a supplier). The legislation does not expose the importer of goods from one EEC member State to another to liability if the goods are defective.

(iv) The supplier of the product but only if the supplier fails to inform the Claimant, after notice, of the identity of the producer, mark owner or importer. Any person in the chain of supply, including the retailer, will be strictly liable unless he can inform the injured party of the identity of the producer or the importer or the person who supplied him with the product. For organisations in the chain of supply greater importance will be on the keeping of records because if a company is unable to identify their source of supply within a reasonable time, strict liability must be assumed.

6.1.7C   Products Covered

Section 1 defines "product" as "any goods or electricity and (subject to subsection (3) below) includes a product which is comprised in another product, whether by virtue of being a component part or raw material or otherwise . . .". The section continues with subsection (3): ". . . a person who supplies any product in which products are comprised, whether by virtue of being component parts or raw materials or otherwise, shall not be treated by reason only of his supply of that product as supplying any of the products so comprised".

In an attempt to unravel this definition, products means goods including not only gas and water but also electricity. Tangible movable property is intended therefore; buildings are not included but the bricks and, for example, electricity sockets in a building would be. Components that are part of a finished product and raw materials are included therefore if there is a defect in a particular component, then both the manufacturer of the final product and the component manufacturer are liable. Subsection (3) referred to above is not clear, but it refers to supply of the product and seems to imply that, for example, a person who supplies a forklift truck is not regarded as having supplied the tyres. Primary agricultural products and game are specifically excluded unless they have undergone an industrial process.

6.1.7D   Meaning of "Defect"

Section 3(1) states: ". . . there is a defect in a product for the purposes of this Part if the safety of the product is not such as persons generally are entitled to expect; and for those purposes "safety", in relation to a product, shall include safety with respect to products comprised in that product and safety in the context of risks of damage to property, as well as in the context of risks of death or personal injury".

The courts are to take into account all the circumstances when determining "what persons generally are entitled to expect" when determining whether a product is defective. These circumstances are listed in Section 3(2) and include:

(a) The manner in which a product is marketed, its get-up and any instructions or warnings that are given with it,

(b) what might reasonably be expected to be done with the product; and

(c) the time when the producer supplied the product to another.

The last circumstance (c) brings into play two factors:

(i) the fact that because safety standards improve, goods put into circulation a number of years ago might not when new have been as safe as comparable goods put into circulation now; and

(ii) goods may become less safe with age due to individual deterioration.

The Section follows closely the wording of the definition of "defect" given in Article 6 of the Directive and it still leaves the issue an objective test. To summarise, a product shall not be considered defective for the sole reason that a better product is subsequently put into circulation. The product must be safe in the light of reasonable use of the product and safe in the way that a person is entitled to expect. What sort of person? Does this mean an expert, a manufacturer or a consumer? It is likely to be a person with no special expertise in relation to the use of that product; the man in the street or perhaps once again "the man on the Clapham omnibus". It may be some time before this wording is tested in the courts.

False and misleading statements, promises and advice provided with the product do not of themselves necessarily make the product defective but they are taken into account in determining the objective expectation of the safety of the product.

6.1.7E   Damage Giving Rise to Liability

Liability arises for:

  (i) death or personal injury

  (ii) loss or damage to any property (including land) and provided the damage exceeds £275 and the property is of a type ordinarily intended for private use, occupation or consumption.

There is no liability for:

  (a) damage to the goods themselves or any composite product of which they form part;

  (b) non-material damage such as pure financial or economic loss.

The claimant is not required to prove negligence and it will be no defence to the defendant to plead that he took all reasonable steps to ensure that no defect occurred. There remains the burden on the claimant to establish that the product was defective, that injury or damage occurred and the causal link betwen the defect and the damage.

6.1.7F   Defences

To escape liability the defendant must establish any one of six possible defences and there can be partial relief by virtue of contributory negligence on the part of the claimant.

The defences listed in Article 7 are set out in Section 4(1) and comprise:

  (a) defect attributable to compliance with an Act of Parliament, EEC regulation or other mandatory regulation e.g. mandatory British Standard. The producer will have to show that the defect was the inevitable consequence of compliance with the regulation;

  (b) the defendant did not at any time supply the product to another. Under this head the defendant would have to show that the product was not intended for sale by him, or supplied in the course of his business. As an example, medicinal materials used in trials before being put on the market.

  (c) the only supply of the product to another by the person proceeded against was otherwise than in the course of a business of that person's. This excludes sale of home made toys to the church bazaar and sales by private individuals of second-hand goods.

  (d) the defect did not exist in the product at the relevant time. Here there is a minor deviation from the Directive wording which requires that "the defect probably did not exist". This could be important in the cases of products accompanied by warnings and instructions which become detached before delivery by the final supplier and also for products with a short life expectancy. It also raises the question of adherence by retailers to the producer's "sell by" date displayed on the goods.

  (e) the state of scientific and technical knowledge at the relevant time was not such that a producer of products of the same description as the product in question might be expected to have discovered the defect if it had existed in his products while they were under his control. This is the "state of the art" defence or development risks defence which was and still is stoutly objected to by consumer groups on the ground that it leaves the product development risk where it was, i.e. with the consumer. Industry on the other hand claimed that to omit this defence would stifle innovation and make the cost of insurance cover prohibitive. There is little justification for the latter contention although in the areas of high risk such as pharmaceuticals exposure would be a serious problem. This defence was optional to EEC member States and pressure from interested parties prevailed upon the UK Government to include it. The Government has indicated that it expects it to be a rare let-off and there is likely to be a heavy burden of proof on the producer to show that the defect could not reasonably have been expected to have been discovered, given the "state of the art" at the time.

The other member States are currently at various stages in the debate on whether to include the defence in their respective legislation and the Reader should update on developments. Denmark, Ireland, the Netherlands and the Federal German Republic will include it. Countries which are likely to omit the defence are France, Greece, Italy, Luxembourg, Portugal and Spain.

6.1.7G   Limitation Period

Articles 10 and 11 deal with limitation periods in respect of recovery of damages. The rules are found in Section 5 and Schedule 1 of the Act. Damage is taken to have occurred at the earliest time at which a person with an interest in the property had knowledge of the material facts about the damage. "Material Facts" include knowledge:

(a) that there was a defect in a product:

(b) that the damage was caused or partly caused by the defect:

(c) that the damage was sufficiently serious to justify the plaintiff in bringing an action to which this section applies on the assumption that the defendant did not dispute liability and was able to satisfy a decree:

(d) of the identity of any defendant liable for the damage.

Actions must be brought within 3 years of knowledge of the material facts unless the claimant is under a disability (e.g. an infant) or there has been fraud or mistake. An action cannot be brought after 10 years from the date of last supply by a producer or importer liable for the defect. It follows therefore that persons injured by products with latent defects which do not appear until 10 years from the date of supply will have no remedy in strict liability under the Act and would have to resort to liability through tort, which would be extremely difficult to establish.

6.1.7H   General

The Act does not put a financial limit on the producer's liability for damages. Article 16 of the Directive permits member States to apply a financial limit which must be a minimum of 70m ECU's (£41m), in respect of liability for death and bodily injury, but this was not incorporated into the UK legislation. Only a minority of the Member States will apply the limit and they are Belgium, the Federal German Republic and Portugal.

It is not possible to exclude liability under the Act by means of any contract term or other provision.

Where two or more persons are liable, for example, a manufacturer of the composite product and a component manufacturer, they will be jointly and severally liable and existing contribution rights in UK law will not be affected. The claimant is likely to sue the party with the greater resource i.e. the "deep pocket principle".

6.1.7I   Consumer Safety

Part II of the Consumer Protection Act, effective from 1st October, 1987, contains a "general safety requirement" and provides that a person shall be guilty of an offence if he supplies consumer goods which are not reasonably safe having regard to all the circumstances. Determining factors would be:

(a) the manner in which, and purposes for which, the goods are being or would be marketed, the get-up of the goods, the use of any mark in relation to the goods and any instructions or warnings which are given or would be given with respect to the keeping, use or consumption of the goods;

(b) published standards of safety applying to the goods;

(c) existence of any means by which it would have been reasonable (taking into account the cost, likelihood and extent of any improvement) for the goods to have been made safer.

"Safe" is defined as reducing to a minimum the risk of death or personal injury by reason of:

(i) the goods;

(ii) the keeping, use or consumption of the goods;

(iii) the assembly of the goods which are supplied unassembled;

(iv) emission or leakage from the goods;

(v) reliance on the accuracy of any measurement, calculation or other reading made by or by means of the goods.

This provision is restricted to goods which are ordinarily intended for private use or consumption other than food and animal feed crops, tobacco, fertilisers, medicines and drugs. Gas and water are also outwith its terms. Goods used in the workplace are already covered by the provisions of the Health and Safety at Work Act. The provision applies to anyone who supplies goods but there is an important defence for retailers — that they neither knew nor had reasonable grounds for believing that the goods failed to comply with the general safety requirement.

Regulation-making powers are included to enable the Secretary of State to act without delay on the grounds of public protection and to make prohibition notices and notices to warn. Enforcement authorities may also serve suspension notices.

Available defences are:

(a) the act or default of another;

(b) the goods were for export;

(c) that when he supplied the goods in the course of retail business he had no grounds to suspect that the goods failed to comply with the general safety requirement;

(d) indication was given to the person acquiring the goods that they were not new goods;

(e) reliance upon information given by another, provided that he shows that it was reasonable in all the circumstances for him to have so relied.

Part II of the Act repeals the Consumer Safety Act, 1978, and the Consumer Safety (Amendment) Act, 1986.

Penalties for an offence under Part II include imprisonment for six months or a fine not exceeding £2,000 or both.

6.1.7J   Misleading Price Indications

Part III has at its centre a general offence which is giving to consumers a misleading price indication about any goods, services, accommodation or facilities and any person who, in the course of a business of his, gives misleading price indications to a customer is liable. This Part will not be considered further in this study. It is expected to come into force early in 1989.

6.1.7K   Product Liability Overseas

Whilst the original aim of the EEC Directive was harmonisation of product liability law in the member States, this will not be achieved, rather it will result in approximation. The extent of approximation will not be known until all the States pass the necessary legislation and a brief review of current law in a number of European countries follows.

6.2   Product Liability in France

France is in the process of implementing the EEC Directive but in practice French law is similar to the provisions of the Directive in any case. Product liability falls under one of three headings: liability for fault, strict liability and quasi-contractual liability.

(i) Liability for Fault. A victim of a defective product must prove that the damage sustained was a direct result of the manufacturer's fault. Because of the difficulties for the plaintiff inherent in this the courts are moving towards placing the burden of disproving negligence on the manufacturer. The manufacturer's duty of care is to the public at large therefore anyone can make a claim. The duty is to ensure that, as far as possible, only safe products are manufactured. The manufacturer and distributor/supplier can be held jointly and severally liable, but as between them liability can be passed up and down the chain of supply if it can be proved that the damage resulted from a particular party's negligence.

(ii) Strict Liability. Under Article 1384 of the Code Civil a person who has a product under his control is liable for all damage caused by the product unless he çan prove that the damage was caused by force majeure (Act of

God). This amounts to strict liability because there is no need for the plaintiff to prove negligence. The question arises as to whether the manufacturer is strictly liable when the product is put into circulation i.e. it is now outwith his control. This issue is not clear.

(iii) Contractual Liability. Article 1645 of the Code Civil renders the seller of a defective product liable to the buyer for any resultant damage, but only if the seller knew of the defect. If not, the seller is liable only to reimburse the costs incurred by the customer. The courts have taken this further. Now the professional seller is presumed to know of the defect and is therefore liable for all the resultant damage. Moreover, liability is restricted to "hidden defects" as distinct from apparent defects. "Hidden defects" are defects which the buyer would not normally notice after having examined the product in the usual way. The standard is an attentive buyer exercising reasonable care and diligence. This liability does not apply in the case of injuries to third parties (other than the buyer). Claims for damages must be brought within one month of the purchaser becoming aware of the defect.

For defects in products there has been developed by means of case law an irrebuttable presumption of fault, consequently any producer or any professional dealer is obliged to compensate an injured party, without being able to exclude liability and not even a "state of the art" defence is possible. A defence of contributory negligence can be offered and also assumption of risk.

Implementation of the Directive is unlikely to include a "state of the art" defence nor a financial ceiling on damages.

6.3   Federal German Republic

In West Germany the civil code is based on fault liability and implementation of the EEC Directive is likely to be introduced by statute.

Product liability law, prior to the Directive, is based on Article 823 of the Burgerliches Gesetzburch whereby there is a duty of care not to manufacture products which may endanger the ultimate consumer. The manufacturer is obliged to provide adequate warnings and accompanying instructions, and to take into account the intended use of the product. The courts have, however, moved from the fault principle to a view that it is not for the plaintiff to prove fault on the part of the manufacturer, but rather for the latter to counter the presumption that the defect was caused by his negligence. This applies to products generally but not in the case of pharmaceuticals. The Pharmaceuticals Act, effective from 1978, provides that the manufacturer of a pharmaceutical product is liable, irrespective of fault, for damage caused by his product. Financial limits of DM500,000 for individual cases and DM200M in aggregate are applicable.

In product liability generally, the injured party must prove that the defect that caused the damage arose in the normal course of events in the manufacturer's sphere of control. The onus is then on the manufacturer to show that the ordinary course of events does not lead to the alleged result. In determining whether specific conditions necessary for liability are met, West German courts distinguish between defective design, defective production, defective instruction and development defect. Defences available are contributory negligence and assumption of risk but the latter does not apply in the case of pharmaceuticals.

In the case of personal injuries, damages are payable for direct financial loss but pure economic loss is not recoverable. Payment is not necessarily on a "once and for all" basis but can be by way of instalments.

Legislation will include a "state of the art" defence and there will be a financial ceiling on liability.

6.3   Italy

The details of implementation of the Directive in Italy are not predictable, but it is likely that development risks defence and financial limits will be left out of the legislation. Ordinarily, Italian law on the liability for dangerous or defective products is based on the principle of fault and the burden of proof rests in the traditional way. The Codice Civile (article 2043) places a duty of care on the manufacturer towards the general public in regard to the safety of his product. The courts, as in the other countries referred to have placed the burden of proof on the manufacturer, obliging him to disprove any negligence on his part. Negligence is presumed unless proof to the contrary is produced.

Everyone in the supply chain bears the common duty of care to prevent the marketing of defective goods, but the responsibilities of each vary according to their functions. A supplier could therefore be responsible solely or be jointly and severally liable with the manufacturer. Within a contract for sale of goods there is a warranty against defects in the goods and therefore the buyer may claim damages for injury or loss suffered in the course of normal use of the product. The supplier is liable unless he can prove that, through no fault of his own, he had no knowledge of the defect.

The defences of contributory negligence and assumption of risk are possible. Damages for personal injuries can include direct financial loss and if caused by a tort, pain and suffering as well.

6.4   The Netherlands

Proposed legislation to implement the EEC Directive is likely to uphold a "development risks" defence but not a financial limit or ceiling on damages. Dutch law on product liability prior to the Directive stems from Article 1401 of the Burgerlizk Wetboek. It is similar in the main to the systems already described with some important differences. One is that it requires more than merely the breach of a duty of care in order to give rise to liability. Other circumstances, such as a statement on the product, inadequate warnings or insufficient instruction must apply in addition. Like the West German rules, the courts classify defects in terms of design, production, instruction and development, thereby assisting the plaintiff in establishing a breach of duty. Dutch law is in line with the French and West German systems in that it has shifted the burden of disproving negligence to the manufacturer, insofar as the latter's negligence is presumed, unless proof to the contrary is produced. The Dutch courts usually accept the plaintiff's allegation of product defect leaving the defendant to show that his product was not defective. Damages for personal injuries include direct financial loss (loss of income, medical expenses etc.) and if it is caused by a tort, pain and suffering also. Defences available are contributory negligence and assumption of risk.

6.5 Belgium

Belgium is expected to continue with its principle of no-fault liability. Implementation of the Directive will not affect this and there will be a "development risks" defence and a financial ceiling on liability.

The "pre Directive" law on product liability is based on the Code Civil and is similar to that applying in France. A manufacturer owes a duty of care to the user at large not to manufacture products which cause loss or injury (Article 1382 of the Code Civil). Article 1384 imposes strict liability on the manufacturer unless he can establish that the damage was caused by force majeure. A cause of action lies with anyone who has suffered injury or damage and the suppliers or distributors as well as the manufacturer may be held jointly or severally liable. There can be a quasi-contractual liability under Article 1645 of the Code Civil under which liability is imposed where there is prior knowledge of the defect. This liability is limited to the contracting consumer only. The contracting consumer may sue the supplier who may have recourse ultimately to the manufacturer. Knowledge of the defect is an essential element here. The limitation period within the scope of contractual liability is one year from the date of conclusion of the contract but Belgian courts tend to treat it as one year from the date that the plaintiff becomes aware of the defect.

In the case of personal injuries, damages are awarded for direct financial loss (medical treatment, loss of income) and if caused by a tort, pain and suffering may be taken into account.

6.6 The Brussels Convention (on judgements and jurisdiction): Civil Jurisdiction and Judgements Act 1982

The implications of multi-state litigation have to be considered when harmonisation or approximation of product liability laws has been achieved. The courts when coming to interpret the legislation will have the broader view of the European Community in mind and therefore it is necessary to set out the rules for determining jurisdiction in national courts in claims which involve parties from different States. The Convention on Jurisdiction and Enforcement of Judgements in Civil and Commercial Matters, in force in the six Member States originally comprising the Common Market will be enforced in the remaining Member Countries in due course. In the UK the Civil Jurisdiction and Judgements Act, 1982, implemented by the Brussels Convention with effect from 1st January, 1987. Note that the Convention applies to jurisdiction generally and not merely that involving product liability. The rules for litigation in product liability claims may be summarised as follows:

(i) A defendant may always be sued in the State of his domicile. Companies and other legal persona are regarded as domiciled where they have their seat.

(ii) In tort actions, where the defendant is domiciled in a member State the courts for the "place where the harmful event occurred" also have jurisdiction. This "place" is determined by interpreting the Convention rule to give the plaintiff the option to raise the action either in the place where the wrongful act occurred or in the place where the damage arose.

(iii) In the instance of several defendants, all defendants may be sued in the courts of the State where any one of them is domiciled.

(iv) In the case of a defendant not domiciled in the Community the question of jurisdiction will be determined by the law of the plaintiff's state.

(v) In order to establish whether a defendant is domiciled in the State whose courts are seized of a matter, that court shall apply its internal law. If the party is not domiciled in that State, then the law of that State is the forum for deciding whether the party is domiciled in another Member State. As an example United Kingdom law provides that a person is domiciled if he is resident in the UK. He is presumed to be resident if he has resided in the UK for the three months before court proceedings begin.

As a result of the Convention provisions, therefore, a claimant may sue in any of the States where any of the defendants is domiciled or in any State where the harmful event occurred. If the defendant is not domiciled jurisdiction over him will be determined by the local law of the Court. The result of this is that "forum shopping" is sanctioned by the terms of the Convention, meaning that the plaintiff can opt for the jurisdiction giving him the easiest burden to discharge and the best financial remedy. The following example illustrates the choices of litigation open to a plaintiff.

A German beer manufacturer distributes his canned product in France. It is purchased there by a Belgian tourist who drinks it in Holland and is poisoned. The injured party can sue the manufacturer in Germany. He can also sue the supplier in France or he can sue them jointly in either Germany or France. He can sue the manufacturer and/or supplier in Holland, the country where the "harmful event" occurred.

The rules for determining the system of law applicable vary from State to State. In the UK it is the law of the place of the wrongful act whereas in the case of Germany it does not follow that the German court will apply German laws on product liability but apply another law. The German courts allow the plaintiff to choose the system that best suits him.

The implications for manufacturers whose products are sold within the Community are that they will be exposed to claims in all the Member States. Component manufacturers are similarly exposed. The freedom to "shop" for the best forum means that limited liability or the development defence applicable in a particular State can be avoided by the plaintiff taking his case to a more favourable system. This will make Community-wide insurance cover for the maximum liability imperative.

Importers of products manufactured outwith the community have a similar liability to manufacturers and have to provide themselves with adequate insurance or certain protection by contractual arrangements with the manufacturer.

6.7 Liability in the United States of America

The United States legal system as it affects product liability is comprised of both the federal law and the rulings of the courts of fifty individual states. This is referred to as "concurrent jurisdiction", meaning that a party may bring an action in either a state court or a federal court. The federal court will only hear cases where damages claimed exceed $10,000 and there is also a requirement of "diversity of citizenship" i.e. that the parties are citizens of different states or one party is a citizen of one of the states and the other is a citizen of a foreign state. Appeals go to federal Courts of Appeals of which there are eleven, each one representing a circuit comprised of several states.

In the majority of product lawsuits the plaintiff requests a jury trial. This is one of the fundamental differences between the American system and that of the United Kingdom. In the UK the judge assesses compensation and a judge is much more clearly bound by the rules of law and the opinions of other judges. In the USA the jury decides on quantum and it is much more sympathetically inclined towards an injured party standing there in front of it. The jury is not answerable to anyone as to how much compensation is awarded; it does not have to explain why it has reached its decision. A jury is capable of awarding an inordinate sum of money and if the defendant businessman or producer wishes to appeal that involves further expenditure and time to bring the case through the mire of legal proceedings. The jury's sums will be affected by the matter of attorney's fees. It is usual in the USA that you pay your own side's fees, win or lose, whereas in the UK the loser pays all. The lawyer is usually working on a contingency fee basis, that is to say he has an arrangement with his client whereby if they lose the lawyer gets nothing but if they win he is paid a proportion of the award, say, one third. The jury, knowing this automatically adds on another one third or even up to fifty per cent to what it would ordinarily consider appropriate. These factors and another important one, that of punitive damages which is dealt with later, caused exporters to the USA and their insurers to think seriously about whether to enter the market at all.

6.7.1   Strict Liability

The basis of product liability law in the USA is strict liability. It is the result of case law conventionally dating back to the case of Greenman v Yuba Power Products Incorporated, 1963, and the rules are now stated in Section 402A of the American Law Institute's Restatement (Second) of Torts. The Restatement should be explained at this point. Because there are courts in fifty states constantly arriving at their own judgement decisions it is necessary from time to time to take stock of what the judges have decided for the purpose of articulating a basic statement of common law provisions. The Restatement does precisely that. It is not the law, however, but merely an expression of what the more prominent members of the legal profession regard as the current law. It incorporates both case law and relevant statutory provisions. The Restatement has persuasive influence on both federal and state courts.

Basically, strict liability for products means that the seller is liable for any defect in or unreasonable danger of his product which threatens the consumer's or user's safety. This eliminates any question of reasonable care and negligence. In Elmore v Americal Motors, 1969, the plaintiff victim of a car crash could not firmly show the cause of the accident but there were two possible explanations: (i) that the driving shaft had come loose or (ii) that there was metal fatigue. The court ruled that it does not matter which cause operated, the car was unfit; it was not reasonably safe.

Section 402A provides:

(1) One who sells any product in a defective condition unreasonably dangerous to the user or consumer or to his property is subject to liability for physical

72

harm thereby caused to the ultimate consumer, or to his property if
  (a) the seller is engaged in the business of selling such a product; and
  (b) it is expected to and does reach the user or consumer without sub-
      stantial change in the condition in which it is sold:

(2) The rule stated in subsection (1) applies although
  (a) the seller has exercised all possible care in the preparation and sale of
      his product, and
  (b) the user and consumer has not bought the product from or entered into
      any contractual relation with the seller.

Points (2)(a) and (b) above are crucial because (a) rules out arguments on negligence and (b) applies the seller's strict liability not only to the buyer but also to any user.

The plaintiff ordinarily must prove the identity of the seller and that is usually an easy matter. Where however in, say, instances of multiple manufacturers of generic products a particular manufacturer cannot be identified the courts can assist the plaintiff by allocating liability on a market share basis. In effect a group of defendants who in aggregate control a substantial share of the market will each be liable for the portion of damages represented by his share of the market unless he can demonstrate that his product could not have been the offending one. This shifts the burden of proof as well as apportioning the damages. A plaintiff who cannot identify the manufacturer can sue the most attractive target.

The plaintiff must prove that the product was defective and often expert opinion is brought to bear on the matter. The mere fact of an accident does not necessarily imply that the product was defective, e.g. a tyre bursts when it hits a large stone on the road. If the defendant argues that his product was constructed in compliance with mandatory Governmental standards and was therefore not defective this may not be a defence. Courts regard these standards as minimal standards and that is not necessarily enough. Wear and tear considerations may arise when determining a product is defective. The plaintiff has to show that the product was defective when it left the defendant. For example a drive-shaft fell out of a car after 24,000 miles and the court said this was not evidence that the car was defective when it left the manufacturer.

6.7.2   Defences

Having identified the defendant and proven the defect there is the possibility of the seller offering one of a number of defences to strict liability. The defences rarely succeed. They are:

  (a) comparative fault,
  (b) misuse of the product,
  (c) alteration of the product,
  (d) Idiosyncrasy of the user, and
  (e) assumption of risk.

  (a) Comparative fault. Where there is more than one party causing the injury
      the principle of comparative fault imposes liability for damages in proportion
      to the relative fault of each party.

  (b) Misuse. A manufacturer has no duty to design a product in anticipation of
      a "misuse" and is not therefore liable if the product becomes dangerous due

to that misuse. Abnormal use is also misuse. In McCready v United Iron and Steel Corporation, 1959, the court held that the manufacturer of steel casement windows was not liable for an accident to a workman who fell whilst using a casement as a ladder. The casement's cross bar failed to support the man's weight. A product is not misused merely because the manufacturer intended that it be used in a different manner to the actual use which caused the mischief. The manufacturer must show that the use which caused the injury was not reasonably foreseeable and this can be difficult for him. In LeBouef v Goodyear Tyre & Rubber Co., 1978, the defence of misuse failed in a claim relating to an alleged fault in a tyre which burst in use. The plaintiff had been driving at over 100 miles per hour and the manufacturer maintained that the product had not been constructed for use at such speed. The court found for the plaintiff on the ground that no adequate warning had been given by the manufacturers.

(c) Alteration to the product. The defendant must show that the alteration is "substantial" and must also prove that the alteration caused the injury. In some States' juridsictions this defence is inapplicable where such alteration is "reasonably foreseeable".

(d) Idiosyncrasy of user. No liability attaches where the user is allergic or unusually susceptible to harm from the product so long as the manufacturer or seller has no knowledge that some people may be exposed to injury by its use or where it appears that only a small number of people are likely to suffer injury. This defence is no longer dependable. It usually revolves around cases of alleged inadequate warning by the manufacturer. In Grau v Proctor and Gamble Co., 1963, the plaintiff had an allergy to Crest toothpaste. The court ruled that such an allergy was not sufficiently common to warrant a warning of danger. On the other hand in Tomer v American Home Prod. Corp., 1976, the court said that a manufacturer of an anaesthetic had a duty to warn when he has the knowledge of danger of serious injury to persons even if they are few in number.

(e) Assumption of risk. Available where the plaintiff voluntarily exposes himself to a known and appreciated danger. The courts have to be convinced that the plaintiff knew of the specific defect involved and that his was actual conscious knowledge of it. The fact that he should have known is not enough to support this defence.

6.7.3   Parties Who May Be Sued

Under USA laws the plaintiff has a wide choice of possible defendants to sue. The chain of supply may include a manufacturer, a component manufacturer, wholesaler, distributor, importer, retailer, used product seller or repairer and any of these may be brought into an action. Usually the manufacturer is sued mainly because he will have the most resources, i.e. the "deepest pocket". It can be argued that he is the party who boasts of the quality of the product, who advertises it and who puts it on the market. The importer is also strictly liable and his standard approaches that of the manufacturer. Wholesalers and distributors have the strict liability doctrine applied to them also. In a number of states the retailer is liable only in negligence in the absence of warranties of fitness and whilst this may yet become applicable in all states, in the majority the retailer is strictly liable at present. The maker of a component part has the same strict duty as the manufacturer. For example let us suppose the faulty component is an altimeter fitted to an aircraft. Whilst the component manufacturer is strictly liable the plaintiff would sue the aircraft manufacturer because the later is bigger and has more capital (the deep pocket) and this would leave the manufacturer to seek indemnity from his supplier. The seller of second-hand goods probably is not strictly liable but there is no certainty about this. In a number of instances sellers were held liable including one seller of a used motor vehicle with defective brakes, the defect arising after the vehicle left the manufacturer's control.

6.7.4 Compensatory Damages

Compensatory damages for injury arising from defective products include compensation for bodily injury, property damage (not the product itself in some jurisdictions) but not for pure economic loss. Until recently claims for emotional harm were allowed only where caused by some physical "impact" to the body of the plaintiff. Now there is a tendency to allow damages for emotional harm to, say, a bystander not in personal physical danger but who was nevertheless affected by someone's negligence. In Culbert v Sampson's Supermarkets, 1982, a mother of an infant recovered damaged for the emotional distress she suffered when she witnessed her child choking on a foreign object from a jar of baby food.

6.7.5 Punitive Damages

In the UK we do not have punitive damages, we simply compensate for the plaintiff's injury but American courts sometimes go further than this. If there is a suggestion that the injuries were caused by wilful or wanton disregard of safety considerations then there is not only compensation but the courts will award extra damages as a warning to others. The basis sum of damages may be multiplied five, ten or even twenty times by sympathetic juries. In negligence actions punitive damages serve to curb conduct which on occasion may border on the criminal but there can be no logic in applying such punishment in cases falling under Section 402A when the state of mind of the defendant is irrelevant.

6.7.5 Law Reform

In view of the onerous liabilities which the system has placed on manufacturers, importers, etc., there are now substantial moves to change some aspects of the law and thus control and limit product liability in the USA. Punitive damages awards are being given attention, for instance. Tort reform bills have been passed in more than thirty of the fifty state legislatures. One example is the reform of the principle of joint and several liability where the plaintiff could collect from the most affluent of the wrongdoers irrespective of his degree of fault. Now in some states juries are required to reduce awards in accord with collateral sources of funds for the plaintiff. In some states the plaintiff's lawyer's fees are restricted by a sliding scale. Other changes are anticipated.

Chapter 7

DEFECTIVE PRODUCTS AND INSURANCE COVERS

7.0   Insurance cover for the liabilities arising from defective products was first provided for ptomaine poisoning resulting from supply of foodstuffs containing deleterious matter. The insurance market gradually developed products cover to encompass a wide range of products to meet the growing needs of industry especially after Donoghue v Stevenson. The following list of product failures will serve to demonstrate the diverse nature of the liability:

ADHESIVES: used in tiling the floor of a food factory; the obnoxious smell from the adhesive rendered all products useless.

ANIMAL FOOD MANUFACTURERS: Zinc oxide used in the manufacture of dairy cake in mistake for magnesium oxide.

AGRICULTURAL MERCHANTS: Crops damaged by a weed killer applied in accordance with the maker's instructions which were incorrect owing to a wrong label having been inadvertently fixed to the goods.

CATERING CONTRACTORS: A contaminated container used by the firm to transport eggs in liquid form caused various dishes composed of the eggs to be poisonous. As a result several hundred guests at a banquet were taken ill, some seriously.

CONCRETE BEAMS: Defect in load-bearing concrete beams causing the building to collapse.

FINISHING SLABS: Green slabs fitted to the side of a building had to be replaced because sulphate used to create the colour caused cracking.

HEATING ENGINEERS: A defective heating system fitted in a timber-built boiler house caused a fire destroying thousands of day-old chicks.

MARMALADE: Supplied in containers marked "Apricot Jam". There is nothing wrong with the marmalade but the buyer cannot sell swiss rolls made with marmalade.

SYNTHETIC LEATHER: Supplied to a shoe manufacturer as a soling material. The material is defective and the shoes are useless.

TILE-MAKING MACHINE: The machine is found to be faulty in that the pressure it achieves leaves the materials unconsolidated. The faulty products have to be broken down for reuse, at considerable extra cost.

Note that some of these examples involve injury to persons or damage to the property of others, whilst others result in damage to the product itself or to another product of which the component is a part.

Failure of materials can affect a wide variety of structures and components and occasionally with disasterous consequences. Examples are air crashes and catastrophes like Flixborough. In order to reduce the chances of material failures the manufacturer must have good quality standards for design, manufacture, installation and final inspection, preferably to British Standard BS5750.

7.1 Insurance Cover

There is no standard approach by insurers to the matter of offering cover for products liability. Insurers have differing views on the scope of cover to be given and this does not always coincide with the needs of those requiring protection. The latter may be faced with claims arising not only from defects in goods, but from faulty storage, misleading instructions for use, faulty or inadequate containers, delivery of the wrong product, delivery of the correct product to the wrong address and inherent design fault. An example of the consequences of perfect goods being delivered to the wrong address is the case of Philco Radio Corporation Ltd. v J. Spurling Ltd., 1949, where film was wrongfully delivered and the unsuspecting recipient opened the packing case while smoking a cigarette and an explosion occurred. Products insurance may be provided by a special policy or, more usually as part of a combined policy document which includes other forms of liability insurance cover such as employers' liability and general liability insurance. This is a convenient "package" policy which has advantages over the system of issuing separate covers. A specimen Product Liability Policy wording is given as an appendix to this Chapter, although in practice it is uncommon to find the cover provided by the issue of a separate policy. However, for the purpose of interpreting the cover it may be helpful to look at the Products cover separately. Cover for risk of legal liability for bodily injury or damage to third party's property caused by defect in the product is termed Product Liability Insurance whereas insurance cover for the cost of replacing the faulty product, the cost of the work involved, or for product recall is called Product Guarantee Insurance.

7.1.1 The Product Liability Policy

The policy wording given in the appendix to this Chapter is typical of wordings in use but policies to vary and the Reader should endeavour to examine other specimens. The policy covers the legal liability of the policyholder for damages and legal costs and expenses for bodily injury or damage to property caused by the goods. This will cover not only defective products but also risks resulting from the sale of the wrong goods, delivery of perfect goods to the wrong address and incorrect labelling. In some policies the words "arising out of any defect in the goods" are used, in which case sale of the wrong goods and wrongful delivery would not be covered. Note also from the definition of "Goods" that cover is given in respect of containers, faulty labelling, instructions or advice. The word "accidental" is used but in some policy wordings it is omitted and this may seem to widen the scope of the cover but nevertheless cover is usually dependent upon an element of accident.

The bodily injury or damage must occur during the period of insurance but the injurious goods need not have been manufactured during that period. Often the goods will be in existence and possibly in circulation before the commencement of the policy period. There must be some actual damage or injury to a third party: there is no cover for mere failure of the goods to meet the purpose. The damage or injury caused is covered and also any consequential loss for which there is a liability at law. Cover is given for goods manufactured, etc. from any premises of the Insured in Great Britain, Northern Ireland, the Isle of Man and the Channel Islands. If the Insured manufactures from a plant anywhere outwith these territories he would have to obtain products cover locally or as part of a multi-national programme. However a products policy usually gives world-wide cover to accommodate manufacturers who export or whose product may eventually reach other parts of the world (sometimes excluding exports to the USA and Canada). General Definition No.3 "Property shall mean material property" restricts the cover by excluding non-material forms of property such as plans, copyright, patents, trade marks and the like.

The limit of indemnity is expressed in two forms. There is an accident or incident limit and in addition an aggregate limit applicable to the whole period of insurance. The aggregate limit is applied by the insurer because of the potential catastrophe risk in products. A faulty batch of goods could produce hundreds of claims. From the manufacturer's point of view this is only one accident but it could be argued that each faulty item produces an accident and therefore arguments may arise as to interpretation. The aggregate limit serves to protect the insurer and it is up to the insured ot obtain a realistic aggregate limit.

7.1.2   Policy Exceptions

The risks not covered are listed as Exceptions and these will now be considered:

(a) Replacing defective goods. The policy does not guarantee the actual goods therefore the cost of replacing faulty goods is not covered. This cost is the subject of Product Guarantee Insurance which will be referred to later.

(b) USA exclusion. In view of the difficulties experienced by insurers due to factors favouring the plaintiff in litigation, insurers in this Country often exclude the cover in order that they may negotiate with the policyholder the terms for acceptance, if at all.

(c) Goods in the custody or control of the Insured The effect of this exception is that cover for the product liability applies only after the goods leave the custody of the Insured. Until then any liability is the subject of other policies such as public liability or motor insurances.

(d) Aircraft. The potential catastrophe risk is apparent here and most insurers exclude it. Note the operative term "knowingly supplied" which means that if a product found its way to an aircraft without the Insured's knowledge it would be covered. In effect the supply of any component part to an aircraft is excluded but the risks of, say, supplying food and drink for consumption on an aircraft is covered, the latter not being concerned with the safety of the aircraft.

(e) Contractual liability. Insurers often exclude liability assumed by the insured by agreement until they know exactly the terms of any relevant agreement entered into by the policyholder. However any contractual liability arising out of a condition or warranty upheld by law is not excluded, for example the warranty of "merchantable quality" under the Sale of Goods Act.

(f) Radioactive contamination. Insurers do not cover this potentially catastrophic risk.

(g) Employers liability. The risk of injury to employees of the Insured is excluded because it is the province of a more specific policy, the Employers Liability Policy.

(h) War, etc. These risks are not normally insurable.

Other exceptions. Some product liability policies exclude liability for defective products resulting from faulty design or formula or the unsuitability of the goods for the purpose for which they were designed. Faulty design will mean that all units of the product will be likely to cause injury or damage and not merely a single "rogue" item. Insurers term this a professional risk more suitable for a Professional Indemnity Policy.

Some policies contain a clause whereby the Insurer attempts to limit claimants to the jurisdiction of this Country but as the Student will have gleaned from the summary of EEC legislation "forum shopping" is likely to be widely used in future and this clause will have little practical benefit to the Insurer.

7.1.3   Other Persons Insured

Product policies usually indemnify not only the Insured named in the Schedule but also persons working for the insured and officers or members of the firm's social sports or welfare organisations. This is convenient from the Insured's point of view. In addition the Legal Personal Representatives of all of the persons indemnified are in turn indemnified. This is in recognition of the legal position following death, i.e. any action for or against a deceased person continues on behalf of or against his estate (see Chapter 4, 4.4.2).

7.1.4   Policy Conditions

The Conditions give the Insurer the right to control the conduct of any claims as well as regulating the behaviour of the Insured. Condition 4 (Discharge of Liability) gives the Insurer the right to abandon the claim to the policyholder after paying the amount due under the policy, in the event of the claim exceeding the amount of indemnity. This would be invoked only in exceptional circumstances, where, say, the policyholder insists on defending the claim against the advice of the insurer.

The insurer may not wish to be involved in protracted litigation and may opt out and pay also any costs incurred up to the date of such discharge.

If there is more than one insurance covering the liability there is no cover, except for the excess of liability beyond the scope of any other policy or policies (Conditon 5). It is likely that any other policy will bear a similar clause in which event the insurers contribute.

7.2   Product Guarantee Insurance

A manufacturer who holds a Product Liability insurance policy may have protection for liability for injury or damage caused by his product but he retains the risk of financial loss resulting from failure of his product to perform to the specification required by his customer. Supposing he supplies electrical machinery to a factory to generate power and the machinery failed to function properly resulting in temporary closure of the factory. This loss would be purely a financial one, in the absence of damage, and it would not be covered by his Product Liability policy. This type of loss and the cost of repairing or replacing the machinery is the subject of a class of insurance termed Product Guarantee insurance which is a full insurance of the product guaranteed and the consequential losses which arise if the product fails. The market for such cover is very restricted and when available a measure of self insurance is necessary because it is regarded by insurers as a trade risk.

This cover is arranged to specifically cover the cost of the removal, repair, alteration, treatment or replacement (including any consequential loss arising therefrom) of any product necessitated by its defective nature or which fails to perform the function for which it was manufactured, designed, supplied, sold, installed, repaired, altered, treated or recommended by the insured. The policy is issued on a "claims made" basis and bears an aggregate limit of indemnity. The period of cover is normally for one year and this does not normally relate to any guarantee period which may be given by the insured.

7.3   Recall of Product Insurance

The cost of calling in a whole range of products which have been widely distributed through the trade channels to individual purchasers may be very heavy. Costs may include advertising in the press and on television. A component or ingredient may make a manufacturer's finished product unsafe and cause him to undertake an expensive recall. It is essential for the organisation to have a product recall plan. This will not remove the risk but it should reduce the impact. The plan should include traceability of the products which is the means by which the product is coded at the production process and any ingredients added later such as packaging should be identifiable. In the absence of a means of tracing individual units a recall becomes a blanket withdrawal and therefore expensive.

Insurance cover is very restricted and usually applies only to accidental causes and not to faulty design, yet the majority of failures result from design. The policy will not cover recall of kindred products, necessary when you cannot identify the defective product and it may not cover the cost of destroying the defective product. A possible alternative to insurance is transfer of the risk of recall by the terms of the contract of purchase or sale. At best this may amount to some reduction in the risk and not a total transfer and such a measure needs expert drafting.

7.4   Consequential Loss Insurance

It may be possible to obtain insurance cover for financial loss sustained by any person even if not accompanied by loss of or damage to property, where such purely financial loss results from defective products or their failure to perform their function. For example, tiling manufacturers supply and install flooring tiles in a supermarket which after cleaning reveal imperfections in the colour of the tiles and as a result the overall contract is delayed and the opening of the supermarket is postponed. The financial loss attributable to the delay would be covered by a consequential loss policy effected by the tiling manufacturers.

7.5   Product Liability Risk Retention

The insistence by the insurance market of substantial deductibles, especially in product guarantee business, unavailability of cover and high premiums for primary cover when written has led to organisations self-funding their risks, if not in full then up to high retention levels. Selection of a liability retention level may be determined on the basis of a percentage of net working capital, perhaps from 1 per cent to 5 per cent. Alternatively the limit could be determined as a percentage of current retained earnings, or for firms with a high cash turnover, as a percentage of sales. Large corporations may arrange their own insurance by means of a Captive Insurance Company, established off-shore, and backed up by reinsurance.

APPENDIX

PRODUCT LIABILITY POLICY

The Company (The Insurer) in consideration of the Insured having paid or agreed to pay the premium and on the basis that any information provided in connection with a proposal form made to the Company shall be incorporated into the contract WILL SUBJECT TO THE TERMS EXCEPTIONS CONDITIONS ENDORSEMENTS AND LIMITS OF INDEMNITY OF THIS POLICY INDEMNIFY THE INSURED AGAINST

(A) All sums which the Insured shall become legally liable to pay as damages and in addition claimants' costs and expenses in respect of accidental Bodily injury or accidental loss of or damage to Property as defined in this Policy occurring anywhere in the world during the period of insurance and caused by any Goods and which arises in connection with the Business as specified in the Schedule.

(B) All costs and expenses incurred with the written consent of the Company in respect of any claim against the Insured which may be the subject of indemnity under this Policy.

(C) The payment of the solicitor's fees incurred with the Company's written consent for representation of the Insured at
   (i) any Coroner's Inquest or Fatal Accident Inquiry in respect of any death
   (ii) proceedings in any Court of Summary Jurisdiction arising out of any alleged breach of statutory duty resulting in Bodily Injury or loss of or damage to Property which may be the subject of indemnity under this policy.

GENERAL DEFINITIONS

1.   BUSINESS shall include the provision of catering social sports and welfare facilities for the Insured's Employees ambulance fire and first aid services and private work undertaken with the consent of the Insured by an employee for a director partner or Employee of the Insured.

2.   BODILY INJURY shall include death illness or disease.

3.   PROPERTY shall mean material property.

4.   EMPLOYEE shall mean

(a) any person under a contract of service or apprenticeship with the Insured

(b)   (i) any labour master or person supplied by him or any person supplied by a labour only sub-contractor
   (ii) any self-employed person
   (iii) any person hired by the Insured from another employer subject to an agreement under which the person is deemed to be employed by the Insured
   (iv) any person participating in any Government or other authorised work experience training study exchange or similar scheme while engaged in working for the Insured in connection with the Business.

5.   GOODS shall mean any goods or products (including containers labelling instructions or advice provided in connection therewith) sold supplied erected repaired altered treated or installed by the Insured in the course of the Business in or from Great Britain Northern Ireland the Channels Islands or the Isle of Man.

AMOUNT OF INDEMNITY

Any One Event
The liability of the Company for all compensation payable to any claimant or number of claimants in respect of any one occurrence or all occurrences of a series consequent on one original cause shall not exceed the sum stated in the Schedule as the Amount of Indemnity for any one event.

Any One Period
The liability of the Company for all compensation payable in respect of all occurrences happening during any one Period of Indemnity shall not exceed the sum stated in the Schedule as the Amount of Indemnity for any one Period of Indemnity.

EXCEPTIONS

The Company shall not indemnify the Insured against liability

(a) in respect of loss of or damage to or any costs or expenses incurred in repairing replacing recalling or making any refund in respect of the Goods

(b) arising from or in connection with any Goods to the knowledge of the Insured sold supplied erected repaired altered treated or installed by the Insured in or for delivery or use in the United States of America

(c) caused by any Goods in the custody or control of the Insured

(d) caused by Goods installed in an aircraft which have been knowingly supplied by the Insured for that purpose and are directly concerned with the safety of such aircraft

(e) which is assumed by the Insured by agreement (other than liability arising out of a condition or warranty of goods upheld by law) unless such liability would have attached in the absence of such agreement

(f) for whatsoever nature directly or indirectly caused by or contributed to by or arising from (i) ionising radiations or contamination by radioactivity from any nuclear fuel or from any nuclear waste from the combustion of nuclear fuel (ii) the radioactive toxic explosive or other hazardous properties of any explosive nuclear assembly or nuclear component thereof

(g) in respect of Bodily Injury sustained by an Employee of the Insured which arises out of and in the course of his employment or engagement by the Insured

(h) for any consequence of war invasion act of foreign enemy hostilities (whether war be declared or not) civil war rebellion revolution insurrection or military or usurped power.

84

INDEMNITY TO OTHERS

The Company will indemnify in the terms of this policy

(a) at the request of the Insured
  (i) any director partner or Employee in respect of liability for which the Insured would have been entitled to indemnify if the claim had been made against him
  (ii) any officer member or Employee of the Insured's canteen social sports and welfare organisations or ambulance fire or first aid services in his respective capacity as such

(b) in the event of the death of the Insured his legal personal representatives in respect of liability incurred by him.

Where the Company is liable to indemnify more than one party the total amount of indemnity to all such parties including the Insured shall not exceed the Amounts of Indemnity.

CONDITIONS

1. Interpretation

This Policy and the Schedule shall be read together as one contract and any word or expression to which a specific meaning has been attached in any part of this Policy or of the Schedule shall bear such specific meaning wherever it may appear.

2. Notice of Claims

The Insured shall immediately report to the Company in writing all accidents claims and civil proceedings. Where the Insured has any knowledge of any impending civil proceedings he shall immediately advise the Company in writing. Every letter claim writ summons process or other document must be sent to the Company immediately.

3. Control of Claims

No admission of liability or offer promise or payment shall be made without the Company's written consent. The Company is entitled to take over and conduct the defence or settlement of any claim in the name of the Insured and at the Company's discretion and to prosecute at its own expense and for its own benefit any claim for indemnity or damages against any other persons and the Insured shall give all information and assistance required.

4. Discharge of Liability

The Company may at any time pay the maximum amount of indemnity payable under this policy in respect of any occurrence or any lesser sums for which any claim or claims can be settled and shall then be under no further liability in respect thereof except for the payment of costs and expenses incurred prior to such payment.

5.   Non-Contribution

If any claim under this Policy is also covered in whole or in part by any other existing insurance the liability of the Company shall be limited to any excess beyond the amount which would have been payable under such other insurance had this Policy not been effected.

6.   Alteration of Risk

The Insured shall give immediate notice of any alteration which materially affects the risks covered by this Policy.

7.   Adjustment

The premium for this Policy having been calculated on estimates furnished by the Insured the Insured shall keep an accurate record containing all relevant particulars and shall at all times allow the Company to inspect such record and following the expiry of each period of indemnity shall supply to the Company a correct statement so that the premium for that period shall be calculated and the difference paid by or allowed to the Insured as the case may be.

8.   Cancellation

The Company may cancel this Policy by sending thirty days notice by recorded delivery to the Insured at his last known address and in such event the Company will return a pro-rata portion of the premium adjusted in accordance with Condition 7.

9.   Reasonable Precautions

The Insured shall take and cause to be taken reasonable precautions to prevent Bodily Injury or loss of or damage to Property.

10.   Observance of Conditions

The due observance of the terms provisions conditions and endorsements of this Policy by the Insured or any persons claiming indemnity or benefit in so far as they relate to anything to be done or complied with by the Insured or such persons and the truth of the statements and answers and information supplied on or in connection with the said proposal shall be conditions precedent to any liability of the Company to make any payment under this Policy.

Signed on behalf of the Company

....

THE SCHEDULE

Date of Proposal   Policy No.

Agent   Renewable on:

Branch

The Insured:

Address:

Business:

Period of Insurance | from | to
(Both dates inclusive)

or any subsequent period for which the Company accepts renewal of this Policy

Amount of Indemnity

(1) Any One Event: £

(2) Any One Period of Indemnity: £

First Premium £   Annual Premium £

Chapter 8

EMPLOYEE CLAIMS

8.0   Legal liability for bodily injury or disease incurred by employees in the course of employment is a major risk exposure for many employers. A feature of this risk is the close interaction between people in the workplace over long time periods. Jean-Paul Sartre's view that "hell is other people" finds some credibility when considering the risks of common employment. The matter of compensation for injury has not been left to the respective bargaining powers of the parties, rather, State intervention and to some extent trade unions have shaped modern employers' liability law. This area of social concern has attracted its share of legislation and this will be summarised here and the extent of insurance cover will also be reviewed. The factors which constitute a master and servant relationship are outlined in Chapter 1 para 1.5.1 and "servant" or employee in this context means not only any person under a contract of service or apprenticeship with the employer but includes labour only sub-contractors, self-employed persons, employees of other companies hired in or borrowed under an agreement to the effect that they are deemed to be employees of the company, and persons engaged in work experience.

8.1   The General Nature of the Duty of an Employer

The authoritative text, *Employer's Liability* (tenth edition 1985) by John Munkman, LL.B, published by Butterworths, describes the general nature of the duty of an employer thus:

> "It is the duty of an employer, acting personally or through his servants or agents, to take reasonable care for the safety of his workmen and other employees in the course of their employment. This duty extends in particular to the safety of the place of work, the plant and machinery, and the method and conduct of the work: but it is not restricted to these matters."

Munkman in support of this quotes, inter alia, two cases:

In Paris v Stepney Borough Council 1951 AC 367, Lord Oaksey said:

> "The duty of an employer towards his servant is to take reasonable care for his servant's safety in all the circumstances of the case."

In Davie v New Merton Board Mills Ltd. 1958, 1 QB 210 Parker L. J. said:

> "The duty owed by a master to his servant at common law can be stated in general terms as a duty to take reasonable care for the safety of his servants . . . if the master delegates . . . the performance of that duty to another he remains liable for the failure of that other to exercise reasonable care . . . this principle holds good whether the person employed by the master is a servant, a full-time agent or an independent contractor."

This duty exists whether the employment is inherently dangerous or not: inherent danger makes the duty more severe. The principle is that if the danger cannot be avoided, e.g. use of explosives in quarry, reasonable care must be taken to reduce it as far as possible.

The student who desires a more detailed study of this area of law is recommended to the above named Text.

The liability of an employer towards his servants can be considered to arise from three sources:

(1) In contract
(2) At common law
(3) By statute.

8.2   Liability Arising in Contract

According to Munkman, liability rests upon tort rather than on contract: the latter being relied upon only where there are special advantages. For instance in Matthews v Kuwait Bechtel Corpn, 1959, 2 QB 57 a workman under an English contract injured abroad, was held entitled to base his claim on contract to bring it within the jurisdiction of the English courts. It is an implied term of a contract of employment that the employer shall exercise reasonable care to protect his employees from harm but because the burden of proving the breach of contract is the same as proving negligence, the latter course is the more common.

8.3   Liability at Common Law

The general duty at common law outlined in 8.1 can be broken down into specific sources, these being:

1. Safe place of work
2. Safe plant and machinery
3. Safe system of work
4. Competent and suitable fellow servants
5. Employer's own actions.

8.3.1   Safe Place of Work

The employer's duty at common law, limited to the exercise of reasonable care, is to provide and maintain a safe place of work, including safe means of access to and from it. In Cole v De Trafford (No.2) 1918, 2 KGB 523 Scutton L. J said "(The Master) is bound to use reasonable care to provide safe premises and appliances for his servants to work in and with, and to use reasonable care to keep them safe". In some instances the danger in the workplace cannot be removed and the employer is not expected to ensure that the premises are safe in all circumstances. His duty is to take reasonable precautions for the safety of the employees. Examples of reasonable precautions are a safety rail for work on a ledge over a steep drop: a handrail where steps are steep or irregular: fencing of an open hatchway between decks of a ship: a line of demarcation on a roof over which a ropeway runs.

In instances of work undertaken out of doors in rough country the employer cannot be expected to protect employees against ordinary natural risks (McGinlay v Nutall & Sons, 1956).

In Latimer v A.E.C. Ltd., 1953, AC 643 a limit to the employer's liability is illustrated. A factory floor was flooded after an exceptional storm and the floor was rendered slippery by rainwater and a mixture of oil. A workman slipped and was injured whilst wheeling a trolley. The House of Lords held that there was no liability at common law there being no negligence for failing to send the workmen home until the condition of the floor improved. The danger was not sufficiently grave for this step to have been taken but circumstances such as the structure of the building being made unsafe by a fire would be sufficient.

Employees often work in premises belonging to third parties and the employer's duty of care follows them but the extent of the duty varies according to circumstances, mainly dependent upon the degree of control that the employer can be said to exercise over those premises. In the case of McQuilter v Goulandis Bros Ltd., 1951, an employee who had to walk along an unlighted deck fell into a hatchway and was killed. Finding for the plaintiff Lord Guthrie said:

"The fact that the work had to be carried out on the premises of a third party did not absolve an employer from his duty of exercising reasonable care for the safety of his workmen. The duty must still be fulfilled, although its scope is circumscribed by the fact that the work was being done on premises not within the possession and control of the employer. As the structure of the premises is outwith his control, and any defects therein beyond his power to rectify, his care for his men could only be exercised within the limits imposed by those circumstances. But he was still under the duty of exercising reasonable care to safeguard them against dangers which he should anticipate and which he had power to avert."

The custom of trade may have a bearing on what is expected of an employer whose employees work away. For instance, employers who are stevedores are in general entitled to rely upon shipowners for safety and window cleaners must take precautions against loose sashes.

8.3.2   Safe Plant and Machinery

"Plant" in this context means all manner of things used in the course of the work. It comprises for example such widely divergent objects as ladders and car heaters. The employer must take reasonable care to provide and maintain proper plant and machinery. Note that it is not enough to provide necessary plant but the plant must be kept in good order. It is a continuing obligation and the employer will be vicariously liable for negligence of fellow workmen in maintenance or in the selection or use of plant.

8.3.3A   The Provision of Plant

The provision of plant may be considered under three heads.

(i) Failure to provide necessary plant.
Necessary equipment may be wanting, causing employees to improvise. In Lovell v Blundells & Crompton & Co. Ltd., 1944, KB 502 a workman instructed to service a boiler, was not supplied with planks for staging and scrounged some materials which proved defective. The employer was liable. There is sufficient grounds for an action if the need for the plant is obvious or a reasonable man would recognise it to be necessary.

(ii) Failure to provide sufficient plant.
In Vaughan v Ropner & Co. Ltd., 1974, a wire rope on a ship's hoist was

damaged and no suitable replacement wire rope was available. An accident occurred after a makeshift rope of odd pieces of fibre was substituted. Defendants liable because a ship at sea should carry enough spares to last a voyage.

(iii) Providing defective or dangerous equipment.

The Employers Liability (Defective Equipment) Act, 1969, has an important bearing in that it imposes a strict liability on the employer in respect of defective equipment and this will be considered after the common law position is outlined. The employer will not be liable at common law unless he knew or ought to have known of any defect or danger. Before the Act came into force the employer could rely upon a reputable supplier or manufacturer and was not expected to examine the equipment for latent defects. In Davie v New Merton Board Mills, 1958, 1 ALL E.R. 67 the House of Lords decided that an employer was not liable for damage caused by a defective implement purchased from a reputable manufacturer. The defect was not apparent on inspection and no intermediate inspection by the employers between the time of its delivery and its use was reasonably to be expected. The employee was therefore left to sue the manufacturer and this could present difficulties if, say the manufacturer had gone out of business or could not be identified. Now the above Act provides that an employee who is injured because of a defect in his employer's equipment can recover damages from the employer if he can show that the defect is due to the fault of some person, e.g. the manufacturer but if no one is at fault damages are not recoverable. Employees' rights under this Act are in addition to common law rights therefore the employee can sue a manufacturer, if say, the employer is insolvent, but the latter circumstances are unlikely in view of compulsory insurance. Any agreement by an employer to contract out of the statutory liability is void.

8.3.3B   Maintenance of Plant

The employer's duty is to take reasonable care to maintain his plant and machinery in proper condition and he will be liable for the negligence of his servants and the negligence of independent contractors to whom maintenance is entrusted. Various aspects of the risk are:

(i) Failure to remedy known defects. Liability will attach where the employer had ample time to put matters right but on occasion delay might be considered reasonable.

(ii) Discovery of unknown defects: inspection and testing. Generally there is a duty on the employer to inspect plant. Frequency and methods of testing must depend upon the circumstances. In Webb v Rennie, 1865, a scaffolding had been erected for shipbuilding and the poles had been left in the ground for two years. As the scaffolding was being dismantled one of the poles snapped and fell upon a workman. The employers were held liable for not inspecting the poles before work began.

(iii) Failure or delay in carrying out repairs. The time factor is important and an employer will not be held liable unless he has had time and opportunity to repair the defect after it came (or ought to have come) to his knowledge. A

92

skilled workman is expected to repair his own tools and in Pearse v Armitage, 1950, the Court of Appeal said that even an unskilled workman should be expected to tighten a slack rope on a safety device.

(iv) Selection of plant. The selection of plant is the responsibility of the employer whether he chooses personally or acts through his servants. However this principle is qualified. If the selection of equipment is properly left to the plaintiff himself who is competent and experienced the employer will not be held negligent.

8.3.4   Safe System of Work

The employer has a duty to exercise reasonable care in providing a proper and safe system of work. Munkman describes "system of work" in this way:

"The employer is responsible for the general organisation of the factory, mine or undertaking; in short, he decides the broad scheme under which the premises, plant and men are put to work. This organisation or "system" includes such matters as the co-ordination of different departments and activities; the lay-out of plant and appliances for special tasks; the method of using particular machines or carrying out particular processes; the instruction of apprentices or inexperienced workers; and a residual heading, the general conditions of work, covering such things as fire precautions. An organisation of this kind is required — independently of safety — for the purpose of ensuring that the work is carried on smoothly and competently: and the principle of law is that in setting up and enforcing the system, due care and skill must be exercised for the safety of the workmen. Accordingly, the employer's personal liability for an unsafe system — independently of the negligence of fellow servants — is not founded on an artificial concept, but is directly related to the facts of industrial organisation."

A master cannot escape liability by delegating performance of the duty to someone else. In Wilson and Clyde Coal Co. v English, 1938, AC 57 a miner on a morning shift was leaving the pit when the haulage plant was put into operation and he was crushed against the side of the road by the hutches before he had time to reach a refuge hole. Although the employers had delegated their duties to a qualified manager they were held liable on the grounds that it was an unsafe system for the haulage plant to be operated while the morning shift was leaving work. The employer should plan the work in advance with due regard for safety and this principle applies whether the work is of a permanent or settled character or whether it varies from time to time or is even a single isolated task.

Allowance for infirmities or inexperience of individual workmen will be expected in planning a safe system of work. In Paris v Stepney Borough Council, 1951, the duty owed to workmen of known peculiarities is demonstrated. A one-eyed workman was engaged in hammering a rusty bolt on a motor vehicle when a chip of metal flew into his eye and blinded him. Protective goggles ought to have been provided for him, even though it was not the practice to make such provision for persons of normal sight engaged in similar work.

8.3.5   Competent and Suitable Fellow Servants

The employer has a duty to employ competent employees but the relevance of this duty, which was at best a question of taking reasonable care in their selection, has now diminished with the abolition of the defence of common employment. The employer is now liable for the negligence of fellow employees and it is on this ground that an action is likely to be raised rather than on an allegation of carelessness in selection.

An action under this head is possible, for example, an employee, although skilled, may not have sufficient skill to deal with a situation which the employer should have foreseen (Butler (or Black) v Fife Coal Co. Ltd., 1912, AC 149). In the United States a number of actions have succeeded where the employers had recruited vicious or dangerous fellow-servants.

8.3.6 Employer's Own Action

The employer's personal negligence resulting in injury to an employee requires little comment. Ordinarily this is a minor risk factor unless the employer is a working master.

8.4 Breach of Statutory Duty

There are several Statutes passed for the benefit of workmen and generally these place upon the employer certain duties in respect of the health, safety and welfare of his employees. If the duties are not performed in accordance with statutory requirements and injury results, this will invariably give the injured employee a right of action, provided he can establish that the breach was the direct cause of his injury. Most employee claims are therefore based upon breach of statutory duty rather than on failure by the employer to exercise reasonable care at common law, just described. The statutory route is normally the easier one for the claimant, because failure to comply with a statutory regulation is enough proof in itself and there is no necessity to prove negligence. In Groves v Wimborne, 1898, 2 QB 402 the action was against an employer for failing to fence dangerous machinery in accordance with the requirements of the Factory and Workshop Act 1878. Vaughan Williams LJ observed:

"It cannot be doubted that where a statute provides for the performance by certain persons of a particular duty, and some one belonging to a class of persons for whose benefit and protection the statute imposes the duty is injured by failure to perform it, prima facie and if there be nothing to the contrary, an action by the person so injured will lie against the person who has so failed to perform the duty."

The employer remains liable for any breach even where he has delegated responsibility to an employee or to an independent contractor. Liability is not dependent upon proof of negligence and contravention of statutory regulations automatically establishes liability. The plaintiff employee must prove three things in an action alleging breach of a statutory duty, namely:

(i) that the statute imposes upon the defendant a duty, which is intended to protect the plaintiff against harm of some kind;

(ii) that the defendant had failed to perform his duty;

(iii) that this breach of duty has resulted in harm to the plaintiff, which is of a kind contemplated by the statute.

8.4.1   Defences To Actions for Breach of Statutory Duty

The defendant may deny that there was a duty imposed on him, or that there was a breach of duty, or he may allege that the duty was not as wide as alleged. Alternatively, the defendant may deny that the plaintiff was within the benefit of the statute, or that the accident was of the kind that the statute was designed to prevent. Contributory negligence (see Chapter 2, 2.4.10) can be an important factor but Volenti Non Fit Injuria (2.1.1) cannot, as a general rule, be pleaded by an employer in an action for breach of a statutory duty. This defence may be applicable, however in the case of a breach of statutory duty by the employee himself, which results in his own injury.

The difficulty with statutory liability is that some duties are mandatory and absolute whereas in other instances it is expressed as "so far as practicable" which is less strict. Even less definitive is the term "so far as reasonably practicable", which is also used in some statutes. Therein lie other possible defences. In the Factories Act, for example, some of the duties are absolute whereas others are qualified by the above terms. The General Duties of the Health and Safety at Work Act, 1974, have to be carried out "so far as is reasonably practicable" but the Act does not define this term and therefore resort to judicial interpretation is necessary. In Edwards v National Coal Board, 1959, 1 AER 743 it was held that "reasonably practicable" is a narrower term than "physically possible". This interpretation implies that a quantitative judgement or balance has to be made between the extent of risk, which is placed on one scale, and the sacrifice, either in money, time or trouble taken with measures to avoid the risk, placed on the other side of the scale. If it is demonstrated that there is a gross imbalance between them and the risk is insignificant compared to the sacrifice, the employer upon whom the duty is laid discharges the burden of proving that compliance was not reasonably practicable.

In Marshall v Gotham Co. Ltd., 1954, AC 360 the House of Lords opined, "If a precaution is practicable it must be taken unless in the whole circumstances that would be unreasonable. And, as men's lives may be at stake, it should not lightly be held that to take a practical precaution is unreasonable . . . the danger was a very rare one. The trouble and expense involved in the use of the precaution, while not prohibitive, would have been considerable. The precautions would not have afforded anything like complete protection against the danger and their adoption would have had the disadvantage of giving a false sense of security".

To summarise, the statutory liability is absolute where the wording is unqualified and is less so in the case of the "so far as practicable" wording. This is still more strict than the position at common law. With the "as far as reasonably practicable" wording the liability is still more onerous than common law, for apart from any other consideration the onus of establishing it is on the defendants.

8.5   The Health and Safety at Work Act, 1974

The Health and Safety at Work Act, effective from 1st April 1975, provides the most comprehensive ever system of law covering the health and safety of people at work and the public at large who may be effected by the activities of people at work. It is an enabling Act and contains a whole range of basic provisions to be converted into specialist provisions. Current health and safety legislation is being progressively repealed and replaced by improved and updated regulations made under the new Act and by approved codes of practice. Therein is the framework for promotion, stimulation and encouragement of high standards for health and safety at work.

8.5.1   Duties of Employers

The general duties of employers to their employees are set down in Section 2 of the Act.

Section 2(1) "It shall be the duty of every employer to ensure, so far as is reasonably practicable, the health, safety and welfare at work of all his employees".

Section 2(2)(a) "the provision and maintenance of plant and systems of work that are, so far as reasonably practicable, safe and without risk to health". This is a general requirement covering all plant, which the Act defines as including machinery, equipment and appliances used at work. It does not supersede the more detailed and specific provisions covering certain equipment contained in existing legislation, but it goes beyond such provisions in requiring a more wide ranging assessment of risk.

Section 2(2)(b) "arrangements for ensuring, so far as is reasonably practicable, safety and absence of risk to health in connection with the use, handling, storage and transport of articles and substances". This subsection is concerned with the materials and substances, whether in solid or liquid form or in the form of gas or vapour, so that the subsection covers everything used at work and in all work activities.

Section 2(2)(c) "the provision of such information, instruction, training and supervision as is necessary to ensure, so far as is reasonably practicable, the health and safety at work of his employees".

Section 2(2)(d) "so far as is reasonably practicable as regards any place of work under the employer's control, the maintenance of it in a condition that is safe and without risks to health and the provision and maintenance of means of access to and egress from it that are safe and without such risks".

Section 2(2)(e) "the provision and maintenance of a working environment for his employees that is, so far as is reasonably practicable, safe, without risks to health, and adequate as regards facilities and arrangements for their welfare at work".

Section 2(3) "Except in such cases as may be prescribed, it shall be the duty of every employer to prepare a written statement of his general policy with respect to the health and safety at work of his employees". This statement is the blueprint on which the employer's entire health and safety at work policy, organisation and activity are based. The employer cannot pass on the responsibility for the compilation of the statement to employees, their appointed safety representatives or to safety committees. However, it would be sensible for an employer to consult his employees, through their safety representatives and to heed the advice of the safety committees, where these exist, in order to ensure that the best arrangements and organisations for safety and health are evolved, maintained and where necessary improved.

8.5.2 Duties to Persons Other Than Employees

Section 3(1) "It shall be the duty of every employer to conduct his undertaking in such a way as to ensure so far as is reasonably practicable, that persons not in his employment who may be affected thereby are not thereby exposed to risks to their health and safety".

Section 3(3) places a duty on an employer, in circumstances which will be prescribed, to give information about such aspects of the way in which he conducts his undertaking to persons who are not his employees as might affect their health or safety. Regulations will need to be made prescribing the circumstances and the information required.

8.5.3 Duties Relating to Premises

Section 4 of the Act lays down duties with respect to health and safety on those who are in control of any non-domestic premises, where people who are not their own employees may work, or where such people use plant or substances provided for their own use there.

8.5.4 Duties of Manufacturers and Suppliers

Section 6 of the Act places duties on persons who design, manufacture, import or supply any article for use at work. They are required to ensure as far as is reasonably practicable that any plant, machinery, equipment or appliance is so designed and constructed as to be safe and without risk to health, when properly used. They must also carry out any testing or examination necessary to achieve this and they must ensure that adequate information will be available about the use for which it was designed and about any conditions necessary for its safe use. If they cannot carry out such testing they must arrange for it to be carried out. A person who erects or installs such plant etc. must ensure that the installation is not unsafe or a risk to health. A person who manufactures, imports or supplies any substance for use at work must ensure that, as far as is reasonably practicable, it is safe and without risk to health and there are requirements for testing and examination and research. He must also ensure that there is adequate information available about this and about any conditions necessary to ensure that it will be safe and without risks to health when properly used.

8.5.5 Duties of Employees

As regards "employees" it should be noted that members of management may be "employees" within the meaning of the Act and will therefore have duties under it. The duties of employees are set out in Section 7 which is quoted below.

Section 7 "It shall be the duty of every employee whilst at work:

(a) to take reasonable care for the health and safety of himself and other persons who may be affected by his acts or omissions at work, and

(b) as regards any duty or requirement imposed on his employer or any other person by or under any of the relevant statutory provisions, to co-operate with him so far as is necessary to enable that duty or requirement to be performed or complied with".

Section 8 "No person shall intentionally or recklessly interfere with or misuse anything provided in the interests of health and safety and welfare in pursuance of any of the relevant statutory provisions".

Note that the question of whether a person is an "employer" or an "employee" will depend on the facts of a particular situation.

8.5.6 Enforcement of the Act Provisions

If an inspector discovers a contravention of one of the provisions of the Act he can issue a prohibition notice if there is a risk of serious personal injury, to stop the activity giving rise to this risk, until the remedial action specified in the notice has been taken. The notice can be issued whether or not there is a legal contravention, and it can take effect immediately or at a later time. It can be served on the person undertaking the activity, or the person in control of it as the notice was served. Alternatively the inspector may issue an improvement notice in the event of a contravention, to remedy the fault within a specified time.

The inspector can prosecute any person contravening a relevant statutory provision instead of, or in addition to, serving a notice. Contravention of some of the requirements can lead to prosecution summarily in a Magistrates' Court or equivalent in Scotland. Contravention of other provisions can result in prosecution either summarily or on indictment in the Crown Court in England and Wales or the equivalent court in Scotland. The maximum fine, on summary conviction, for certain offences is £1,000. There is no limit to the fine on conviction on indictment. Imprisonment for up to two years can be imposed for certain offences in addition to an unlimited fine. In addition the Court may make an order requiring the cause of the offence to be remedied. The inspector may seize, render harmless or destroy any substances or articles that he considers to be the cause of imminent danger or serious personal injury.

8.5.7 Fire Prevention and Precautions

The Fire Precautions Act, 1971, is amended by the 1974 Act so that general fire precautions at most places of work can be dealt with under the 1971 Act by the fire authorities and the Home Office Departments. The Health and Safety at Work Commission and Executives will, however, remain responsible for control over "process" risks, that is, risks of outbreak of fire associated with particular processes or particular substances. The fire provisions in the Offices Shops and Railway Premises Act and the Factories Act are expected to be repealed. Fire certificates issued under those Acts will continue in force as if issued under the 1971 Act, and also as if they include certain requirements concerning fire precautions at present contained in the repealed sections.

8.5.8 Effect of the Act on the Liability of an Employer

It should be noted that to breach the Act is a criminal offence and not in itself a civil matter. Conversely, nothing in the Act shall be construed as conferring a right of action in any civil proceedings imposed by Sections 2 to 7 or any contravention of Section 8. However, as discussed in 8.4 above, where breach of statutory duty results in injury or illness, this is normally enough proof in itself without the necessity for negligence to be established.

8.6   The Factories Act 1961

The Factories Act, 1961 regulates matters pertaining not only to safety but also to such matters as welfare (e.g. canteens and washing facilities), the employment of women and young persons and their hours of work. Some of the administrative provisions of this Act have been repealed by the regulations under the Health and Safety at Work Act, 1974, and eventually the Factories Act may be superseded by regulations under that Act. Section 175 of the Factories Act gives a complex definition of a "factory", and only part of that definition will be quoted here.

". . . the expression "factory" means any premises in which or within the close or curtilage or precincts of which, persons are employed in manual labour in any process for or incidental to any of the following purposes, namely —

(a) the making of any article or part of any article; or
(b) the altering, repairing, ornamenting, finishing, cleaning or washing, or breaking up or demolition of any article; or
(c) the adapting for sale of any article;
(d) the slaughtering of cattle, sheep, swine, goats, horses, asses or mules; or
(e) the confinement of such animals as aforesaid while awaiting slaughter at other premises, in a case where the place of confinement is available in connection with those premises, is not maintained primarily for agricultural purposes within the meaning of the Agricultural Act, 1947, or, as the case may be, the Agricultural (Scotland) Act, 1948, and does not form part of premises used for the holding of a market in respect of such animals; being premises in which, or within the close or curtilage or precincts of which, the work is carried on by way of trade or for purposes of gain and to or over which the employer of the persons employed therein has the right of access or control . . .".

The section goes on to list a wide range of premises used for specified activities.

Generally the occupier of a factory is responsible for seeing that the Act provisions are complied with: he need not necessarily be the employer of the persons working therein: the test is control of the premises.

General safety requirements laid down include regulations relating to:

(a) condition of factory premises;
(b) lifting tackle and lifting machines;
(c) cranes and other lifting machines;
(d) fencing of vats containing dangerous liquids;
(e) fumes in confined spaces;
(f) explosive and inflammable dust, gas or substance;
(g) steam and compressed air plant;
(h) water sealed gasholders;
(i) fire precautions;
(j) fencing of machinery;
(k) dust, fumes and humidity;
(l) poisonous and harmful processes;
(m) protection of eyes;
(n) lifting heavy weights and
(o) washing and drinking facilities.

Additional regulations relate to specified industries including iron and steel foundries, shipbuilding and docks, building and engineering operations, electricity stations and railways.

The chief objective is the protection of employees of the occupier of the factory but others come within the protection of the Act. In Lavender v Diamints Ltd., 1949, 1 KB 585 occupiers were held liable to a window-cleaner for failing to provide safe means of access to the premises. In most instances the duties laid down are absolute and it is not a matter of the employer merely exercising reasonable care; he must ensure that the requirements of the Act are observed to the letter. An example is the absolute duty to fence all prime mover machinery, transmission machinery and other dangerous parts of any machinery (Sections 12 to 16). These parts of machinery must be securely fenced, except that in certain cases fencing may be dispensed with if the position or construction of the machine gives the same degree of safety as fencing must give. It is no defence to say that it is impracticable to fence the machine, or that the machine, if securely fenced, will become useless.

Failure to comply with the Act provisions can result in prosecution and where breach of the regulations results in injury this will assist the plaintiff in pursuance of his claim for compensation, as in the case of the 1974 Act.

8.7   The Agriculture (Safety, Health and Welfare Provisions) Act, 1956

Some parts of this Act have been repealed or modified and it now takes effect within the framework of the Health and Safety at Work Act, which has wider powers to make safety regulations in the agriculture industry where, formerly, safety standards had been less stringent than in other industries.

Section 1 authorises the making of regulations to protect workers employed in agriculture against risks of bodily injury or injury to health "arising out of the use of any machinery, plant, equipment or appliance, the carrying on of any operation or process, or the management of animals". The regulations also require safe places of work and safe means of access, and protection from falls through apertures and from ladders, staircases and other places. Regulations on maximum weight of any load consisting of a sack or bag to be carried are effected. A young person under 18 is not to be employed "to lift, carry or move a load so heavy as to be likely to cause injury to him". There are regulations in respect of ladders, tractor cabs, circular saws, fencing of stationary machinery, threshers and balers, field machinery, the safety of children and poisonous spraying.

8.8   The Offices, Shops and Railway Premises Act, 1963

This Act also now takes effect within the framework of the 1974 Act and it covers places of work not covered by the Factories Act. Most of the administrative provisions (regulations, prosecutions, exemptions) have been repealed or modified to conform to the 1974 Act and future regulations will be made under the latter.

The three types of premises to which the Act applies, namely, offices, shops and railway premises are defined in detail but here broad outlines only are necessary.

Office premises includes either an entire building or part of a building, whose sole or principle use is for "office purposes".

Shop premises include not only shops in the ordinary way but all buildings or parts of them used for retail trade. The latter includes sale of food or drink for immediate consumption, meaning restaurants and pubs etc.

Railway premises means a building or part of a building used for railway purposes and adjacent to the railway track, but excluding offices and shops, hostels for railway workers, hotels and electricity stations. Since railway workshops are "factories" there is very little left. Possibly only buildings such as signal boxes qualify.

The Act does not apply to premises where only relatives of the employer work and therefore it excludes many small family run retail shops. It does not extend to the protection of customers. Floors, steps, passages and gangways require to be in proper condition and free, as far as reasonably practicable, from obstruction and slipperiness. Protection is required from open staircases and floor openings. Fencing of dangerous parts of machinery and restrictions on the cleaning of machines by persons under 18 are provided for. Welfare requirements relate to cleanliness, overcrowding, temperature, ventilation, lighting, sanitary and washing facilities, drinking water, cloakrooms, seats for sedentary work or resting and facilities for eating.

Responsibility for complying with the Act rests primarily with the occupier as in the case of factories, but in some instances others may be liable, for example the owner of the building for, say, the condition of the common stairway or for lighting.

8.9   The Mines and Quarries Act, 1954

Like the statutes already referred to which are specific to particular places of work this Act also takes effect within the framework of the 1974 Act and will be replaced, in time, by regulations under the latter. The Act lays down very detailed precautions necessary for the safety and system of working of employees in mines and quarries. The safety requirements for coal mines are more strict than those for other types of mines such as shale or fireclay. All mines must be specifically checked for safety of roofs and sides and the operation of winding apparatus.

Quarry workers must be safeguarded against danger from falls and quarry faces must be inspected to ensure safe working conditions.

8.10   The Employment Protection Act, 1975

This statute deals with the rights of employess in the contract of employment. Part I deals with the Advisory Conciliation and Arbitration Service (ACAS), trade union recognition, the duty of employers to disclose information for collective bargaining. Part II covers guarantee payments, suspension on medical grounds, maternity, trade union membership, time off work, insolvency of employer, written statement of reasons for dismissal, remedies for unfair dismissal, itemised pay statement, working hours and pay, and the Employment Appeal Tribunal.

Part III deals with, inter alia, wages councils and statutory joint industrial councils, Part IV with procedure for handling redundancies and Part V covers miscellaneous and supplementary provisions.

It is pertinent to look at the Act provisions on remedies for unfair dismissal (Sections 71 to 80). These Sections provide for:

(a) improvements to the remedy of reinstatement or re-engagement for unfair dismissal. Industrial Tribunals will now have to consider if reinstatement or re-engagement is practicable and if the employee wants this remedy as a first step. If an employer fails to comply with an order for reinstatement or re-engagement the tribunal can make a further award of compensation of between 13 and 52 weeks pay,

(b) compensation for unfair dismissal to be calculated as a basic award related to years of service plus a compensatory award which will take account of any loss suffered by the employee,

(c) in certain cases where dismissal was related to membership of an independent trade union or to taking part in its activities, a Tribunal may give interim relief to the complainant by way of an order for the revival or continuation of the employee's contract.

8.11   Sex Discrimination Acts 1975, and, 1986

The 1975 Act bans discrimination on grounds of sex, in the selection of employees or in their promotion, transfer or dismissal. Discrimination is lawful still, only where "sex is an essential qualification for the job".

Section 1(1) "A person discriminates against a woman in any circumstances relevant for the purposes of any provision of this Act if —

(a) on the ground of her sex he treats her less favourably than he treats or would treat a man, or

(b) he applies to her a requirement or condition which he applies or would apply equally to a man but —
    (i) which is such that the proportion of women who can comply with it is considerably smaller than the proportion of men who can comply with it, and
    (ii) which he cannot show to be justifiable irrespective of the sex of the person to whom it is applied, and
    (iii) which is to her detriment because she cannot comply with it.

(2) If a person treats or would treat a man differently according to the man's marital status, his treatment of a woman is for the purposes of subsection (1)(a) to be compared to his treatment of a man having the like marital status".

Section 2 of the Act deals with discrimination against men in similar terms with such modifications as are requisite.

The Sex Discrimination Act 1986 is not yet fully in force but relevant sections already in force include:

Section 1 which extends the 1975 Act to employers of five or fewer employees and partnerships of five or fewer partners and limits to some extent the previous exemption for employment in a private household.

Section 6 extends Section 75 of the 1975 Act (which makes void any term of a contract leading to discrimination which is unlawful) to provisions of collective agreements, employers' rules and the rules of trade unions, employers' associations, professional organisations and qualifying bodies.

Section 7 amends the Factories Act and the Mines and Quarries Act by removing restrictions on women working shifts, overtime restrictions and maximum hours limitations.

Mental or emotional distress to a victim of discrimination, resulting in the person suffering injury to feelings could result in an action against the employer for "bodily injury".

8.11.1   Sexual Harassment in the Workplace

A new potential liability is emerging as a result of recent court decisions on alleged sexual harassment and to date the litigants have been women. The Equal Opportunities Commission says it gets about six complaints a month regarding sexual harassment and that this is only the "tip of the iceberg" of the problem. Complaints make up 5 per cent of all enquiries made to the EOC about employment (*The Guardian* 11/8/86). Sexual harassment includes not only unwelcome acts which involve physical contact of a sexual nature, but also behaviour falling short of such physical acts. The Trades Union Congress defines sexual harassment as "repeated unwanted sexual advances, sexually explicit derogatory statements, or sexually discriminatory remarks made by someone in the workplace which are offensive to the worker involved and cause the worker to feel threatened, humiliated, patronised or harassed, or which interferes with the worker's performance". The Sex Discrimination Acts do not specifically outlaw sexual harassment but in the opinion of the EOC the decision in Porcelli v Strathclyde Regional Council, 1984, (Industrial Relations Law Reports 1984 p. 467) places the risk firmly within the scope of the Sex Discrimination Acts. In this case a Scottish Industrial Tribunal accepted the plaintiff Mrs. Porcelli's account of the sexual harassment to which she was subjected by two male colleagues, that the defendant employers Strathclyde Regional Council were vicariously responsible and that the treatment to which she was subjected was to her detriment. However the Tribunal concluded that, had Mrs. Porcelli been a man whom the two employees disliked, they would have treated him just as unfavourably. The Plaintiff took her case to the Employment Appeal Tribunal which held that the Industrial Tribunal had erred in law in dismissing her complaint and therefore allowed the appeal. As a result of a final Law Lords ruling the matter was referred back to the Tribunal which ordered the defendants to award Mrs. Porcelli £3,000 in compensation for the "act of discrimination". Lord Emslie's opinion was that "sexual harassment is a particularly degrading and unacceptable form of sex discrimination which it must have been the intention of Parliament to restrain".

Employers are becoming aware of the risk. A booklet from the Society of Civil and Public Servants issued to 150,000 civil servants warns that if offenders harass co-workers they could face legal action.

8.12   Random Examples of Accidents at Work

The following is a list of accidents spanning a range of work, resulting in claims against employers:

- failure to provide a guard on a car repair lift resulted in a young woman being scalped: her hair caught in a giant screw operating the lift

- miner had leg amputated below the knee after being caught in a conveyor belt
- defective brakes and gears on a shovel loader used by a brick company caused the death of an employee
- a railway shunter was crushed between a wagon and a platform
- a worker contracted pneumoconiosis from inhaling dust whilst working on operations on iron and steel castings
- four workmen were killed when a construction cradle cable snapped and the cradle crashed to the ground
- a farmworker was electrocuted while washing down the walls of a farmhouse using a pressure washer: the electricity supply socket was not earthed
- a roofing worker was electrocuted while using a 240-volt electric saw
- whilst washing a tea-cup an employee sustained injuries when she slipped on duckboard
- an employee who persisted in practical jokes injured a fellow workman as a result: employer was liable for failing to take necessary measures to prevent
- nervous shock suffered by a train driver following a fatal accident to a passenger
- horseplay by a fork-lift truck driver who shunted his machine against a duckboard upon which a colleague was standing, causing him injury
- employee's hearing impaired by employer's failure to contain noise level in a ship repair yard.

8.13   Latent Diseases

Claims by employees for personal injury from latent or insidious diseases present special problems because symptoms often become apparent perhaps many years after causation and the employer (and therefore his insurer) is faced with claims which are not anticipated and for which no reserve funds have been set aside. Where there have been several employers over the causation period there is also the problem of allocation of responsibility. In the last decade, for example, claims for asbestosis and hearing impairment have caused employers to look for retrospective insurance cover. Changes in the limitations periods for bringing personal injury claims mean it is now increasingly difficult for any point of limitation to be taken as a defence by the employer. The law relating to occupational deafness is still developing. Hearing impairment caused by exposure to noise is actionable at common law as from 1963, this being the date of publication by the Factory Inspectorate of *Noise and the Worker*. Some claimants may have been employed by more than one previous employer and some attempt has to be made to apportion liability, usually on the basis of successive periods of exposure.

Because many employers' liability insurance covers were on a "claims occurring" basis this can mean involvement by the different insurers of several previous employers in apportionment of the liability. An agreement has been entered into by two insurers and two large trade unions whereby compensation is guaranteed for all deafness claims, avoiding the uncertainty of litigation and thereby relieving the trade unions of the high cost of litigation. This is tantamount to a "no-fault" compensation agreement. Claims falling within the scope of the agreement (in the iron trades) are those arising from alleged over-exposure to noise of at least one year's duration between 1963 and 1978 and provided there is medically confirmed occupational deafness of at least 10 decibels. Damages awards, which were modest up to 1982, increased considerably following the decision in Heslop v Metalock (GB) Ltd., 1982, where the plaintiff was awarded £7,750 for hearing impairment from exposure to noise over a period of 24 years. Liability for hearing impairment has developed considerably world wide. There has been considerable litigation in the USA of course and in Europe. Employees in South Africa are some of the latest to follow the trend in demanding damages for impairment to hearing.

The "long tail" type of liability claim has been a problem in the form of lung disease even before deafness claims arrived. The Pneumoconiosis etc. (Workers Compensation) Act, 1979, allows sufferers of any of five dust related diseases specified in the Act (as amended) to claim lump sum compensation from the Government if former employers are no longer in business. Latent diseases claims are likely to persist, as people become more aware of opportunities given by legislation to pursue their cases. Moreover, employer responsibility for other occupational hazards such as occupational stress from overwork could develop in future.

8.14 Research on Employee Claims

The Rehabilitation Studies Unit at Edinburgh University has carried out research into employee claims and the following statistics are extracted from a study entitled *A Screening of Employers' Liability Claims Files* by Hugh M. Bochel and Paul Cornes. This is a review of 209 cases and relates to claims of £5,000 or over:

- 93% of claimants were male
- 46% were employed in skilled manual occupations and tended to be injured in accidents involving machinery they operated
- 32% were unskilled manual workers, many suffering from sprains and strains from lifting or handling heavy objects
- 1% of claimants were in management/supervisory positions
- 8% were skilled non-manual workers
- 13% were semi-skilled manual workers

The highest proportion (23%) were employed in the construction industry, followed by engineering (19%), distribution and catering (16%) and heavy industry (15%).

Chapter 9

COMPULSORY EMPLOYER'S LIABILITY INSURANCE

9.0   Employer's Liability Insurance

With few exceptions, insurance of the legal liability of the employer for bodily injury to his employees is compulsory in the United Kingdom. Before the Employer's Liability (Compulsory Insurance) Act, 1969, not every employer insured the risk and in some instances an injured employee had little chance of obtaining compensation from an impecunious employer, even where he had a valid claim in law. The Act took effect from 1st January 1972 and the Employers Liability (Compulsory Insurance) Regulations, 1971, also apply and give the detail upon which the Act relies. Now an employee with a valid claim for damages is confident in the knowledge that an insurer is providing the funds to satisfy any successful claim. The Act further assists the claimant by prohibiting insurers from avoiding payment on the ground of breach of certain contractual conditions by the employer.

9.1   The Employers Liability (Compulsory Insurance) Act, 1969

By the terms of the Act, employers in Great Britain are required to effect insurance against their legal liability for bodily injury or disease to employees sustained during the course of their employment. Certain exceptions apply. It is not necessary for members of the insured's family to be covered therefore a business employing only family members does not require to effect insurance cover, unless the business has been incorporated as a limited company. Exempted also are certain corporations which are backed by central government funding, including nationalised industries, local authorities, police authorities (and by later Regulations) London Transport Executive, Water Authorities, and the Commission for New Towns.

The Act is precise in the matter of interpretation of key terms. For instance, the risk must be covered by an "approved policy" which means a policy not subject to any conditions or exceptions prohibited by regulations. (This will be considered later.) The policy must be issued by an authorised insurer, meaning a person or body of persons lawfully carrying on in Great Britain insurance business of that class in accordance with the provisions of the Insurance Companies Act, 1982. "Business" includes a trade or profession and includes any activity carried on by a body of persons whether corporate or unincorporate. "Employee" means an individual who has entered into or who works under a contract of service or apprenticeship with an employer whether by way of manual labour, clerical work, or otherwise, whether such contract is expressed or implied, oral or in writing.

Compulsory insurance applies to employees not ordinarily resident in Great Britain but who visit in the course of employment for a continuous period of not less than fourteen days.

Whilst the Act does not in any way modify or effect the legal liability of the employer outlined in Chapter 8, it does impose on the employer a statutory obligation to insure that liability. The penalty for failure to insure is a fine not exceeding £200 for each day of failure and directors, officers or managers who wilfully fail to comply are also liable to proceedings.

Northern Ireland, the Isle of Man and the Channel Islands have similar, but separate legislation for the compulsory insurance of this risk.

9.1.1 The Employers' Liability (Compulsory Insurance) Regulations, 1971

The Regulations set out in detail the actual requirements of the Act. Provisions include:

(a) any limit of indemnity for any one occurrence under an insurance policy must not be less than £2 million. Few insurers impose a limit of indemnity.

(b) a certificate of insurance must be issued by the insurer not later than thirty days after the date on which the insurance commences or is renewed.

(c) the certificate of insurance must be displayed at the place of business or where there is more than one location, at each place of business.

(d) the employer must produce the certificate or policy for inspection by anyone having reasonable grounds for requesting it.

(e) certain conditions in policies are prohibited. These are conditions which state that no liability shall arise under the policy or that any such liability shall cease:
  (i) in the event of some specified things being done or omitted to be done after the happening of the event giving rise to a claim under the policy;
  (ii) unless the policyholder takes reasonable care to protect his employees against the risk of injury or disease in the course of their employment;
  (iii) unless the policyholder keeps specified records or provides the insurer with or makes available to him information therefrom.

In effect the insurer is prevented from repudiating claims in certain instances, for example, late notification by the employer of a claim (i) or where the employer fails to ensure that a guard on a machine is in place (ii) or where the employer fails to provide the insurer with information on, say, wages for the purposes of calculating the premium (iii). Because the objective of this legislation is to ensure, as far as possible, that there will be resources to satisfy an injured employee's claim, it is desirable to limit the freedom of insurer's to contract out of liability once cover is effected. In the event of an insurer having to pay a claim by virtue of the Regulations above, there is a right of recovery from the employer of the amount paid and this statutory right is usually reinforced by an express clause in the policy wording.

It is important to appreciate that not all restrictive conditions in an employer's liability insurance are ineffective, but only those in the categories listed above. Trade endorsements are in use and are not prohibited by the Regulations. In fact, these endorsements control the underwriting and the insurer may, for example, exclude the use of power-driven woodworking machinery or exclude work above a certain height or below a certain level.

The Offshore Installations (Application of the Employers' Liability (Compulsory Insurance) Act, 1969) Regulations, 1975 brings all offshore workers in the UK sector of the Continental shelf within the compulsory insurance legislation. Insurance requirements apply to foreign employers and employees as well as those from the UK, but in the case of foreign employees the person has to be in the locus for more than seven days before insurance is necessary.

9.2 Insurance Cover for Employer's Liability

The scope of the usual employer's liability policy (refer to the Appendix to this Chapter) covers the. Act requirements besides giving a measure of contractual liability cover in respect of any principal. Cover includes liability for accidents to or illness of employees temporarily employed abroad and there is no apparant restriction on the meaning of "temporarily". "Bodily injury" includes death. The word "accidental" is not used in the operative clause because this presupposes one readily identifiable incident and this is not always possible, for instance, in the cases of gradually operating causes of diseases. Moreover, the possibility of deliberate injury, like an assault by a fellow employee, must be taken into account and therefore the words used are sufficiently wide to include this cause of injury.

The words "any person under a Contract of Service or Apprenticeship" is wide enough to include:

(i) any labour master or labour only sub-contractor or a person supplied by them

(ii) self-employed persons working for the insured provided that work is undertaken under the immediate supervision and control of the insured

(iii) "hired-in" labour

(iv) persons under work experience schemes.

By the traditional wording insurers provided indemnity in respect of events that happened during the period of insurance, irrespective of the date that the claim is made. For cover to operate under this "claims occurring" wording the injury or disease must be "caused" during the period of insurance and not merely become manifest during that period. In the case of some diseases, such as pneumoconiosis referred to in Chapter 8, it may take years for the effect to show and therefore the use of the word "caused" is enough to bring into operation a policy which has lapsed. A movement in the insurance market in the UK and in the USA especially towards a policy on the basis of "claims made" instead of "occurring" basis has lost some momentum and may well not become an acceptable norm. The "claims made" wording gives indemnity in respect of claims intimated during the period of insurance which may have been caused either during the period or prior to it. The consequences of this alternative wording will be discussed later.

The bodily injury or disease must "arise out of and in the course of employment". These words have a special meaning in the law of master and servant (Chapter 1, 1.5.2) and mean that any injury or disease resulting from what the employee is employed to do and those things incidental to it, such as dining in the company's canteen or being given fire drill for example, is covered by the policy.

The words "liability at law" include both common law and statutory liabilities.

"Claimants costs and expenses" include the costs and disbursements of solicitors, fees of counsel, medical fees and fees of other experts, incurred by the claimant. Expenses include other costs incurred in the necessary prosecution of the claim by the claimant.

9.2.1   Indemnity to Principal

Liability attaching solely by virtue of contract or agreement is not covered but certain contractual cover is given in (B), but only in the relationships of employer/principal. An indemnity is given to the Principal in his own name in respect of the Principal's liability for injury or disease to the Insured's employees. For example, a main contractor who is a principal will often be involved in proceedings because his name is the one appearing on a site entrance and if by the terms of the contract the Insured gives an indemnity to the principal, then the policy accommodates this contractual obligation. In any event the risk covered is only that of liability for injury/disease to the Insured's employees. The contractual cover is subject to provisos. Radioactive contamination and explosive nuclear assembly risk is not included in this limited contractual liability cover (proviso i). The Principal is bound by the terms and conditions of the policy and the Insured has to arrange for the conduct and control of claims to be vested in the insurer as they would be in the case of claims against the Insured (proviso ii). The Principal, as beneficiary, must comply with the terms and conditions of the policy, just as the Insured must (proviso iii).

9.2.2   Solicitors' Fees for Representation

The cover includes solicitors' fees for representation of the Insured at any Coroner's Inquest or Fatal Accident Enquiry or Court of Summary Jurisdiction. Only the solicitor's fee is covered; counsel briefed would be at the Insured's expense unless the Insurer in its own interest felt it advisable to brief counsel in view of possible civil proceedings to follow. The fee payable in any Court of Summary Jurisdiction is covered but subsequent or alternative proceedings in the High Court would not be included.

9.2.3   Other Persons Indemnified

In the event of the death of the Insured the Company will indemnify the Insured's legal personal representatives in the terms of the policy. This cover is necessary because of the provisions of the Law Reform (Miscellaneous Provisions) Act, 1934 (Chapter 4, 4.2) whereby rights of action or liability no longer cease on the death of either party to an action. An employer's liability insurance policy being a personal contract between two parties would automatically cease on the death of either party to it were it not for this clause and therefore the provisions of the 1934 Act would be defeated.

Although there is no indication from the wording of the specimen form of policy provided here it is usual for the combined form of policy to expressly provide indemnity to:

(i) any director partner or person under a contract of service or apprenticeship with the Insured in respect of liability for which the Insured would have been entitled to indemnity under the policy if the claim had been made directly against the Insured

(ii) the officers committees and members of the Insured's canteen, social, sports and welfare organisations and first aid, fire and ambulance services in their respective capacities as such

(iii) any director partner or employee for whom with the consent of the insured an employee is undertaking private work.

The cover therefore extends to give personal indemnities to various people relating to the risks of injury or disease to fellow employees.

9.2.4   Avoidance of Certain Terms and Right of Recovery

The prohibition of certain restrictive conditions in an Employer's Liability policy (outlined in 9.1.1(e) above) causes insurers to place a clause in the policy to draw the attention of the Insured to the right an insurer has to recover from the Insured any monies paid solely by reason of the regulations.

For example, if the Insured is in breach of the Notice of Claims Condition in the policy by not reporting an accident until, say, one year later, the Insurer cannot plead breach of contract to avoid making a payment to the injured employee. Having settled the claim the Insurer is entitled to recover the payment from the Insured.

9.2.5   General Conditions of the Policy

1.   Interpretation Condition. This condition makes it unnecessary to repeat the definition of any word or expression once defined. The policy wording and the schedule are formally linked as a single contract.

2.   Notice of Claim Condition. It is essential for the Insurer to be informed of an accident or possible claim early enough to arrange adequate investigation. The insurer may be prejudiced by late reporting of an accident.

3.   Control of Claims Condition. The Insurer assumes absolute control over conducting the claim and in the event of any other party being at fault the insurer may join that party in litigation before settling with the claimant.

4.   Other Insurances. Double insurance is unusual but could occur where there is a take-over or merger involving the policyholder. In circumstances of two or more insurance policies operating, each would contribute proportionately to the cost of any claim.

5.   Adjustment of Premium. Where the premium is on the basis of a rate per cent of wages paid during the risk year it is important from the insurer's point of view that an accurate account of wages paid is kept and is available for inspection if necessary. The condition also draws the Insured's attention to the possible adjustment of premium retrospectively.

6.   Alteration to the Risk. This condition protects the Insurer against any material increase in the risk and provides the opportunity for adjustment to the premium and conditions, if warranted.

7.   Reasonable Precautions. The Insured has a common law duty to take reasonable precautions to avoid accidents and this condition merely emphasises this. Obviously in many instances accidents are caused by failure in this duty and it would be unrealistic for the insurer to attempt repudiation of liability on this ground, unless it was a case of blatant disregard of reasonable precautions. In any case this is another of the conditions prohibited by the legislation.

8.   Cancellation. Not all policies contain a cancellation clause and even where it is expressed in the policy it would be applied only in extreme circumstances, e.g. bad moral hazard. In the event of cancellation by the Insurer a return of premium would be given, probably adjusted on wages up to the date of cancellation.

APPENDIX

SPECIMEN EMPLOYER'S LIABILITY POLICY

(The student should note that a separate policy for the E.L. risk is unusual: more likely the cover will form part of a combined liability policy and specimens of the latter should be examined. Insurers have simplified the wordings used according to their own styles but in this specimen of a separate policy form the traditional wording is used.)

(The preamble is followed by the following operative clause):

"The Company agrees that subject to the terms exceptions and conditions contained herein and of any endorsement hereon if any person under a contract of service or apprenticeship with the Insured (hereinafter called "an employee") shall while employed in or temporarily outside Great Britain Northern Ireland the Isle of Man or the Channel Islands sustain bodily injury or disease caused during the period of insurance and arising out of and in the course of his employment by the Insured in the Business the Company will

(A)   Indemnify the Insured against liability at law for damages and claimant's costs and expenses in respect of such bodily injury or disease other than liability attaching by virtue of a contract or agreement which would not have attached in the absence of such agreement except as provided in (B)

(B)   Where any contract or agreement entered into by the Insured with any public authority company firm or person (hereinafter called "the principal") so requires

1.   Indemnify the Insured against liability arising in connection with and assumed by the Insured by virtue of such contract or agreement.

or

2.   Indemnify the Principal in like manner to the Insured in respect of the Principal's liability arising from the performance of such contract or agreement but only so far as concerns liability as defined in this policy to an employee of the Insured PROVIDED THAT

(i) the Company shall not be liable in respect of any legal liability of whatsoever nature directly or indirectly caused by or contributed to by or arising from ionising radiations or contamination by radioactivity from any nuclear fuel or from any nuclear waste from the combustion of nuclear fuel

(ii) the Insured shall have arranged with the Principal for the conduct and control of all claims to be vested in the Company

(iii) the Principal shall as though he were the Insured observe fulfil and be subject to the terms exceptions and conditions of this Policy in so far as they can apply.

The Company will also

(1) Pay all costs and expenses incurred with its written consent

113

(2) Pay the Solicitor's fee incurred with its written consent for the representation of the Insured at any Coroner's inquest or Fatal Accident enquiry or proceedings in any Court of Summary Jurisdiction in respect of any act or omission causing or relating to any event which may be the subject of indemnity under this Policy

(3) In the event of the death of the Insured the Company will in respect of the liability incurred by the Insured indemnify the Insured's personal representatives in terms of the policy provided that such personal representatives shall as though they were the Insured observe fulfil and be subject to the terms exceptions and conditions of this policy so far as they can apply.

AVOIDANCE OF CERTAIN TERMS AND RIGHT OF RECOVERY

The indemnity granted by this Policy is deemed to be in accordance with the provisions of any law relating to compulsory insurance of liability to employees in Great Britain Northern Ireland the Isle of Man or the Channel Islands.

But the Insured shall repay to the Company all sums paid by the Company which the Company would not have been liable to pay but for the provisions of such law.

CONDITIONS

1.   This Policy and the Schedule shall be read together as one contract and any word or expression to which a specific meaning has been attached shall bear such specific meaning wherever it may appear

2.   In the event of any occurrence which may give rise to a claim under this Policy the Insured shall

(a) without delay give notice and full particulars thereof in writing to the Company

(b) retain anything connected therewith for such time as the Company may reasonably require

(c) immediately forward to the Company upon receipt every letter claim writ summons or process

(d) immediately notify the Company when the Insured has knowledge of any impending prosecution inquest Fatal Accident or Ministry enquiry

3.   No admission offer promise payment or indemnity shall be made or given by or on behalf of the insured in connection with any claim without the written consent of the Company. The Company shall be entitled to take over and conduct in the name of the Insured the defence or settlement of any claim or to prosecute in the name of the Insured for its own benefit any claim for indemnity or damages or otherwise and shall have full discretion in the conduct of any proceedings and in the settlement of any claim the Insured shall give all information and assistance as the Company may require

4.   If the liability which is the subject of a claim under this policy is covered by any other insurances the Insurers will not pay more than their rateable proportion

5.   The premium for this Policy having been calculated on estimates furnished by the Insured the Insured shall keep an accurate record containing all particulars relative thereto and shall at all times allow the Company to inspect such record. The Insured shall within one month from the expiry of each period of insurance furnish such particulars and information as the Company may require and the premium for such period shall thereupon be adjusted and the difference paid by or allowed to the Insured as the case may be subject to any minimum premium required

6.   The Insured shall give immediate notice of any alteration which materially affects the risks covered by this policy

7.   The Insured shall take all reasonable precautions to prevent accidents and disease

8.   This Policy may be cancelled by the Insurers sending seven days' written notice by recorded delivery to the last known address of the Insured

For and on behalf of the Company

....

Chapter 10

GENERAL LIABILITIES OF THE ENTERPRISE

10.0   Up to this point the particular liabilities relating to the product and those of potential claims by employees have been reviewed. In this Chapter the objective is to identify liabilities in the wider spectrum of the business's activities, as they affect members of the public at large, arising out of occupation of premises and work and activities away from premises, but leaving aside until later the liability arising from negligence in a professional capacity.

Legal liability can arise in tort, considered at length in the beginning of this Course, and through breach of contract. The student of risk management is expected to have an appreciation of these risks which may threaten the profitability of the enterprise, but the range is so wide that it is not possible to deal with more than a limited selection of commercial and industrial activities. Sampling should enable a realistic application of the principles to most practical situations.

10.1   Examples of Claims by the Public

The major disasters which occur, such as those at Flixborough, Bophal, Chernobyl, Zeebrugge, Kings Cross Underground and the Occidental Oil Rig awaken public awareness, temporarily at least, to the threats presented by technology, but the risk manager must be constantly on the alert to prevent or minimise the effects of events which, whilst hopefully do not have the potential of the foregoing, nevertheless may have serious implications for the business. The following incidents resulted in legal liability:

- The widow of a fireman killed whilst fighting a fire was awarded damages against a property owner for alleged failure to provide a safe means of escape for firemen.
- A mental patient at a hospital recovered £8,500 damages against the hospital authority for failure to take an elementary precaution to prevent her from jumping from an upper floor window.
- A five year old boy died when he tried to have a swing on an electric cable. Damages were awarded and in addition the defendant firm was fined £300 for negligence under the Health and Safety at Work etc. Act, 1975.
- A woman was awarded £10,000 (in 1981) against a local authority after falling into a hole in a pavement.
- A one-ton compressor rolled off a lorry and injured a 54-year-old man. Damages were £75,000 (1982).
- An actress won substantial damages against a magazine for libel.
- A road tanker crashed in a village causing extensive damage to houses. Claims exceeded £200,000 (1976).
- A woman was awarded substantial damages for injuries received when she was trapped in a lift.
- A gas explosion in a row of shops killed 21 people and caused widespread property damage (1970).
- The owner of a suitcase recovered compensation from a carrier for loss of the suitcase during transit.

10.2   Premises Risks

Occupancy or ownership of premises is an area of potential liability for injury to persons and damage to property and before considering the legal aspects it is worth listing a few incidents from records:.

- a stevedore was injured when he tripped over a wire on the deck of a ship.
- a pedestrian fell on a railway crossing because of the state of the crossing and as a result she was injured by a passing train.
- collapse of a ceiling resulted in a visitor suffering nervous shock.
- a child fell through the balustrade of a staircase and was injured.
- damage to a car resulted from collapse of a chimney.
- a salesman visiting premises was injured when he slipped on oil spilled on the floor.
- a contractor's workman fell through a faulty roof.

10.2.1   Common Law and the Statutory Duty of Care

You would expect that the occupier's duty to take reasonable care not to cause injury to his neighbour would be one aspect of the general duty of care founded upon Lord Atkin's dictum in Donoghue v Stevenson, 1932, (see 2.4.2) but, for reasons mainly historical, the liability of an occupier of premises developed separately. At comon law the extent of the duty owed by an occupier was determined by the legal status of the person on the premises: the categories being "invitee", "licensee", and "trespasser". It was long recognised that the occupier should have some responsibility for the safety of persons entering his premises with his permission. In Commissioner for Railways v McDermott (1967) 1 AC 169, Gardner, L C said "Occupation of premises is a ground for liability and is not ground for exemption from liability. It is a ground of liability because it gives some control over and some knowledge of the state of the premises and it is natural and right that the occupier should have some degree of responsibility for the safety of persons entering his premises with his permission . . . there is a "proximity" between the occupier and such persons and they are his "neighbours". Thus arises the duty of care . . .".

The common law distinction drawn between the different categories of visitors lead to hard cases and bad law and eventually reform by statute. The Occupiers Liability Act, 1957 remedied the confusion. Section 2(1) provides:

"An occupier of premises owes the same duty, the comon duty of care, to all his visitors, except in so far as he is free to and does extend, restrict, modify or exclude his duty to any visitor or visitors by agreement or otherwise."

There is no definition of "premises" in the Act and therefore the word is assumed to have the same meaning as at common law. This includes houses, buildings, land or "places and strucures of all sorts upon which persons may be invited to come". The Act abolishes the distinction betwen invitees and licensees and substitutes the category of "visitor" to represent all who come on premises by the occupier's invitation or permission. The Act does not concern itself with the duty owed to trespassers, this being left to the common law.

The duty of care to all visitors is defined in Section 2(2) as: "a duty to take such care as in all the circumstances of the case is reasonable to see that the visitor will be reasonably safe in using the premises for the purposes for which he is invited or permitted by the occupier to be there". It is a question of fact in any particular case whether the occupier has observed the standard of care required by the Act. This is similar to the principle of negligence at common law and factors such as the obvious nature of the danger, sufficiency of warnings, lighting, fencing, the visitor's purpose and his conduct and the knowledge of the occupier would determine whether the requisite standard of care was applied. Note that the duty is owed only so long as the visitor is using the premises for the purposes for which he is permitted. If he goes beyond the scope of his authority he falls into the category of a trespasser and in that event a much lower duty of care is owed by the occupier.

The common duty of care owed to visitors is qualified by the Act in respect of two special classes of visitors, namely, children and visitors who exercise some special calling. Section 2(3) provides:

"The circumstances relevant for the present purpose include the degree of care, and want of care, which would ordinarily be looked for in such a visitor, so that (for example) in proper cases —
(a) an occupier must be prepared for children to be less careful than adults; and
(b) an occupier may expect that a person, in the exercise of his calling, will appreciate and guard against any special risks ordinarily incidental to it, so far as the occupier leaves him free to do so".

In (a) above the duty is made more stringent, whereas by (b) the occupier's duty of care is less burdensome in respect of special risks incurred by, for example, visiting service engineers. The more onerous duty towards child visitors exists at common law in any case and this clause in the statute does not add anything to it. It is obvious that a child, by virtue of inexperience and curiosity, may well be placed in a position of danger in circumstances which would ordinarily present no risk to an adult.

In Glasgow Corporation v Taylor, 1922, A C 44 a seven-year-old boy died after eating poisonous berries from a bush growing in a public park. The bush was inadequately fenced from the public who were not warned of the danger and the Corporation was held liable. In Moloney v Lambeth B.C., 1966, 64 LGR 440 the plaintiff, a four-year-old was injured when he squeezed through the balustrade of a staircase and fell below. Although it was an accident that could not have happened to an adult, it was held that the occupiers should have anticipated the risk to a child and taken measures to prevent it. The extent of the duty owed to child trespassers will be considered later.

With regard to the special provision in (b), relating to risks incidental to a person's calling, examples are a clerk of works using scaffolding to inspect roof repairs, a window cleaner using window sashes for support or a stevedore standing near the edge of overhanging cargo. In Roles v Nathan, 1963, W L R 1117 Lord Denning M.R. said:

"When a householder calls in a specialist to deal with a defective installation on his premises, he can reasonably expect the specialist to appreicate and guard against the dangers arising from the defect. The householder is not bound to watch over him to see that he comes to no harm".

The risks contemplated under (b) are not those ordinary risks incidental to the premises, such as a broken floor board or the movement of a fork-lift truck, but special risks incidental to the visitor's calling, for example the risk presented to an electrician by a "live" wire.

10.2.2   Coexistent Duties of Occupier and Employer

Where the injured visitor to premises is an employee of the occupier there are coexistent duties of master to servant and of occupier to visitor to be considered. It may transpire that the claimant has a remedy both under the Occupiers Liability Act and by virtue of the duty owed to him by his employer at common law and under one of the various statutory regulations described in Chapter 8. Usually the duty owed under the latter is a higher one and therefore the injured employee/visitor will choose to pursue his claim on the ground of breach of the strict duty imposed on the employer.

10.2.3   Independent Contractors on the Premises

The occupier of premises is not ordinarily responsible for injury or damage caused by the negligence of independent contractors engaged by the occupier to work on the premises. This follows the rule on vicarious liability, i.e. a principal is not liable for the acts of his independent contractor, with certain exceptions. Section 2(4) provides:

"In determining whether the occupier of premises has discharged the common duty of care to a visitor, regard is to be had to all the circumstances, so that (for example) . . .
(b) where damage is caused to a visitor by a danger due to the faulty execution of any work of construction, maintenance or repair by an independent contractor employed by the occupier, the occupier is not to be treated . . . as answerable for the danger if in all the circumstances he had acted reasonably in entrusting the work to an independent contractor and had taken such steps (if any) as he reasonably ought to satisfy himself that the contractor was competent and that the work had been properly done".

The occupier is relieved of liability provided:

(i)   it was reasonable for the occupier to have employed an independent contractor;

(ii) he takes reasonable care in his selection of a competent contractor and

(iii) he takes reasonable care in checking, where possible, that the work has been properly carried out by the contractor.

In instances where the work is of a technical nature, supervision and inspection may be delegated by the occupier, for example, to a naval architect in the case of ship repairs.

10.2.4   Visitors by Virtue of Contractual Provisions

A person who has rights to visit premises given by the terms of a contract between the occupier and another party is owed the same duty of care by the occupier as applies to other visitors. An example is the employee of a contractor, who is not privy to the contract with the occupier. Section 3(1) provides:

> "Where an occupier of premises is bound by contract to permit persons who are strangers to the contract to enter or use the premises, the duty of care which he owes to them as his visitors cannot be restricted or excluded by that contract . . ."

A visitor of a tenant will therefore be entitled to the common duty of care owed by the landlord, who cannot exclude his liability to the visitor in his contract with the tenant. If the occupier extends or increases his duty of care to his contracting party for the benefit of that party (an unlikely course) all visitors who enter the premises by the right given by that contract are also entitled to the benefit of the additional obligations.

10.2.5   Defences Available to an Occupier

Contributory negligence can be a viable defence in an action against an occupier under the Occupiers Liability Act. Voluntary assumption of risk is provided for in the Act. Section 2(5) states:

> "The common duty of care does not impose on an occupier any obligations to a visitor in respect of risks willingly accepted as his by the visitor (the question whether a risk was so accepted to be decided on the same principles as in other cases in which one person owes a duty of care to another)".

In Simms v Leigh Rugby Football Club Ltd., 1962, 1 Lloyds Rep. 440 the plaintiff, a participant in a rugby league match was injured, allegedly by colliding with a concrete wall positioned about seven feet from the playing area. The proximity of the wall did not violate the rules of the Rugby Football League. The plaintiff suffered a broken leg when he was tackled and thrown towards the wall. The court was not satisfied that the injury was caused by contact with the wall and even if that had been the case, a claim for breach of duty under the Act would have failed said the Judge, who stated further: "anyone who plays professional Rugby League football accepts . . . the risks incidental to playing on a field which satisfies the bye-laws of the governing body of the sport". An adequate warning to the visitor of the danger may exonerate the occupier from liability. Section 2(4) states: "Where damage is caused to a visitor by a danger of which he had been warned by the occupier, the warning is not to be treated without more as absolving the occupier from liability, unless in all the circumstances it was enough to enable the visitor to be reasonably safe". Essentially, the warning must be enough to enable the visitor to be reasonably safe, in the circumstances of the case.

Contracting out of the duty of common care by the occupier may effectively relieve him of liability. To repeat the proviso in Section 2(2): ". . . except in so far as he is free to do so and does extend, restrict, modify or exclude his duty to any visitor or visitors by agreement or otherwise". However, it must be borne in mind that the Unfair Contract Terms Act, 1977 prohibits certain terms in contracts which purport to relieve one party from responsibility for death or bodily injury caused by his negligence. To some extent the restrictions by the above Act have been removed by Section 2 of the Occupiers Liability Act, 1984, which excludes from the ambit of "business liability", liability incurred in the course of business occupancy to persons visiting in pursuit of recreational or educational purposes, rather than the actual business of the occupier. By way of illustration, a farmer for

121

example is free to exclude his liability to hikers or to parties of geologists whom he permits on his land, whereas he could not exclude liability for bodily injury caused by his negligence to, say, a visiting vet or salesman.

10.2.6   The Duty to Trespassers

A trespasser is a person "who goes on the land without any invitation of any sort and whose presence is either unknown to the proprietor or, if known, is practically objected to" (Addie v Dumbreck, 1929, A C 358). Even a person who is on land involuntarily or who does not realise that he is trespassing is a trespasser nevertheless. Trespass can occur when a person who is on premises lawfully remains there after his licence to be there has run out, or where, as a visitor, he enters part of the premises or land which is beyond his permitted area. Permission for a person's presence may be withdrawn by the occupier and provided reasonable notice has been given and a reasonable time has elapsed the visitor becomes a trespasser. Before looking at statutory modification, the common law position on the duty of care should be reviewed. At common law an occupier of premises owes no common duty of care to adult trespassers, to see that his premises are safe or to give warning of danger, concealed or otherwise. Generally, the only duty owed to a trespasser is not to set traps for him, or injure him wilfully or through reckless disregard for his presence. The principle is one based on humanitarian grounds. The trespasser therefore comes on the premises at his own risk, unless there is some act done with the deliberate intention of doing him harm or some act done with reckless disregard for his presence.

Court decisions in cases involving children trespassing on premises have established a distinction between child and adult trespassers, in terms of the duty of care owed to them. In Cooke v Midland Great Western Rail Co. of Ireland, 1909, A C 229 Lord Atkinson said: ". . . young children and boys are of a very inquisitive and frequently mischievous disposition, and are likely to meddle with whatever happens to come within their reach". If an occupier, knowing that children are likely to trespass on his land, makes no reasonable attempt to prevent such trespass, by say, keeping fences in repair and a child is injured by something on the land which is specially alluring to children, then the occupier is generally held to be liable. In Herrington v British Railways Board, 1971, 2 W L R 477 the Court of Appeal held that by allowing the fence bounding a live electrified railway line to fall into disrepair, the Board had shown a reckless disregard towards a child trespasser who went on to the line and was injured. The master at the local railway station knew that children had been seen on the line but had not inspected the fence. Again in Southern Portland Cement v Cooper, 1974, All E R 87, a quarrying company tipped waste on its land adjacent to posts which carried a high tension electric cable at a site where children frequently played. On the occasions when they were observed they were warned off but on one occasion the plaintiff, a boy of 13, was injured when his arm came in contact with the electric cable. The defendant occupiers were held liable. Since it was expected that children would be attracted to play on the heap the company should have taken steps to prevent the danger from arising. There are circumstances, in the case of children of tender years where responsibility may rest with the parent rather than the occupier. In Phipps v Rochester Corporation, 1955, 1 Q B 450, Devlin, J commented that an occupier should not be liable when children enter unto land at such a tender age that their unaccompanied presence is unforeseeable, with the assumption that the parents of such children will be exercising control over them. In Simkiss v Rhondda Borough Council, 1983, 31 L G R 460, a seven year old plaintiff was injured when sliding down a steep slope on a blanket. It was stated that the occupier was entitled to asume that prudent parents would take steps to warn their children of such obvious perils. The claim against the occupiers failed.

The common law on the duty of an occupier to unlawful visitors has been changed by the Occupiers Liability Act, 1984.

An occupier of premises will owe a duty to trespassers if he is aware (or ought to be) of danger, knows (or has grounds to believe) that the trespasser is or may be in the vicinity of the danger. He has a duty to take such care as in all the circumstances is reasonable to see that the trespasser does not suffer injury. The duty may be discharged by giving appropriate warnings of the danger and it does not apply to damage to property.

Interestingly, Section 1 of the Guard Dogs Act, 1975, states that: "A guard dog is not permitted to be used in premises unless under the control of a handler while being used except whilst it is secured so that it is not at liberty to go freely about the premises. A warning that a dog is present must be clearly exhibited at each entrance to the premises".

This provision is as much to protect the trespasser as the lawful visitor and results from public concern about numerous instances of injury to persons of both categories.

10.2.7   Landlord's Liability

Landlord's liability relates to two categories of claimaints, the tenant and third parties. The landlord is not liable in tort to a tenant in respect of injury to the tenant arising out of defects in the premises once the premises have been passed to the tenant. Any remedy the tenant has will depend upon contract, i.e., the terms of the lease. Third parties are not privy to such a contract. In Cavalier v Pope, 1906, A C 428, it was held that the wife of a tenant could not recover damages in respect of a landlord's breach of a covenant with the tenant as she had no privity of contract.

The landlord's liability to third parties is shaped by the common law (in tort) and by Section 4 of the Defective Premises Act, 1972. At common law a landlord owed no duty of care to third parties who were injured on the premises; the liability rested primarily with the occupier and it did not matter whether the defect in question existed at the commencement of the lease or developed during the term of the lease. By virtue of Section 4 of the Defective Premises Act a landlord who is under an obligation to the tenant for the maintenance or repair of the premises, either by an express term of the tenancy agreement or lease or by virtue of the provisions of the Housing Acts, 1936-61, the landlord owes to all persons who might reasonably be expected to be affected by defects in the premises a duty to take such care as is reasonable in all the circumstances to see that they are reasonably safe from personal injury or damage to their property caused by a defect resulting from his failure to carry out his obligation to the tenant for the maintenance or repair of the premises. The duty is owed if the landlord knows (whether as the result of learning from the tenant or others) or if he ought in all the circumstances to have known of the relevant defect provided there is an obligation or right of entry to repair the defect. This duty operates in favour of third parties generally, i.e., visitors, neighbours, passers-by, etc. Liability also attaches to the landlord for injury or damage to third parties resulting from defects in parts of a property over which the landlord retains control. Examples are the common stairway, lifts and services in an office block where there are several tenants.

Where a landlord lets premises which are in a dangerous condition, without taking measures to effect repair or taking from the tenant a covenant to repair he will be liable to third parties.

Where furnished premises are let there is an implied warranty that they are fit for occupation at the beginning of the tenancy therefore a landlord can incur liability for injury, etc. resulting from defects in this respect.

10.2.8   Defective Premises Act, 1972

The Defective Premises Act, 1972, is concerned with liability, following sale, for newly-built, converted or adapted dwellings as well as the landlord's liability outlined in 10.2.7 above. The Act gave effect to the recommendations in the Law Commission Report on the Civil Liability of Vendors and Lessors for Defective Premises (Law Commission No.40). At common law the vendor of a building could not be held liable for defects; the remedy, if any, lay in contract or in misrepresentation. The basic principle is "caveat emptor"; there is no implied term in the sale of land that the property on the land is free from defects. The purchaser can have it surveyed to satisfy himself about its condition or suitability for his purpose. The 1972 Act places on the vendor or lessor of premises liability for injury or damage to persons caused by defects in premises.

By Section 1 a person taking on work for or in connection with the provision of a dwelling (whether by erection, conversion or enlargement of a building) and a person who in the course of a business which consists of or includes providing or arranging for the provision of dwellings (including local housing authorities) arranges for another to take on work for or in connection with the provision of a dwelling, owes a duty to see that the work is done in a workmanlike or, as the case may be, a professional manner, with proper materials and so that, as regards that work, the dwelling will be fit for habitation when completed. The duty is owed by builders, sub-contractors, site-developers, architects, and housing authorities. The same applies to public utility companies. The duty is owed not only to original purchasers but also to anyone acquiring an interest in the building such as successors in title.

By the provisions of Section 2 dwellings built under approved schemes are exempt from the above provisions of Section 1. These include those under the National House Builders' Registration Council scheme by which the builder, backed by guarantee, will remedy any major structural defects occurring in the 10 years following certificated completion.

By Section 3, where a duty is owed because of the doing of work of construction, repair, maintenance or demolition, to persons who might reasonably be expected to be affected by defects caused in the premises by the doing of the work, that duty shall not be abated by the subsequent disposal of the premises.

10.3   Pollution Liability

Legal liability for environmental pollution is not new but it has become more onerous since the early 1970's. Clean air legislation dates back to the fourteenth century and a person was hanged in that era for burning sea coal in London and for causing excessive smoke. Clean air and water pollution legislation was enacted in the last century and the late 1960's saw increasing public concern over environmental abuse in developed countries, which was expressed at the Stockholm Conference on the Environment in 1972. A UK Government White Paper in May 1970 set out proposals on protection of the environment and in 1974 the Control of Pollution Act was enacted but much of this is yet to be enforced. Under the Health and Safety at Work Act anyone operating a registered works is required to "use the best practical means for preventing the emission into the atmosphere from the premises of noxious or offensive substances . . ." The term "best practical means" is the air pollution touchstone for standards in the United Kingdom. Referring to practicable control of noise the Control of Pollution Act 1974 defines "practicable" as "having regard amongst other things to local conditions and circumstances, to the current state of technical knowledge and to the financial implications". This implies considerable tolerance and even the question of whether the business can afford measures of control. Environmentalists argue that whilst the Clean Air Act resulted in reduction of the amount of visible pollution such as smoke there is little control over the emissions of any other pollutant of the urban air. In addition the EEC took measures to harmonise regulations.

The main causes for concern may be classified as:

(i) Pollution of the Air
        Causes: — lead
                — pollution by domestic smoke
                — industrial pollution
                — lead in petrol
                — aircraft emission

(ii) Pollution by Noise
        Causes: — aircraft
                — supersonic aircraft
                — traffic
                — industrial noise

(iii) Pollution of Fresh Water
        Causes: — industrial liquid waste
                — pesticides
                — sewage

(iv) Pollution of the Land
        Causes: — pesticides and fertilisers
                — waste disposal
                — antibiotics

(v) Pollution of the Sea and Beaches
        Causes: — oil
                — industrial liquid waste
                — sewage
                — nuclear waste.

The nature of the pollution risk means that claims, when they occur, will often be large. Seepage may continue undetected for a long period or a leak from an underground pipe may not be detected by metering devices. By the time it is detected it may have contaminated the ground and the water table and an expensive clean up operation will be required. Effluent may be well dispersed before its harmful effects are noticed and if one person is injured others are likely to be and in the area of chemical contamination especially, the financial consequences for the business could be serious. There is the added problem of a possible long time lag between cause and effect, which may create difficulties for the business in ascertaining which past liability insurer should foot the bill, assuming there was cover.

10.3.1   The Control of Pollution Act, 1974

The Act makes regulations for waste disposal, water pollution, atmosphere pollution, air pollution, noise and public health. Section 1, once it is implemented, will impose a comprehensive disposal duty on authorities in respect of controlled waste which becomes situated in their areas and all such waste likely to be so situated.

Section 3 provides that persons may not either deposit controlled waste on any land, or cause or knowingly permit its deposit, or use any plant or equipment, or cause or knowingly permit such use, for purposes of disposing of such waste . . . unless the relevant land is occupied by the holder of a "disposal licence". For contravention of this section the penalty may be imprisonment for up to five years. Liability for injury or damage resulting from depositing poisonous, noxious or polluting waste arises under the Act and also at common law under the rule in Rylands v Fletcher. The Act strengthens the powers of local authorities to control noise from fixed premises. For example, within a Noise Abatement Zone the local authority may seek a reduction in noise levels where these levels are not acceptable and where such a reduction would afford a public benefit and would be practicable at reasonable cost.

10.4   Builders and Contractors

Builders' risks vary considerably and can be wide-ranging. The size of the operation may vary from the small jobbing contractor to very large firms building estates and civil engineering firms specialising in larger construction projects. Possible liability risks can include:

- injury to employees.
- injury to employees of principal and sub-contractors.
- injury to third parties and damage to property of third parties.
- use of plant, whether owned or hired in.
- acts of sub-contractors.
- advice given.
- goods supplied.
- damage to surrounding property by weakening or undermining foundations.
- removal of load bearing walls.
- fire.
- damage to property in the ground.
- pollution.

A building contractor may be in breach of his common law and/or statutory duty to exercise due care, resulting in an action against him for damages. Apart from these obvious responsibilities falling upon him for his own acts, the acts of his servants and in some situations the acts of his sub-contractors, he may be required to assume additional burdensome responsibilities by reason of the terms of contracts. Contractors are frequently required to provide principals with indemnities in respect of certain liabilities.

The complexities of relationsips between parties involved in building projects have led to the practice of using standard forms of contract which attempt to set out clearly the duties, rights, powers and obligations of the contracting parties. The advantages of standard wordings are that the terms are well known to the parties, expense of drafting is minimised and variations can be seen by amendments and deletions to the printed wordings. There are many contract forms in use; the following are the most common:.
- Standard Form of Building Contract for the Joint Contract Tribunal (JCT).
- General Conditions of Contract for Works of Civil Engineering Construction.
- I Mech E/IEE Model Form of General Conditions of Contract.
- General Conditions of Government Contracts for Building and Civil Engineering Works — Form GC/Works/1.

10.4.1   Standard Form of Building Contract JCT 80

When a principal employs a contractor to carry out work on his behalf he is in a position to transfer to the contractor responsibility for certain risks by means of contract conditions and to demand indemnities from the contractor. From the various standard forms of contract, the Standard Form of Building Contract JCT 80 is selected here to examine the effect of such risk transfer affecting liability for bodily injury to third parties and damage to property. This Form is used in relation to the construction of new buildings and the extension, alteration and repair of existing buildings. By means of "indemnity clauses" one party to the contract is required, in certain circumstances, to indemnify the other party, against all claims for personal injury or damage to property. These clauses may make the party to be bound responsible not only for the acts of his servants but also for the actions of his sub-contractors.

Clause 20.1 relating to liability of the contractor for personal injury or death and indemnity to the employer is as follows:

"The Contractor shall be liable for, and shall indemnify the Employer against, any expense, liability, loss, claim òr proceedings whatsoever arising under any statute or at comon law in respect of personal injury to or the death of any person whomsoever arising out of or in the course of or caused by the carrying out of the Works, except to the extent that the same is due to any act or neglect of the Employer or of any person for whom the Employer is responsible including the persons employed or otherwise engaged by the Employer to whom clause 29 refers".

In effect the employer (the principal) obtains an indemnity from the contractor for any claim for personal injury to or death of any person unless the employer, his servants, agents or sub-contractor is at fault. "Any person" in line four of the clause includes the contractor's employees, the sub-contractor's employees,

employees of the employer in the contract and any other person. "Any person for whom the Employer is responsible . . . to whom Clause 29 refers" means other people engaged by the employer to carry out work which is not part of the contract and which the employer must complete, e.g. carpet layers or decorators, who are not regarded as sub-contractors.

The risk is transferred to the contractor but only if the contractor is unable to prove that the injuries were due to an act or neglect of the employer or those for whom he is responsible. Thus it comes down to onus of proof which rests with the contractor, if he is to avoid providing an indemnity.

Clause 20.2 relates to liability of the contractor for damages to property and indemnity to the employer. It reads:

"The Contractor shall, subject to clause 20.3 and, where applicable, clause 22C.1, be liable for, and shall indemnify the Employer against, any expense, liability, loss, claim or proceedings in respect of any injury or damage whatsoever to any property real or personal in so far as such injury or damage arises out of or in the course of or by reason of the carrying out of the Works, and to the extent that the same is due to any negligence, breach of statutory duty, omission or default of the Contractor, his servants or agents or of any person employed or engaged upon or in connection with the Works or any part thereof, his servants or agents or of any other person who may properly be on the site upon or in connection with the Works or any part thereof, his servants or agents, other than the Employer or any person employed, engaged or authorised by him or by any local authority or statutory undertaker executing work solely in pursuance of its statutory rights or obligations."

Under this Clause the contractor indemnifies the employer against loss or damage to property to the extent that it is due to any negligence, breach of statutory duty, omission, or default on the part of the contractor, or any person employed upon, or in connection with the works, or any person who may properly be on the site in connection with the works. The onus of proof switches to the employer who, in order to obtain the benefit of the indemnity has to show that damage was the fault etc. of the contractor or other person for whom the contractor is responsible. The indemnity does not apply to acts or omissions on the part of the employer, and those persons for whom the employer is responsible. The indemnity from the contractor does not include damage to the works, works executed and/or site materials up to and including the date of the issue of the Certificate of Practical Completion (Clause 20.3).

The reference to Clause 22(C)1 at the beginning means that the contractor's indemnity for property damage is subject to the contractor effecting insurance for the existing structures and contents against specified perils; the policy to be in the joint names of contractor and employer. The contractor is not therefore liable for negligently damaging the employer's existing premises because insurance is in force and the insurers will not be able to recover from the negligent contractor because he is the policyholder (jointly).

The employer next requires the contractor to effect insurance to cover the indemnities he has extracted from the contractor under Clauses 20.1 and 20.2. Under Clause 21 the contractor has to effect and maintain employer's and public liability policies and is obliged, when requested by the employer, to send to the architect for inspection by the employer documentary evidence of such insurances.

Let us examine how the indemnity given to the employer by Clause 20.1 in respect of bodily injury stands in relation to the Unfair Contract Terms Act, 1977. Section 2(1) of that Act provides "a person cannot by reference to any contract term or to a notice given to persons generally or to particular persons exclude or restrict his liability for death or personal injury resulting from negligence". The Court of Appeal in the case of Thompson v T. Lohan (Plant Hire) Ltd. and Hurdis (*The Times* 12/2/87) had to consider an indemnity given to the owner of an excavator by the hirer under the Contractors' Plant Association Conditions (Clause 8) which makes the operator supplied by the owner effectively the servant of the hirer and which continues ". . . the Hirer . . . who alone shall be responsible for all claims arising in connection with the operation of the plant by the said drivers or operators".

The circumstances were that the plaintiff's husband was killed as the result of negligent operating of the excavator by the driver, a Mr. Hill. The excavator had been hired out to Mr. Hurdis by Lohan with Mr. Hill as the operator. The Court held that Clause 8 did not exclude or restrict liability: it merely transferred the financial responsibility for the liability to another party. The plaintiff was not prejudiced by the contract condition and there was no violation of the Unfair Contract Terms Act. Clause 20.1 is therefore not contrary to the spirit of the legislation.

Strict liability in nuisance at comon law for damage to land by removal or weakening of support (see Gold v Patman and Fotheringham Ltd., 1958, 2 All ER 497 . . .) falls on the principal and not the contractor, unless the latter has been negligent. To protect the employer against this type of liability Clause 21.2.1 of the Standard Form of Building Contract provides:

"Where it is stated in the Appendix that the insurance to which Clause 21.2.1 refers may be required by the Employer the Contractor shall, if so instructed by the Architect, take out and maintain a Joint Names Policy for such amount of indemnity as is stated in the Appendix in respect of any expense, liability, loss, claim or proceedings which the Employer may incur or sustain by reason of injury or damage to any property other than the Works and Site Materials caused by collapse, subsidence, heave, vibration, weakening or removal of support or lowering of ground water arising out of or in the course of or by reason of the carrying out of the Works excepting injury or damage."

This insurance covers the employer against the risk of damage to adjoining property by the perils specified which will be his responsibility even though the work was carried out by an independent contractor. If the contractor is at fault the employer obtains indemnity under Clause 20.2 but if he is not at fault the insurance under 21.2.1 covers the liability of the employer. The former is an indemnity clause whereas the latter is an insuring clause.

The indemnities given by a contractor are of little use if the contractor does not have the financial resources to meet his obligations under them. Employment of contractors can present high risks of injury or damage and it is advisable for the employer to make sure that this contractors' insurance policies are adequate. This means checking the actual insurance documents and in practice this is not always done. The employer may not have implemented a system of vetting contractor's insurances or it may be regarded as too troublesome. Very high limits of insurance indemnity are a necessary precaution where the work presents a high risk of damage such as the use of oxyacetylene cutters, blow torches and the like.

Chapter 11

INSURANCE OF GENERAL LIABILITIES

11.0   Unlike employer's liability, insurance of the general third party liability risk is not compulsory by law, with certain special exceptions, but these liability risks usually present a greater threat to the stability of most businesses because there is no limit to the amount of damages that can be awarded for bodily injury or damage to property. It is necessary to provide some form of funding and this may be by means of an internal fund or the establishing of a captive insurance company or by transferring the risks to an insurer. The insurance cover available on the market is extensive in scope but certain risks are excluded although for some of these cover may be negotiated. Limits of indemnity apply and if a court award exceeds the policy limit the business will have to call upon assets to make up the difference. It is important therefore to ensure that the limit of indemnity is realistic or that an "excess layer" cover is in force to fully protect the enterprise against catastrophe.

A summary of insurance cover available will be undertaken here and a specimen policy wording is provided as an appendix to this Chapter.

11.1   The Public Liability Policy

The typical cover for the general public liability risk provides indemnity to the insured for all sums which he may become liable to pay as damages in respect of accidental bodily injury to any person or accidental loss of or damage to property of third parties happening in connection with the business and occurring during the period of insurance.

The policy is concerned only with ACCIDENTAL injury or damage. The insurer does not intend to pay for injury or damage deliberately caused or which is inevitable. The term "accidental" is not defined, although the word refers to something fortuitous, unexpected and of sudden onset. Some insurers omit reference to "accidental" but in that case it is usual to specifically exclude inevitable damage and deliberate act, which, in effect, brings the cover back to the limits of "accidental" events. A legal decision involving interpretation of this concept is Gray v Barr, 1971, 2 All E R 949. A household policy covered the insured for public liability risks. The policyholder, jealous of his wife's affections for another man and suspecting that she may be at the friend's house, went there to look for her, taking with him a loaded shotgun. He met her friend, grappled with him and the loaded shotgun went off killing the friend. The policyholder was tried for murder and manslaughter but was acquitted. In a civil action however, the wife of the deceased sought damages against him and he looked to his insurer for indemnity, but the insurers disputed that the incident was an "accident". The judge in the lower court thought it was. The insurers appealed and the judges in the Court of Appeal were not unanimous on the issue but they decided that as a matter of public policy the policyholder was not entitled to be indemnified under an insurance policy.

The activities associated with the type of business described in the policy schedule are covered and in addition the policy includes the risks of ancillary activities such as staff welfare, canteens, sports, etc. and even private work for directors and senior

131

officials involving employees. The business is exposed to liability claims where there are such activities and it is convenient to have the cover provided here with the main business risks.

Note in Definition 3 of the specimen wording that the meaning of "property" is construed as "material property" only. In law the word has a wider meaning than is intended here and includes intangible forms such as patents, copyrights, design rights, trade marks and trade names. Insurers intend to cover liability for loss of or damage only to tangible property such as damage to stock, buildings, machinery, motor cars and the like.

The policy always expressly limits the indemnity and the wording shown makes it clear that the limit applies per "occurrence". Insurers protect themselves against the possibility of several consequences of a single accident being interpreted as separate accidents and the limit of indemnity thus being deemed as applicable to each one. A series of injuries, say, from one cause will be subject in aggregate to the indemnity limit, for example, if an explosion results in accidental injury to a number of people.

11.1.1   Risks Not Covered

Cover is not available for risks that are considered uninsurable and the policy does not cover employer's liability, products and motor vehicle liabilities because these are the subject of more specific insurance covers. Other risks not covered may be included by negotiation.

Exclusion 1(a) refers to road vehicles which require compulsory insurance under the Road Traffic Acts. The liability risk in respect of other mechanically propelled vehicles is covered by this policy, for example fork-lift trucks or mobile plant. It should be clear that the motor insurance policy carries the road vehicle risk. Exclusion 1(b) ensures that risks covered by aviation and marine insurance are not included here, but the policy does cover the relatively non-hazardous hand propelled craft (rowing boats presumably). Exclusion (c) does not appear in every public liability policy. Here the boiler and lifting apparatus risks are covered so long as they are inspected and maintained according to regulations. These risks can be the subject of more specific insurance classified as "Engineering" which ordinarily provides an inspection service as well.

Exclusion 2 removes contractual liability. The reason is that insurers would not know the extent of their obligations, so varied and extensive are the liabilities that it is possible for a business to assume by contract. The exclusion is often modified at the request of the insured to include some degree of contractual liability (see 11.1.3 below) and in fact in some industries, contractual liabilities assume a standard form and without the necessary cover the policy would be rejected. An example is the construction industry, dealt with in Chapter 10. It should be appreciated that when cover is given it is still confined to accidents as described in the policy and will not encompass indemnities given by the insured in respect of say, financial penalties for time loss, failure to meet delivery dates, fines, proceedings etc.

Exclusion 3 excludes the product liability risk and avoids overlap with the more specific policy for this risk. Whilst the faulty product is still in the premises of the policyholder the risk is borne by the public liability policy.

Exclusion 4 restricts cover for pollution liability. The cover provided by this policy relates only to accidental pollution as, for example, the unexpected breakdown of the effluent plant. Deliberate pollution and the gradually operating risk is not covered, but cover is given for defective sewers or sanitary arrangements. Insurers will usually make enquiries before providing the cover particularly in those industries where the risk is heavy, such as chemicals.

Exclusion 5 refers to an excess (or deductible) if any applies. In this case the possible excess applies to claims arising from work or activities away from the premises of the Insured. The amount of the excess may depend upon the previous claims record of the insured business or the hazardous nature of the work.

Exclusion 6 removes the risk covered by an employer's liability policy.

Exclusion 7 is property in the charge of or in the custody or control of the Insured. Thus the liability of a bailee as a watch repairer, a launderer or a warehouseman for loss or damage to goods left with him would not be covered. The insurers' reasoning is that the property should be covered under material damage policies such as Fire and Theft insurances. Excepted from the exclusion wording and therefore specifically covered are:

(i) employees property, for example an employee's car in the firm's car park or tools or clothing belonging to him.

(ii) the belongings of visitors whilst they are on the premises.

(iii) building which the insured may occupy for the purposes of cleaning, maintenance or repair.

(iv) premises leased, hired or rented to the Insured. In this case there is a proviso that such premises must be insured against fire and any additional liability assumed under an agreement between the landlord and the tenant is not covered. There is an excess applicable to the cover for liability for damage to rented premises unless the cause is fire or explosion.

Exclusion 8 restricts public liability cover outside of the territorial limits of the policy to that attaching to visits abroad by directors and non-manual employees. This may not suffice with the growth of international business activities, especially by the advent of the EEC and extension of cover can be arranged which must meet the requirements and the local conditions of each country.

Exclusion 9 deals with uninsurable risks such as war, civil strife, etc.

Exclusion 10 removes from the scope of the cover the nuclear risks comprising in (a) the nuclear reactor establishment risk and in (b) the nuclear war-head risk. It should be noted that the wording does not exclude the radioactivity risk arising from industrial use of radioactive isotopes and such risks are covered as a matter of course, provided usage is declared on the insurance proposal form.

11.1.2   Costs and Expenses

The solicitor's fee for representation of the Insured at any Coroner's Inquest or Fatal Accident enquiry will be met, which not only provides the Insured with indemnity but ensures that proper representation is provided thus assisting the insurer in preparing the ground for any subsequent claim which may be brought against the Insured. Likewise, it is in the interests of both parties that legal representation be provided when proceedings are taken against the Insured for any alleged breach of statutory duty which has resulted in, say, bodily injury to a third party. If the Insured can avoid being convicted this will often make the claimant's task of proving negligence against the Insured more difficult.

11.1.3   Policy Extensions

Contractual liability cover can be given for some risks assumed by agreement. Extension 1 gives indemnity to any Principal with whom the Insured enters into a contract where the terms of the contract require the Insured to provide the Principal with indemnity. In effect the cover applies to the Principal's potential liabilities for third party bodily injury or damage to property arising out of the work being carried out by the Insured on behalf of the Principal. As mentioned earlier, the cover is confined to accidents as described in the policy and will not extend to indemnities given by the Insured in respect of risks not covered by the policy such as liability for liquidated damages or under penalty clauses. The policy may also exclude certain types of work such as demolition, use of explosives, pile driving, etc. but the indemnity demanded by the Principal may encompass accidents arising out of such activities. The Risk Manager should be alert to the possibility that the indemnity given to the Principal may therefore be much wider than the scope of the liability policy cover. By this extension the Principal becomes a party insured under the policy but only if his contract with the Insured requires such indemnity and subject to the provisos that he complies with the terms and conditions of the policy and permits the Insurer full control over the conduct of the claim.

Extension 2 provides indemnity to several categories of persons connected with the business who may be personally liable and accountable for bodily injury or damage. Indemnity is given to, say, a director or employee who is sued by a third party or who is a co-defendant with the Insured as a joint tortfeasor. Persons carrying out ancillary services connected with the business, for example, members of the firm's voluntary fire fighting squad, are exposed to liability risk and it is convenient to have the cover included in the main business policy. This has become part of the public liability cover now being offered by most insurers. The legal personal representatives of the Insured and of all of the additional persons covered are indemnified in the event of the death of any such person.

Extension 3 provides cover in respect of the risks associated with premises disposed of and outlined in 10.2.8 (Defective Premises Act cover).

11.1.4   Policy Conditions

Those policy conditions which are common to the Employers Liability policy (Appendix to Chapter 9) require no further comment. Because the indemnity given by this policy is limited in amount the condition wording (or similar) quoted in the Appendix to this chapter is deemed necessary by insurers. In the event of a claim exceeding the limit of indemnity the Insurer may exercise a right to discharge its obligations to the Insured by paying up to the limit plus costs and expenses incurred up to the date of discharge and thereby relieve itself of the claim and any further liability under the policy. This would leave the Insured to deal with the remainder of the outstanding amount due. It is to be hoped that an insurer would not take this rather drastic step but continue in partnership with the policyholder in an endeavour to assist as much as possible in the negotiations with the third party. A reputable insurer would only apply the condition where, for example, the policyholder was insisting on defending an action which it considered was defenceless and therefore a waste of money, or where the policyholder was being difficult or obstructive.

11.2 Cross Liabilities

IN the cae of a holding company with several subsidiary companies it is quite possible that two separate subsidiary companies may be joint defendants in an action by a third party or there may even be an action in liability by one subsidiary against another company which is a member of the same group. If the public liability insurance is arranged in the name of the holding company to cover all of the group's member companies or, alternatively, in the joint names of all and the normal policy wording is in use this would effectively deny indemnity for inter-company claims and therefore provide less cover than would be available if each subsidiary company effected its own separate policy. Insurers will remedy this by attaching a "Cross Liabilities Clause" to the group policy. The wording will be along these lines:

> "In the same manner and to a like extent as though this Policy was issued in the name of one of them only this Policy shall indemnify the Insured in respect of claims made by any one of them (or their servants or agents) against any other of the Insured. Subject otherwise to the terms exceptions limitations and conditions of this Policy."

The clause if often applied to policies issued in the joint names of a principal and a contractor and would therefore admit a claim by one insured against the other.

11.3 Contingent Liability Cover

Circumstances sometimes arise where a business, faced with a certain liability risk, looks to some other party for its protection, consequently that other party may arrange insurance in their joint names or a policy endorsed to indemnify the business which requests the cover. Such a need often arises in the construction industry where the employer may look to the contractor for his insurance protection. A tenant, for example, could look to the landlord's policy for protection. When cover is dependent upon others effecting insurance there can be no absolute certainty that when a claim arises the cover will always be effective. The premium may not have been paid on time or the policyholder may be in breach of a policy condition or guilty of non-disclosure of a material fact rendering the cover void. The business relying on cover at second hand has still retained a measure of risk, i.e. the possibility that the insurance protection expected may not materialise. The contingency of exposure to a liability claim because insurance is ineffective can be insured by extending the business's own public liability policy or by a separate contingent liability insurance policy. This form of insurance is a second line of defence and will be brought into operation only in the event of the primary policy being inoperative. The business can minimise the risk by constantly reviewing the cover taken out by, say, a contractor but if it is employing a large number of contractors frequently it will be difficult to maintain a satisfactory system of checking and contingent liability insurance may be the most satisfactory answer to the problem.

11.4   Cover for Pollution

The insurance buyer experiences different attitudes by insurers on the matter of providing cover for pollution or environmental impairment. Some are prepared to give cover whilst others are not. Where cover is available it relates only to accidental injury or damage as, for example, the unexpected breakdown of an effluent treatment plant. Deliberate pollution is not ordinarily considered insurable and the problem of obtaining cover is world-wide.

In the late 60s and early 70s following the major marine pollution disasters of the *Torry Canyon* and *Amoco Cadiz*, liability insurers reacted by introducing to their policies a pollution exclusion. This removed all cover for seepage and pollution but reinstated cover for liability for bodily injury and damage to property caused by sudden or accidental pollution. From 1974 Environmental Impairment Insurance was available in this Country giving world-wide cover and two years later similar cover was available in the USA. National pools also began to be introduced in European Countries in the late 70s. The subject of environmental impairment has received an enormous amount of publicity in the last two decades and reaction from pressure groups has caused industries most at risk to seek cover. This selection against insurers and the levels of public awareness has caused insurers' attitudes to harden and E.I.L. cover availability is sparing and restricted. The demand for cover in the USA is further increased by Government imposition of a financial responsibility requirement on waste disposal businesses and there is the possibility of similar requirements for operators of waste generators and underground tanks.

The wording of the specimen form of policy provided would admit claims in respect of accidental pollution only and not gradually operating or deliberate pollution and of course cover is restricted to liability for bodily injury and damage to property. There is always the possibility that a court may construe pollution as "accidental" where the insured can argue that it was unintended and unexpected from his point of view.

APPENDIX

SPECIMEN PUBLIC LIABILITY
(OR THIRD PARTY LIABILITY) POLICY

(As noted in the Appendix to Chapter 9 a common practice by insurers is to issue a combined liability policy. This Appendix is a specimen form of a separate public liability policy and is produced here for purposes of illustrating the scope of that form of insurance. There is no standard wording but the following is typical of the cover given.)

The Preamble is followed by the Operative Clause:

"The Company will subject to the terms exclusions conditions and limitations contained herein or endorsed hereon indemnify the Insured in connection with the Business against liability at law for damages and claimants costs and expenses in respect of

(1) accidental bodily injury to or disease contracted by any person

(2) accidental loss of or damage to material property occurring during any period of insurance

DEFINITIONS

1.   BUSINESS shall include the ownership of premises and the provision and management of canteen social sports and welfare organisations for the Insured's employees first aid fire and ambulance services and private work carried out with the consent of the Insured for any director partner or senior official of the Insured by any employee of the Insured

2.   BODILY INJURY shall include death illness or disease

3.   PROPERTY shall mean material property

LIMIT OF INDEMNITY

The liability of the company under this policy for damages in respect of one occurrence or all occurrences of a series consequent on or attributable to one source or original cause shall not exceed the sum stated in the schedule.

EXCLUSIONS

The Company shall not be liable under this policy in respect of

(1)   liability arising directly or indirectly by or through or in connection with the ownership possession or use by or on behalf of the Insured of any:

(a) mechanically propelled vehicle but this exception shall not apply in respect of bodily injury or loss of or damage to property arising in circumstances where compulsory insurance or security in respect of any such vehicle is not required by any relevant law and the Insured is not entitled to indemnity under any other policy

(b) aircraft hovercraft or watercraft (other than hand propelled watercraft)

(c) pressure vessel lifting apparatus or other item of plant
 (i) owned by the Insured or
 (ii) the maintenance for which the Insured is responsible which has not been inspected to the extent required by statutory regulations

(2) any liability which attaches because of an agreement but which would not have attached in the absence of that agreement

(3) injury disease loss or damage caused through anything which the Insured or an employee has manufactured sold supplied repaired serviced tested or processed whilst elsewhere than on any premises occupied by the Insured

(4) injury disease loss or damage caused through air or water pollution unless proved to have been caused by immediate discharge consequent upon an accident or unless due to defective drains sewers or sanitary arrangements

(5) the excess being the sum stated in the Schedule for which the Insured is responsible in respect of each and every occurrence of loss of or damage to property caused through the carrying on of any trade process by the Insured or an employee elsewhere than on the premises

(6) bodily injury to or disease contracted by any of the following:

 (a) any person under a contract of service or apprenticeship with the Insured when such injury or disease arises out of and in the course of his employment by the Insured

 (b) any labour master (or Labour only sub-contractor) or person supplied by him and/or any self employed person for labour only whilst engaged on behalf of the Insured

(7) loss of or damage to

 (a) property belonging to the Insured

 (b) property held in trust by or in the custody or control of the Insured or of an employee other than
 (i) employees property
 (ii) visitors property whilst temporarily on or about the premises other than for servicing cleaning alteration repair or inspection
 (iii) buildings (together with the contents thereof) temporarily occupied by the Insured or an employee for the purpose of cleaning maintenance or repair
 (iv) any premises leased hired or rented to the Insured provided that
  (A) such premises are insured against fire
  (B) the Company shall not be liable for any liability which attaches to the Insured by reason of an express term of any contract unless such liability would have attached to the Insured notwithstanding such term
  (C) the Company shall not be liable for the first £ of each and every occurrence of loss or damage unless due to fire or explosion.

(8) legal liability occurring outside Great Britain Ireland Northern Ireland the Channels Islands or the Isle of Man but this exclusion shall not apply to liability arising out of business visits by directors and non-manual employees normally resident in any of those countries

(9)   any consequence whether direct or indirect of war invasion act of foreign enemy hostilities (whether war be declared or not) civil war rebellion revolution insurrection or military or usurped power

(10)   any legal liability of whatsoever nature directly or indirectly caused by or contributed to by or arising from   .

  (a) ionising radiations or contamination by radioactivity from any nuclear fuel or from any nuclear waste from the combustion of nuclear fuel

  (b) the radioactive toxic explosive or other hazardous properties of any explosive nuclear assembly or nuclear component thereof

COSTS

The Company will also pay all costs and expenses including a solicitors fee for

  (a) representation at a Coroners Court Fatal Accident or Ministry Inquiry

  (b) the defence in a Court of Summary Jurisdiction of proceedings arising out of an alleged breach of statutory duty incurred with its written consent and relating to any claim which may be the subject of indemnity under this policy.

POLICY EXTENSIONS

1.   The Company will subject to the terms exceptions and conditions of this Policy indemnify the Insured against liability in respect of bodily injury or loss of or damage to property as follows

To the extent that any contract or agreement entered into by the Insured with any Principal so requires the Company will

  (a) indemnify the Insured against liability assumed by the Insured

  (b) indemnify the Principal in like manner to the Insured in respect of the liability of the Principal arising out of the performance by the Insured of such contract or agreement

    Provided that
      (i) the conduct and control of claims is vested in the Company
     (ii) the Principal shall observe fulfil and be subject to the terms exceptions and conditions of this policy so far as they can apply
    (iii) the indemnity shall not apply to liability in respect of liquidated damages or under any penalty clause

2.   The Company will subject to the terms exceptions and conditions of this Policy indemnify at the request of the Insured

  (i) any director or employee of the Insured while acting on behalf of or in the course of his employment or engagement by the Insured in respect of liability for which the Insured would have been entitled to indemnity under this Policy if the claim against any such person had been made against the Insured

(ii) any officer member or employee of the Insureds social sports or welfare organisation or first aid or ambulance service in his respective capacity as such

(iii) any director partner or senior official of the Insured in respect of private work carried out with the consent of the Insured

(iv) in the event of the death of any person entitled to indemnity under this Policy the personal representative of such person

3.   The company will subject to the terms and conditions of this Policy indemnify the Insured against liability in respect of bodily injury or loss of or damage to property arising in respect of any premises disposed of by the Insured.

CONDITIONS

N.B. The conditions in the Public Liability policy are identical to those in the Employers Liability policy (see appendix to Chapter 9) except that one additional condition is usually included in the former relating to the limit of indemnity and a typical wording is:

"The Company may at any time pay to the Insured in connection with any claim or series of claims the amount of the limit of indemnity (after deduction of any sum or sums already paid as damages) or any lesser amount for which such claim or claims can be settled and upon such payment being made the Company shall relinquish the conduct and control of and be under no further liability in connection with such claim or claims except for the payment of costs and expenses recoverable or incurred prior to the date of such payment"

For and on behalf of the Company

....

SCHEDULE

COMPANY:	POLICY NUMBER	
INSURED	PERIOD OF INSURANCE From Noon To Noon	RENEWAL DATE
ADDRESS		FIRST PREMIUM
	Proposal and Warranty signed	
Carrying on the business of	Policy signed	ANNUAL PREMIUM
and no other for the purpose of this insurance.		

Limit of Indemnity £   any one claim or number of claims arising out of one cause.

The Excess   £

141

Chapter 12

PROFESSIONAL NEGLIGENCE: DIRECTORS AND OFFICERS LIABILITY

12.0 General

The legal consequences of the negligence of the professionally qualified person whilst acting in his professional capacity can involve large sums in damages. The number of actions for professional negligence has increased dramatically in the last twenty years and damages and costs have spiralled, resulting in withdrawal by the insurance market of cover for some professions and escalating costs of insurance cover where it is available. Some professions such as solicitors have called for statutory limitation of professional liability but so far the British Government has not obliged. Insurance premium increases and reduction in insurance capacity has caused some professions to look to other means of protecting their members, mainly by setting up mutual insurance schemes. For the medical profession two bodies, the Medical Defence Union and the Medical Protection Society, cover 200,000 members on a subscription basis. The Law Society which from 1975 up to 1987 provided cover for over 30,000 solicitors under a group insurance policy has launched a mutual scheme. At the present time (1989) there are signs that the specialist professional indemnity insurers are showing more interest in writing the business again.

Factors contributing to the escalating professional liability risk include increasing awareness of the average citizen of his rights, expansion of the duty of care owed outside of contractual duty, higher court awards, access to legal aid and less inhibition in suing a professional person. The situation in the USA is at crisis point where, for example, liability for medical malpractice is so onerous that it is reported that 12% of American obstetricians have stopped delivering babies and many surgeons are avoiding high risk cases. The problem there of liberal liability laws does not only affect medical practice and moves are afoot to bring reform. The Federal Government commissioned the General Accounting Office to research the problem and following several years' work the GAO has proposed several recommendations including a "self-policing" system by the medical profession and co-operation between medical profession and the insurance industry to improve standards of risk management.

12.1 Professional Negligence

A professional person can incur liability both in contract and in tort but at one time the doctrine of privity of contract forbade any party not in a contractual relationship with the professional person from suing him where the third party suffered loss because of negligent advice or services rendered to the client. In cases of a fiduciary relationship (e.g. a trust), there could be liability for wrongful advice even in the absence of a contract.

This restriction of tortious liability was radically changed by the decision in Hedley Byrne & Co. Ltd. v Heller & Partners Ltd. 1963, 2 All E.R. 575, described in 10.1.2 below. In Midland Bank Trust Co. Ltd. and Another v Hett, Stubbs & Kemp, 1978, 3 All ER 571, the Court held a firm of solicitors liable in tort for failing to register an option to purchase a farm, and also liable in contract. Liability in contract is confined to the parties to the contract but liability in tort is wider. Professional persons in giving advice may be liable not only to the client in contract but also to any other party in tort if there is a relationship which is enough to constitute a duty owed. An architect who makes a mistake in supervising building construction will be liable in contract to the party who engaged him, but he owes a duty of care also to any person likely to be injured or damaged as a result of his error. This would include workmen on the site, passers-by, visitors using the building and even subsequent purchasers of the building. The Latent Damages Act, 1986, discussed in Chapter 4 (4.8) extends the architect's liability.

The standard of care expected of a professional person is the standard expected of an average member of his particular profession. The expected degree of care was clearly expressed in the case of Lanphier v Phipos, 1838, 173 E.R. 581, as: "Every person who enters into a learned profession undertakes to bring to the exercise of it a reasonable degree of care and skill. He does not undertake, if he is an attorney, that at all events you shall gain your case nor does a surgeon undertake that he will perform a cure, not does he undertake the highest possible degree of skill. There may be persons who have higher education and greater advantage than he has but he undertakes to bring a fair, reasonable and competent degree of skill". Whilst a considerable degree of skill is looked for, it is not an impractically high standard. In the Midland Bank case it was stated by Oliver J.:

> "Now no doubt the duties owed by a solicitor to his client are high, in the sense that he holds himself out as practising a highly skilled and exacting profession, but I think the court must beware of imposing upon solicitors — or upon professional men in other spheres — duties which go beyond the scope of what they are requested and undertake to do. It may be that a meticulous and conscientious practitioner would, in his client's general interest, take it upon himself to pursue a line of arguing beyond the strict limits comprehended by the instructions. But that is not the test. The test is what the reasonably competent practitioner would do having regard to the standard normally adopted in his profession."

12.1.1 Professional Liability Claims

Tort liability of the professional is less quantifiable than contractual liability because a duty is owed to a much wider range of persons and interests. The following list of professional risks will serve to illustrate this area of potential liability:

Accountants: A firm of accountants who were instructed by a firm of solicitors to examine the accounts of a business and report in order that the solicitors could decide whether or not to advance a sum of money into that business, overlooked an overvaluation in the stock sheets examined. Consequently the solicitors discovered some years later that there had been an overvaluation of 3%. The solicitors sued for failure to report overvaluation but the claim failed on the ground that the accountants had not been engaged to take stock but to make a reasonable and efficient investigation of the accounts, a task which they had carried out adequately. The defendants had not been negligent in the task they had contracted to undertake (Mead v Bal, Baker & Co., 1911, 27 TLR 269). However where an accountant was instructed to check the accounts of a company and failed to discover discrepancies in the figures arising from the dishonesty of an employee, the accountant was held liable (Fox & Son v Morrish Grant & Co., 1928, 35 TLR 126).

Architects: An architect has a contractual responsibility for negligent design and supervision resulting in a flawed structure. He also has tortious liability for personal injury and damage to property. In Clay v A. J. Crump & Sons Ltd., 1964, 1 QB 533, a site owner instructed an architect to plan and supervise the site re-development including engaging demolition contractors to clear the site. A certain wall was specified by the architect for demolition but in conversation with the owner the architect said the wall could remain standing if the demolition contractor thought it was "safe to do so". The architect failed to inspect the wall although he had been to the site on several occasions and subsequently he issued his certificate to the demolition contractors. Later the wall collapsed injuring a workman. The architect was held to be liable jointly with the demolition contractor.

Manufacturers: Professional persons employed by manufacturers to design and test products owe a duty of care to the user of the product under the principle of Donoghue v Stevenson, 1932, and liability would rest vicariously with the manufacturer. The subject is explored in Chapter 6.

Surveyors: A surveyor engaged to inspect property for his general opinion of its condition will be liable if financial loss results from his failure to discover the presence of dry rot, woodworm or settlement. The quantity surveyor's function is to measure the work or the amount due from his employer to a building contractor and if he is in breach of his duty to act fairly in making the evaluation, he can be held liable.

12.1.2   Wrongful Advice

In some circumstances an action in negligence will lie against a professional person for negligent mis-statements even where he has no contractual or fiduciary relationship. In Hedley Byrne & Co. Ltd. v Heller & Partners, 1963, a merchant bank replied to an enquiry from another bank which requested information on behalf of its customer concerning the creditworthiness of a firm. No fee was required for the information. The reply, which was given expressly "without responsibility" was favourable, stating that the firm "was good for its ordinary business engagements". As a result of relying upon this information, the bank's customer lost £17,000 when the company went into liquidation. The action failed because of the disclaimer on the written reply but the importance of the decision is the opinions of the Law Lords that in appropriate circumstances the professional would be liable for negligent mis-statements to persons other than his clients. Before the Hedley Byrne decision the position regarding negligent statements was that a person giving advice or information to another, where there was no contractual or fiduciary relationship, owed no duty of care to the receiver of the advice other than a duty to act honestly. Since the decision it is possible, in certain cases, that a "special relationship" exists between the giver and the receiver of the information and if the information is given negligently, causing a loss to the receiver, an action for damages will lie. Lord Reid found that there was no special relationship which would give rise to a duty of care in this case but he conceded that:

"... if in a sphere where a person is so placed that others could reasonably rely on his judgement or his skill or on his ability to make careful inquiry, such person takes on himself to give information or advice to, or allows his information or advice to be passed on to, another person who, as he knows, or should know, will place reliance on it, then a duty of care will arise."

Certainly the special relationship will not arise when information or advice is given on a purely social occasion nor, where the defendant has not held himself out as possessing the relevant skill or knowledge to give advice in the area in question. An example of the necessary relationship between the parties is the case of W. B. Anderson & Sons v Rhomes, 1967, 2 All ER 850. The plaintiff companies relied upon information from the defendant in reply to inquiries as to the creditworthiness of a third party, who subsequently became insolvent. The defendant was a well established and reputable company dealing in the fruit and vegetable market and the plaintiffs wished to sell potatoes to the third party on credit terms. The court found that a duty of care existed in relation to the representations made by the defendant because they concerned business transactions where it was clear that the other party relied on the information. The opinion was requested in a business connection and was not casual and perfunctory. The conditions for liability for wrongful advice to persons not in contractual or fiduciary relationship therefore are that the professional must know that the other is relying on his skill and the other must in fact rely upon it. The fact that there is no fee involved does not affect liability. A disclaimer will relieve the giver of liability.

Liability for mis-statements during negotiations in a contract is demonstrated by Esso Petroleum Company v Mardon, 1976, 1 All ER 5, a case which applied the Hedley Byrne principle to the pre-contractual situation. In negotiations leading to a contract for the tenancy of a new filling station the petrol company informed the prospective tenant that the estimated throughput in the third year of operation would be 200,000 gallons. The receiver was doubtful but was reassured by the defendants who were the experts, and he accepted the tenancy. By the third year of business the throughput had not exceeded 100,000 gallons per annum and the tenant was in arrears with his rent. The petrol company raised an action against him for recovery of rent and he counterclaimed for breach of warranty and negligent mis-representation. Lord Denning in the Court of Appeal opined:

"It seems to me that Hedley Byrne, properly understood, covers this particular proposition: if a man, who has or professes to have, special knowledge or skill, makes a representation by virtue thereof to another — be it advice, information or opinion — with the intention of inducing him to enter into a contract with him, he is under a duty to use reasonable care to see that the representation is correct, and that the advice, information or opinion is reliable. If he negligently gives unsound advice or misleading information or expresses an erroneous opinion, and thereby induces the other side into a contract with him, he is liable in damages."

And Ormrod L J:

"The parties were in the kind of relationship which is sufficient to give rise to a duty on the part of the plaintiffs. There is no magic in the phrase "special relationship"; it means no more than a relationship the nature of which is such that one party, for a variety of reasons, will be regarded by the law as under a duty of care to the other."

12.1.3   The Misrepresentation Act, 1967

In addition to the tortious remedy for misrepresentation which induces a person to enter a contract, described above, there is a statutory remedy available. Section 2(1) of the Misrepresentation Act, 1967, gives a remedy where the representor

146

cannot prove "that he had reasonable grounds to believe and did believe up to the time contract negotiations were concluded, that the facts represented were true". This statutory route could be an easier one for the plaintiff because he does not have to prove that the representor was negligent: the onus of proof is on the latter. Moreover no proof of a special relationship is necessary. Evidence in support is the Court of Appeal decision in Howard Marine and Dredging Co. Ltd. v A. Ogden and Sons (Excavators) Ltd., 1978, QB 574. A contract for the hire of two barges was effected on the strength of the owners' representation as to the barges' carrying capacity. The representation was incorrect, although not fraudulent and the hirers claimed damages under Section 2(1) of the Act and under the principle in Hedley Byrne. Their case failed under Hedley Byrne because the Court considered there was no special relationship in view of the informal circumstances of that particular representation but succeeded, on appeal, under Section 2(1) on the ground that the owners had not discharged the onus of proof of reasonable ground of belief.

12.2 Coping With The Professional Liability

Coping with the risk means risk reduction measures such as self-regulation by the professional associations, preventative education and providing the resources to meet claims. It is imperative that professionals be conversant with current statute and case law pertaining to their area of expertise. They should be aware of the standards expected of their own profession, the competence of competitors and be up-to-date in their technical knowledge. Contact with fellow professionals through the professional association, where problems arising in practice can be reviewed, is helpful. Sensitive responses to client needs and dissatisfaction are possible by friendly relations and this may preclude an action being commenced.

The risk can be funded by membership of a mutual scheme, a captive insurance company or by conventional insurance.

12.2.1 Professional Liability Insurance

A typical wording of an operative clause of a professional indemnity insurance cover will read:

> "The Company agrees . . . to indemnify the Insured to the limits specified in the Schedule in respect of any sums which the Insured may become legally liable to pay as damages for breach of professional duty as a result of any claim or claims made upon the Insured during the period of insurance arising out of the conduct of the practice or business described in the Schedule as a direct result of any act, error or omission therein committed by the Insured or their predecessors in the practice or business whenever the same was or is alleged to have been committed. The Company will also indemnify any employee of the Insured if the Insured requests in respect of liability for which the Insured would have been entitled to indemnity if the claim had been made against the Insured."

Provided the claim arises during the period of insurance covered it does not matter when the act or omission complained of took place, therefore cover is retrospective. The date the claim is made is relevant and not the date of the occurrence, thus cover is on a "claims made" basis. Indemnity is given in respect of the fault of the predecessors in title because when a practice is taken over the new owner(s) assumes liability for all outstanding liabilities. In this cover claims against the firm only would be covered and not claims against former partners or former owners personally. A claim may be intimated against an employee of the firm alleging personal negligence and in that event cover is available, subject to the insured firm requesting it.

The limit of indemnity is usually expressed as an aggregate figure applicable in any one period of insurance rather than as a limit per claim or occurrence.

The policy may cover claims intimated during a period of, say, three or six months after the date of expiry or lapse of the policy. This "discovery period" covers claims in respect of negligence occurring during the period of insurance which are not made until after the policy period ends.

12.2.2   Exceptions to Cover

Cover is intended to apply to unintentional forms of conduct and therefore does not include dishonest, fraudulent, criminal or malicious acts of the insured, their predecessors in business or employees of the insured. Ordinarily libel and slander is excluded but cover is possible by policy extension and for additional premium.

12.2.3   Extensions of Cover

(i) Dishonesty of employees. This is a risk which is likely to cause financial loss to the employer mainly but on ocasions the employer may incur legal liability to others. The employer can cover the risk of his own financial loss by means of a fidelity guarantee insurance but this type of policy does not cover the liability to third parties. Insurers may be prepared, therefore, to amend the dishonesty exclusion by deleting the reference to dishonesty etc., of employees. Alternatively, the policy can be endorsed to specifically include liability for dishonest, fraudulent, criminal or malicious conduct of employees.

(ii) Loss or damage to documents. The standard cover already covers professional negligence resulting in loss of or damage to documents but the professional person may be liable for loss of documents belonging to others, as a bailee and there is also the risk of loss or damage to own documents. This cover is a mixture of third party and material damage cover. Documents include deeds, wills, agreements, maps, plans, records, books, letters, and certificates but cover will not include bearer bonds, currency notes, money orders, postal orders or other negotiable documents.

(iii) Breach of warranty of authority. The risk covered by this policy extension is that where the professional person acts as an agent of a principal, impliedly warranting that he/she has the authority of the principal, and in fact has not the authority. A third party, acting on the basis of the professional person's supposed authority and suffering loss because of the absence of that authority could bring an action for breach of warranty of authority. As an example, an architect employed by a local authority to supervise the construction of a sports centre may instruct the builder in additional work and expenditure beyond the authority given him. If the local authority (the principal) refuses to ratify this, the architect can be liable to the builder. It is usual to draft the extension wording to the policy to cover "breach of warranty of authority made in good faith" in order to exclude cover in respect of deliberate breaches of warranty of authority.

(iv) Libel and slander. Apart from extension of the above policy the risks of defamation can be covered by the issue of a special policy. Indemnity is possible for legal liability in respect of:

(i) libel

   (ii) slander to title of goods

   (iii) infringement of trademark, registered design, copyright or patent right, arising from matter contained in publications.

In addition to paying damages, the policy will cover expenses in withdrawing the offending publication. Ordinarily, cover will be subject to an excess or to the insured paying a fixed percentage of each and every claim.

12.3   Directors and Officers' Liability

Directors and officers of companies hold positions of trust and therefore they have responsibility to their company, the shareholders, the employees and the public at large. Their liability for damages and legal costs and expenses may be incurred at common law and, increasingly, by virtue of statute law, e.g. the Companies Act, 1985 and the Insolvency Acts, 1985/86. The 1985 Act defines an officer in relation to a body corporate as including directors, managers and secretaries. It can be assumed that "managers" refers only to those to whom the whole of the managerial function of the company has been delegated. In this area of liability claims may arise against directors/officers alleging:

   (i) negligent mis-statements
   (ii) acting beyond the scope of their authority
 (iii) bad advice
 (iv) authorising excessive company borrowing
  (v) making unauthorised payments
 (vi) failure to make statutory payments
 (vii) failure to supervise
(viii) unavoidable conflict of interests.

In Selangor Rubber Estates Ltd. v Cradoc and Others, 1968, 2 All ER 1073, two nominee directors of a public company were held liable for a loss of £232,500 following the bankruptcy of a director responsible for the losses. The nominee directors, who had acted under the control of the bankrupt director, were in breach of their duties as directors and in breach of trust.

In Dorchester Finance Company Ltd. and Another v Stebbing and Others, 1977, a chartered accountant (Stebbing) and two non-executive directors failed to exercise proper care and skill in that they knowingly and recklessly made loans without adequate security. All the defendants were held liable in negligence for damages amounting to £400,000.

Statutory liability is exemplified in the case of British Airways Board v Parish, 1979, 2 Lloyds Rep. 371 CA. The managing director signed a company cheque which omitted the word "Ltd." and this in contravention of the Companies Act. He was held personally liable for £34,000 because the company had gone into liquidation and was unable to meet the cheque. Statutory liability has become more onerous (the Companies Act, 1981, imposed many additional duties on company directors) and shareholders, including institutional investors, are becoming more alert to the possibilities of suing directors. The Insolvency Act, 1985, which was consolidated in the Insolvency Act, 1986, established a new statutory tort termed "wrongful trading". Section 15 provides that if in a winding-up it appears to the liquidator that a director or former director has been guilty of wrongful trading he may apply to the court for an order that the person is liable to make a contribution to the company's assets. Wrongful trading occurs where a director, once he has knowledge that the company can no longer avoid insolvent liquidation, fails to take every step to minimise the potential loss to the company's creditors that he ought to take in the circumstances.

In the USA, Europe and Australasia these liabilities arise under approximately the same principles.

12.3.1 Directors and Officers Insurance Cover

Insurance protection for directors/officers' liability provides indemnity for damages, out-of-court settlements and legal defence costs in respect of civil proceedings and certain criminal actions. Global cover for multi-national companies is written. The policy indemnifies directors and officers of the insured company against loss arising from any claims made against them jointly or severally by reason of any wrongful act in their capacity as a director or officer of the company. In addition the company is indemnified in respect of any payment which they elect to make or are legally entitled to make arising out of any claim made against any director/officer for which the director/officer would otherwise have been entitled to indemnity. Cover is on a "claims made" basis.

The "wrongful act" covered is any actual or alleged breach of duty, neglect, error, mis-statement, misleading statement, omission, breach of warranty of authority or other act wrongfully attempted by the director or officer. Not included in the cover are claims based upon:

  (i) statutory liability for pollution

 (ii) bodily injury or damage to tangible property

(iii) defamation

 (iv) any director or officer gaining any personal profit or advantage or receiving any remuneration to which they are not legally entitled

  (v) failure to effect or maintain insurance on behalf of the company

 (vi) fines, penalties or punitive damages imposed by law

(vii) failure or the effects of any product or failure to render professional services and or professional advice

(viii) payment of commissions, gratuities or any other benefits to political groups, government or armed service officials or directors/officers/employees of or any person having an ownership interest in any customer of the company

 (ix) dishonesty or fraud by any director/officer (but there is cover for costs and expenses of successfully defending any action brought in this connection).

A limit of indemnity is applied and is expressed as an aggregate limit. In common with professional indemnity insurance, a deductible is applied.

The Institute of Directors has launched an insurance scheme which provides directors with protection for liability arising under the Insolvency Act. This covers wrongful trading and also expenses arising from enquiries by the Department of Trade and Industry and other regulatory bodies. Covered also are legal and other costs of disputes with the directors' companies over the terms and conditions of directorships and disputes with the Inland Revenue.

Chapter 13

MOTOR VEHICLES

13.0 General

Liability for injury or damage to property caused by the use of motor vehicles arises in the law of negligence. The user owes a duty of care to those whom he can reasonably foresee might be injured by his failure to exercise care and breach may result not only in civil damages but also in criminal proceedings. In 1985 the number of persons killed on the roads in the United Kingdom was 5,165 and 312,359 persons were injured. This was the lowest figure since 1956 and a higher figure is expected for 1986. Road accidents are a major cause for concern from the point of view of human suffering and the burden imposed on medical services. This concern is reflected in the mass of legislation enacted to regulate the use of vehicles on roads in the UK and to increase road safety. The goods vehicle operator and transport manager has to digest an inordinate amount of statutory regulations dealing with safety, environmental and social matter pertaining to road transport operation.

Occasionally accidents have catastrophic results and court awards approaching one million pounds for single cases of serious bodily injury are known. At Hixon, Staffordshire in 1968 a train travelling from Manchester bound for London smashed at high speed into a 60-ton transporter vehicle carrying a massive 120 ton transformer over a Continental type level crossing. Eleven people died and about forty were injured. The train was wrecked. A public enquiry concluded that the blame rested with the vehicle driver and attendants who failed to follow procedure by using the phone provided to warn the railway signalman. A road tanker over-turned at a village and the resultant fire and explosion caused extensive damage to surrounding property.

13.1 Road Traffic Regulations

Road traffic regulations are to be found in a number of Acts and Regulations which relate to all aspects of the risks of road use involving pedestrians, cyclists, motorists, commercial vehicle drivers and operators. Subjects include construction and use of vehicles, operators' licensing, safety of vehicles and loads, road traffic regulations, compulsory insurance requirements, passenger vehicle operations and international transport operations. In this Text the emphasis will be upon commercial users. Only the Road Traffic Act, 1972 (as amended by the Road Traffic Act, 1974) is outlined here and the Student is not expected to have knowledge of the other complex and numerous regulations pertaining to road transport.

13.1.1 Duty to Stop and Report in Event of Accident

Part I of the Road Traffic Act, 1972, deals with principal road safety provisions, offences connected with the use of motor vehicles on the road, the riding of pedal cycles and with traffic generally. Section 25 requires that in the event of an accident whereby personal injury is caused to a person other than the driver of that motor vehicle or damage is caused to another vehicle or trailer or to an animal . . . the driver shall stop and, if required to by any person having reasonable grounds, give his name and address and also the name and address of the owner and the identification marks of the vehicle. Alternatively the driver shall report the accident at a police station or to a constable as soon as reasonably practicable, and in any case within 24 hours.

13.1.2　Compulsory Insurance of Motor Vehicles

Motor insurance has been compulsory in the UK since 1930 and the extent of insurance requiements are set out in Part IV of the Road Traffic Act, 1972, Sections 143 to 158. The purpose is to make certain, as far as possible, that the victim of a road accident shall recover compensation, subject to legal liability.

Section 143(1) reads thus:

"Subject to the provisions of this Part of the Act, it shall not be lawful for a person to use, or to cause or permit any other person to use, a motor vehicle on a road unless there is in force . . . such a policy of insurance or such a security in respect of third party risks as complies with the requirements of this Part of this Act; and if a person acts in contravention of this section he shall be guilty of an offence."

Note that not only the person using a motor vehicle but also anyone causing (or instructing) or permitting others to use a motor vehicle is responsible to see that the insurance policy or the security is wide enough to cover use by those other persons. "Causing" means any express instruction or order, whereas "permitting" denotes implied as well as express permission. The parting with the control of any vehicle to any person is prohibited unless that person is covered by a policy or security. The consequences of breach of the statutory duty to make certain that insurance or security is effective when causing or permitting someone else to drive a vehicle are that the person permitting may be liable in damages to a third party injured by the vehicle. In Monk v Warbey and Others, 1934, 50 T.L.R. 163, Warbey owned a car which he insured at Lloyd's, the cover being restricted to driving by himself or a member of his family. The car was lent to one, Knowles who in turn permitted May to drive and whilst the latter was driving he negligently injured Monk. Neither Knowles nor May had any means to satisfy the judgement in favour of Monk, consequently Monk brought an action against Warbey on the grounds that he was in breach of duty under Section 143. Monk succeeded and the decision established that there can be a vicarious civil liability on the owner of a vehicle where he permits use in the knowledge that there is no effective insurance. Criminal proceedings will also be a result.

For the purpose of the Act a "motor vehicle" means a mechanically propelled vehicle intended or adapted for use on roads. Section 196(1) defines a "road" as "any highway and any other road to which the public has access, and includes bridges over which a road passes". The test is not whether the members of the public have any right of access but whether it is a fact that the public has access, therefore included would be a private road on which people trespassed. The forecourt of an hotel, the private property of the owners and accessible to the main road was deemed a "road" because members of the public used it as a short-cut from one place to another. To "use a motor vehicle on a road" is interpreted widely and in effect means to have the use of a motor vehicle on a road. The word "use" in the Act is intended to cover a motor vehicle both when it is being driven on the road and when it is not being driven on the road. A motor vehicle left standing could run away and cause injury. In Elliot v Gray, 1959, a car was left on a public road with the battery removed and the petrol in the tank had evaporated, so that it could not be mechanically propelled. Because the car could be moved, though it could not be driven, it was held that the owner had the "use" of the car on a road within the meaning of the Act.

The policy or security must cover legal liability in respect of death of or bodily injury to any person and damage to property (see 13.1.8) arising out of the use of a motor vehicle on a road. There must be cover for emergency treatment given by a medical practitioner at the scene of the accident or by a hospital. Currently the fee is £15.00 per person treated and in addition the medical practitioner is entitled to expenses of £0.29p for each mile travelled in excess of two. The Act is not concerned with liability for death of or bodily injury to an employee of the user or driver where such injury arises out of and in the course of his employment. This is of course legislated for in the Employers Liability (Compulsory Insurance) Act, 1969. There is no compulsion to insure contractual liability.

In order to permit a measure of freedom of choice in providing for the vehicle liability risk financially, the legislation sets out two possible alternatives to conventional insurance cover, namely the security and a deposit. A large organisation operating a fleet of vehicles may consider that savings are possible by creating its own fund to meet the cost of motor claims. A self-funding scheme will usually require some form of catastrophe cover from an insurer and this could take the form of an excess of loss cover, for example the insurer comes on risk when it is in excess of, say, £100,000 any one accident. There may be an aggregate loss cover also. The deposit and security are merely forms of financial guarantee of solvency for a fund and the givers are not called upon to pay third party claims unless the fund proves insufficient. The security must be for a minimum of £25,000 in the case of public service vehicles and a minimum of £5,000 for other vehicles and is available from authorised security givers who are usually insurance companies. A person or company which has deposited with the Accountant General of the Supreme Court the sum of £15,000, is exempt from the requirements of third party insurance or security (Section 144.1) but very few vehicle users utilise this method of complying with the requirements of the Act. Apart from the need for an internal fund, the use of vehicles thus covered seems to be somewhat restricted by the proviso "apply to a vehicle . . . at a time when the vehicle is being driven under the owner's control". It is not absolutely clear whether use by an employee or, say, the spouse of an employee for social purposes, would constitute driving under the owner's control. It depends upon the rules laid down, or instructions as to such use given by the owner. This issue must not be confused with the principle of vicarious liability where the question of use arising out of, or in the course of employment has its own guidelines (see Chapter 1: 1.5.1).

13.1.3   Vehicle Users Exempt from Compulsory Insurance

Section 144(2) sets out a list of users exempt from the compulsory insurance requirements of Section 143(1). They include:

(a) County councils and county districts in the UK.

(b) Police authorities.

(c) Use of Vehicles for salvage purposes pursuant to Part IX of the Merchant Shipping Act 1894.

(d) Vehicles used in pursuance of a direction under the Army Act 1955 or the Air Force Act 1955.

(e) Vehicles owned by the London Transport Executive or by a body which is within the meaning of the Transport (London) Act 1969.

(f) Invalid carriages falling within certain specifications as to size and use.

In the main the exemptions relate to risks funded by the Government or the Crown and therefore there is sufficient financial guarantee and it is unnecessary to compel insurance. Many local authorities, for example, do insure in any case. The Crown accepts liability for damage by vehicles being delivered for requisitioning and the user is deemed to be a servant of the Crown in respect of resulting injury or damage.

13.1.4 Requirement of a Certificate of Insurance or Security

Section 147(1) provides: "A policy of insurance shall be of no effect for the purposes of this part of this Act unless and until there is delivered by the insurer to the person by whom the policy is effected a certificate . . . in the prescribed form and containing such particulars of any conditions subject to which the policy is issued and of any other matters as may be prescribed". There is also a provision for issue of a certificate of security on the same lines as above. The Act also lays down rules for the return of the certificate of insurance or security in the event of cancellation of cover.

13.1.5 Avoidance of Certains Terms and Right of Recovery

The Act restricts the right of an insurer to repudiate liability under a policy in the event of breach of a condition in the same manner as the Employers Liability (Compulsory Insurance) Act (see Chapter 9: 9.2.4). Section 148(1) provides that no insurer shall have the right to decline to meet liabilities compulsorily insurable on the grounds of breach of policy conditions or restrictions relating to the following matters:

(a) the age or physical or mental condition of persons driving the vehicle;

(b) the condition of the vehicle;

(c) the number of persons that the vehicle carries;

(d) the weight or physical characteristocs of the goods that the vehicle carries;

(e) the times at which or the areas within which the vehicle is used;

(f) the horsepower or cylinder capacity or value of the vehicle;

(g) the carrying on the vehicle of any particular apparatus;

(h) the carrying on the vehicle of any particular means of identification, other than any means of identification required by the Vehicles (Excise) Act, 1971.

The Act gives the insurer the right to recover from the insured in the event of a payment being made in respect of bodily injury, where the payment is made solely because of the provisions of this Section.

Section 148(2) provides that any conditions in a policy relieving an insurer from liability from some act or omission after an accident are of no effect as regards claims from third parties for bodily injury, e.g. failure to give prompt notice to the insurer of an accident. Once again a right of recovery is given.

Section 148(3) provides that no contractual agreement between the insured and persons travelling in the vehicle (entering, getting on to, or alighting from) which purports to negative or restrict the liability of the user to passengers shall have effect. In effect, where the passenger voluntarily accepts the risks of travelling, either by understanding or by agreement the vehicle user will still bear the full legal liability.

13.1.6   Duty to Give Information as to Insurance or Security

Section 151(1) provides that a person against whom a claim is made in respect of Act liability shall on demand by or on behalf of the person making the claim give certain information. He must state whether he was insured or had in force a security in respect of that liability, and he must give such particulars as specified in the certificate of insurance or security. This is to assist the third party claimant to further his claim.

Under Section 166 a duty is imposed on the driver in the case of an accident involving injury to another to produce evidence of insurance or security or to report the accident. The driver is required to produce his certificate, not only to a police constable, but alternatively to some person who has reasonable grounds for its production. If this is not done, or cannot be done, then the driver must, as soon as possible, and in any case within 24 hours report the accident at a police station or to a police constable and thereupon produce his certificate. The accident must be reported within 24 hours, but the driver can claim the right to produce the certificate within 5 days after the accident at a police station specified by him at the time he reports the accident.

13.1.7   Compulsory Cover in Europe

The EEC Directive on Insurance of Civil Liabilities arising from the use of motor vehicles (No.72/166/CEE) requires that motor insurance policies issued in a member State give the minimum indemnity necessary to comply with the laws relating to compulsory insurance of motor vehicles in other member States. With effect from 1st January, 1974 all motor insurance policies issued in the UK include this compulsory element of cover. In addition to the eleven member States of the EEC a number of other European countries signed the Directive and are thus participants in this arrangement which facilitates movement of vehicles across frontiers by eliminating the need for documentary proof of insurance.

13.1.8   The Motor Vehicles (Compulsory Insurance) Regulations 1987

With effect from 1st January 1989 legal liability for damage to third party property became a Road Traffic Act compulsory insurance cover, but only up to a limit of

£250,000 for any one accident or series of accidents arising from one cause. In practice, all motor insurance policies include third party property cover with limits of indemnity applying only to commercial vehicle covers, and the cover given is at least £250,000 and in almost all policies is considerably in excess of this.

13.2 International Transport by Road

British hauliers and companies which transport their own products by means of their own vehicles are increasingly operating from the United Kingdom to Europe, the Middle East and Asia. This increases the variety of legal and commercial requirements demanded by the operator. Heavy on-the-spot fines for failure to comply with regulations are risks attaching to foreign use and in serious cases the vehicle may be impounded and drivers imprisoned until legal requirements are satisfied.

The European Agreement concerning the International Carriage of Dangerous Goods (ADR) requires that danagerous goods are packed and labelled in accordance with the Agreement and that the carrying vehicle complies with special conditions of the Agreement. Vehicles must be inspected and certificated in the country of registration to ensure that they conform to ADR requirements. Special stringent regulations apply to the carriage of dangerous goods on ships.

The special difficulties which can arise when dealing with claims at a distance, more especially in the Middle East and Asia, are due mainly to problems of communication with resultant loss of control. Dealing with third party claims at a distance through an intermediary is likely to make the claim more costly. Insurers have to grapple with such problems and on occasions find it necessary to send out their own representative for on-the-spot handling of the matter.

13.2.1 The International Green Card System

The Green Card System came into being in 1953, introduced by an international body known as the Council of Bureaux. The Green Card is an international insurance certificate valid for the period shown thereon in the country or countries specified thereon. For a British vehicle user the Green Card is issued by his home insurer and the card guarantees effective insurance to cover third party liability in the country visited. The Card is thus recognised as evidence of insurance whereas the ordinary certificate of insurance issued by, say, a British insurer would be worthless in a foreign country. The Green Card is valid only in those countries which have their own domestic Bureau and this is the case in nearly all European countries. Where the Green Card is not valid, it is necessary to effect special insurance before entry to that country. Green Cards are valid in some territories beyond Europe including Tunisia, Morocco, Turkey and Israel. The strength of the Green Card lies in the fact that the local Bureau of the country that the vehicle is visiting guarantees it and that Bureau, in turn is guaranteed by the Bureau of the vehicle's home country, thus the local victim of an accident involving a foreign vehicle is sure to obtain compensation, assuming liability of course. In the United Kingdom the Motor Insurers' Bureau provides the guarantee. It should be explained, however, that the motor insurer which issues the Card is liable for the claim in the usual way under the terms of the policy.

Since the United Kingdom became a signatory to the EEC Directive referred to in 13.1.7 above the previous requirement of inspection of Green Cards at frontiers has been dispensed with in respect of those European countries which are signatories to the Directive. This is because the minimum compulsory insurance requirements of those States are now automatically complied with by inter-Government agreement. However, the minimum third party cover now given for foreign use as part of the basic policy is not sufficient for most operators, who deem it essential to have the wider liability cover and indeed own damage protection as well. For this it is necessary to have the policy extended to cover the journey abroad, and insurers continue to issue the Green Card for the "Directive" countries, even through it is not strictly necessary.

To sum up, there are three different situations pertaining to insurance of vehicles for international journeys:

(i) The EEC Directive Countries (17) where minimum cover is already given by the policy and no Green Card is necessary;

(ii) Countries other than those in (i) which have a Bureau. A Green Card is necessary, otherwise insurance has to be specially effected before entry;

(iii) Countries other than those in (i) and (ii) above. A Green Card would not be effective and insurance has to be arranged specially, before entry.

13.3 Spanish Bail Bonds

Difficulties can be encountered by users of vehicles visiting Spain when an accident occurs. The Spanish authorities may detain the driver or his vehicle and in that event release can only be obtained against a guarantee or bail deposit. Insurers issue Spanish Bail Bonds which provide a guarantee, usually for £500 or £1,000 and if the need arises the driver can produce the Bond which will be backed by the insurer's local office or by the Spanish Bureau. This is not a form of insurance but merely the provision of money as bail and if any of the sum provided as surety is forfeited the holder must reimburse the insurer who provided the Bond. The Bond is not compulsory for visiting vehicle users to Spain but it is a wise precaution and must be effected before commencement of the trip. There is a modest premium payable.

13.4 The Motor Insurers Bureau

Certain weaknesses in the operation of the Road Traffic Act, 1930, and subsequent statutes resulted in instances where the victims of road accidents were unable to obtain compensation because vehicles were uninsured or untraced. Following Government expressed concern the motor insurance industry established the Motor Insurers Bureau in 1946. The Bureau (MIB) entered into an agreement with the Ministry of Transport to provide compensation to victims of motor accidents in certain circumstances. The MIB is a body incorporated under the Companies Act, that is, it is a legal person it can bring and defend actions in its own right. The Road Traffic Act, 1974, requires that all insurers in the United Kingdom who transact motor insurance must be members of the MIB. The Bureau is funded by means of a levy on motor insurers, which is in proportion to motor premium of each member. Apart from operating the Green Card system described in 13.2.1 the

Bureau's main function is to fulfil two agreements made with the Ministry of Transport/Secretary of State for the Environment relating to (i) uninsured drivers and (ii) untraced drivers. The agreements apply only to liabilities which are required to be insured under the Road Traffic Acts, which include death or bodily injury and damage to property of third parties:

(i) Uninsured drivers: Where a person is injured by a vehicle and obtains a judgement against the driver who ought to have been insured but is not and is a "man of straw", the MIB will meet the liability, subject to certain requirements.

(ii) Untraced drivers: If the victim of a road accident cannot find a defendant against whom to raise an action, he cannot obtain a judgement. In such "hit-and-run" cases the Bureau undertakes to compensate the victim provided the balance of probabilities point to:
    (a) a motor vehicle having been the cause of injury or death; and
    (b) the motorist, had he/she been known, being held liable by a court to pay damages for the injury or death.

The MIB agreement excludes the first £175.00 of claims for damage to property.

13.5   Goods Carrying Vehicles

Vehicles used for commercial purposes may be classified as goods carrying vehicles, buses and coaches, cars carrying passengers for hire or reward, and vehicles of special construction, many of which are tools of trade. Each category presents special liability risk features.

Goods carrying vehicles range in size from small goods carrying vans to the maximum size permitted on UK roads which is 38 tonnes. The extent of use or mileage will have a bearing on the claims frequency: the higher the road exposure, the greater the risk. There can be a potential catastrophe risk where goods of flammable, explosive, toxic or other dangerous nature are transported and the size of the vehicle and gross weight is also a risk factor. Accidents of horrific consequences have occurred, involving chemical tanker vehicles, in the UK and elsewhere, notably the inferno at a Spanish holiday camp a few years ago. For the UK there is an impressive list of legislation covering transportation by road of explosives, petroleum spirits, radioactive materials, poisons, poisonous waste, dangerous substances and liquefied gases.

General loading and unloading risks have also to be considered.

13.6   Vehicles of Special Construction

There is a wide range of purpose built vehicles of special types such as cranes, excavators, dumpers, mechanical navvies, mobile plant for site clearing and levelling, etc.

Vehicles which operate below wheel base level such as excavators and mechanical navvies may cause damage to electric cables, sewers, or gas pipes and resulting claims can be very expensive. Additional risks are subsidence, flooding, or water pollution. These items of plant are frequently the subject of hire contracts and the risk manager, where plant is being hired in, should be aware of indemnities required by the owners. Contract terms may also determine liability for plant hired out by a company. Special operating risks attaching to the use of mobile cranes are overturning and damage to overhead cables. Here again the matter of hiring agreements is relevant and the Contractors' Plant Association Conditions are often applicable.

13.7 Contingent Liability

Contingent liability risks in general were considered in Chapter 11 (11.3) and in respect of motor vehicles a company may be exposed to claims when someone else is using a vehicle on the company's behalf or where the company has no direct control over the use of vehicles despite the fact that it may own them. Employees who supply their own car for use in their employer's business and who are responsible for insuring the vehicle can involve the company in liability vicariously. Ordinarily, the employee's own insurance policy is relied upon by both parties but there is the possibility that the policy may not operate due to a breach of a policy condition by the employee or where the policy has lapsed. In either event, the employer is exposed to a claim. A company which hires in a vehicle with a driver and relies upon the vehicle owner's insurance cover is similarly exposed to a contingency risk. Likewise firms which hire out vehicles, such as a self-drive hire business, and who require the hirer to effect insurance cover may be faced with an uninsured liability claim. Insurance of the motor contingent liability risk can be arranged under a separate policy or by extending the general liability policy. It is not a Road Traffic Act insurance requirement because the liability of the firm depends upon someone else's insurance being inoperative, therefore no certificate of insurance is necessary.

13.8 Motor Fleets

A fleet of vehicles operated by one organisation may consist of a mere dozen vehicles or there may be thousands of vehicles comprised of private cars and commercial vehicles including items of plant. In practice fleets are usually:

(i) Commercial vehicles owned by haulage contractors, that is, firms carrying the goods of others for reward, with a few private cars used by directors or senior staff;

(ii) Mixed fleets of commercial vehicles and private cars operated by retail traders or manufacturers, consisting of a number of vehicles used for delivery of own goods and a number of private cars mainly used by representatives;

(iii) Self-drive hire fleets;

(iv) Special type vehicles designed as tools and not as load carriers and often used by building and civil engineering contractors;

(v) Public service coaches;

(vi) A combination of more than one of the above.

The potential liability risk in operating a fleet of vehicles is considerable and providing cover for a large fleet is a major item of expenditure, either by means of an internal fund or by paying insurance premiums. In the case of larger fleets owners have the advantage of the law of large numbers and spread of risk when assessing accident frequency and average claims cost, consequently it is more feasible to retain the risk by providing a self-insurance fund. A number of large organisations self-insure their motor fleets and these arrangements often cover not only their own damage losses but the third party liability risks as well. One national corporation in the UK operates 61,000 vehicles ranging from light vans up to 32-ton articulated trucks and in addition, some 7,000 units of engineering plant. The risk is self-insured and the fund guaranteed by a Security given by a leading UK insurer. Catastrophe cover is provided by an insurer in the form of excess of loss insurance, but the excess point is a very high figure. That corporation also operates a fleet of private cars, but this is covered by conventional insurance.

13.9   Insurance of the Commercial Vehicle Liability Risk

For the purposes of reference, a specimen copy of the Eagle Star Group's Fleet Policy is given in the Appendix to this Chapter and the cover relating to third party liability risks only will be given attention here. The specimen form is applicable to fleets and combines cover for both commercial vehicles and private cars in the one policy, but in motor insurance generally it is usual to use separate (and differing) policies.

13.9.1   Liability to Third Parties

The cover follows the formula found in liability insurance covers generally but the special aspects of vehicle operations are expressly referred to in Clause 1. Liability cover for the insured vehicle includes loading and unloading risks, but the latter is restricted by Exception 7 of the Exceptions to Clause 1 to the limits of the carriageway or thoroughfare, although cover is not so limited in respect of the driver or attendant of the vehicle. This is the standard approach by motor insurers, who thus avoid overlapping with the cover provided by the general public liability policy cover.

In Section 2 of Clause 1 cover is provided for the contingent liability risk. Many insurers do not include this as a matter of course, but give the cover as an extension of the policy or under a separate policy. Section 3 of Clause 1 indemnifies in respect of the unauthorised movement of other vehicles.

There is a limit of indemnity of £1,000,000 for any one accident in respect of damage to third party property so far as concerns commercial vehicles or vehicles bearing trade plates. The practice is general and the figure varies, with a limit of £500,000 in some instances. Insurers apply a property indemnity limit because of the greater potential damage claims arising from accidents involving heavy vehicles. The indemnity provided for private cars is unlimited and in the case of all vehicles insured there is no upper limit on the third party bodily injury liability cover.

Section 4 provides indemnity to the legal personal representatives of the persons entitled to indemnity because of the provisions of the Law Reform (Miscellaneous Provisions) Act, 1934 (Chapter 4: 4.2).

13.9.2   Legal Fees and Manslaughter Defence Costs

Legal fees for representation and for defence are paid by the policy as in most other liability covers. In addition the policy pays costs of defence against a charge of manslaughter or causing death by reckless or dangerous driving in the UK if the charge arises out of an accident which is the subject of indemnity under the policy. Defence costs are also provided for an equivalent charge arising in any of the Countries which are signatories to the EEC Directive on the Insurance of Civil Liabilities (see 13.1.7 above).

13.9.3   Exceptions to Third Party Cover

Many of the exceptions to Clause 1 listed are common to liability policies and have been discussed earlier in the Text. Worthy of note are:

(i)   Exception 1: No cover is applicable where the driver is not licensed to drive the vehicle or is suspended from driving. Note however that indemnity would be given to the insured person or firm if the insured had no knowledge of the driver's lack of licence or of his suspension.

(ii) Exception 3(c): Liability for loss of or damage to goods on the vehicle is not covered. A goods-in-transit insurance is more appropaite for this risk.

(iii) Exception 5: This excludes the tool of trade or working risk for special types of vehicles or mechanical plant, e.g. an excavator causing damage to underground cables whilst being operated. However the working risks associated with goods-carrying vehicles, agricultural tractors, self-propelled agricultural machines and fork-lift trucks are covered. In all events, cover for third party injuries required by the Road Traffic Acts and equivalent EEC legislation is provided.

(iv) Exception 6: Excluded are risks of trade plate-bearing vehicles beyond the limits of any road. The intention here is to dovetail cover with that provided by the motor trader's internal risks insurance, and to prevent overlapping.

Exception 8: This is the exclusion of crop-spraying risks in respect of agricultural or forestry machinery. Even when these vehicles are insured under more specific agricultural vehicle policies most insurers exclude the risks. Others exclude crop-spraying only when the farmer is operating on farms other than his own.

(v)   Exception 9: Limiting the cover for unauthorised movement of vehicles to indemnity for movement by the insured or employees and to vehicles not owned, etc., by the insured.

13.9.4   Territorial Limits and Foreign Travel

The geographical scope of the policy is set out in Clause 5 and is typical of almost all policies issued in the UK. The full scope of cover applies to the British Islands and the Channel Islands and whilst the insured vehicles are in transit by sea between any ports in these areas. However, in accordance with the EEC Directive the policy includes cover in respect of the minimum requirements of those European Countries which have signed the Directive.

Provision is made expressly on the policy for foreign travel at the request of the insured and subject to the insurer's agreement. Liability for Customs duty and other charges arising out of damage or loss which is insured by the policy, is covered.

A Spanish Bail Bond for up to £1,000 is provided without additional premium.

13.9.5 Unauthorised Use and Unlicensed Drivers

Clause 6: Drivers employed by the insured or other persons may, unknown to the insured, use an insured vehicle for purposes not included in the description of use, for example, private work or unauthorised social domestic or pleasure use. The policy extends to indemnify the insured in such circumstances and whilst this cover is most likely to apply to accidental damage to the insured's vehicles, it could also be relevant to third party claims against the insured under the head of vicarious liability. The insured's knowledge of or consent to such use outwith the description would render this cover inoperative.

Clause 7: Exception No.1 to Clause 1 is set aside in circumstances where the law does not require a driver to be licensed, for example, where a vehicle is being used off the "road" as defined in the Road Traffic Act. However there is the proviso that the driver must be of an age to hold a licence to drive the particular vehicle, albeit he does not have one. This is a practical approach by the insurer and at the same time the proviso relieves the insurer of the risks of, say, a child driving a heavy vehicle on private premises.

13.9.6 Towing Trailers or Disabled Mechanically Propelled Vehicles

Full third party cover applies whilst the insured vehicles are towing trailers or disabled mechanically propelled vehicles. Third party cover for towing vehicles in an emergency where there is a breakdown is invariably given as standard. This is in recognition of occasional need to give roadside assistance. Insurers do not take on board the risks of liability for damage to the trailer or vehicle being towed nor for the goods carried thereon.

13.9.7 Contractual Liability to Principal

Clause 10 covers the insured in respect of liability assumed by the insured under an agreement with a principal for the execution of work or services. This contractual liability cover only relates to the basic liability cover given by the policy (Exception 2 to Clause 10). For example no cover is given for delay or penalty clauses in the contract. It comes down to indemnity in respect of bodily injury or damage to property caused by the negligence of the insured or a person in the employ of the insured (Exception 5). The principal must agree to the control of all claims being vested in the insurer.

Exception 1 to Clause 10 excludes contractual liability for injury to the principal's employees occurring in the course of employment but of course an action in tort against the insured or his driver by an employee of a principal would be a third party claim and is covered by the policy.

164

Exceptions 3 and 4 effectively exclude more onerous contractual terms which may require the insured to provide the principal with compensation for pure economic loss, for example, or where the contract requires replacement of damaged property by new property without adjustment for wear and tear.

13.9.8   Policy Conditions

The conditions in the fleet policy are similar to those examined in the various liability policies looked at earlier and most require no further comment.

Clause 12, Condition 8, dealing with property damage claims has the same effect as in other liability policies where there is a limit of indemnity (see Chapter 11: 11.1.4).

Condition 9 (Joint Insured) has the effect of covering cross liabilities (see 11.2).

APPENDIX

Eagle Star Group

Fleet Policy

The Insured having

1. made to Eagle Star Insurance Company Limited (the Company) a written proposal and declaration which are the basis of and form part of this contract, and
2. paid or agreed to pay the premium as consideration,

the Company will provide the insurance detailed in this Policy during the Period of Insurance stated in the Schedule and during any further period for which the Company may accept payment for renewal.

For and on behalf of the Company

A. R. N. Ratcliff
Chief Executive

Eagle Star Insurance Company Limited
Head Office
1, Threadneedle Street, LONDON EC2R 8BE

INTERPRETATION

The Certificate of Motor Insurance, the Schedule, the Schedule of Vehicles, the Appendices and any endorsements are incorporated in this Policy and any word or expression to which a specific meaning has been attached in any part bears the same meaning wherever it appears.

DEFINITIONS

In this Policy

1 "Insured Vehicle" means any vehicle or trailer as defined or described below:
   (a) "Private Car" means any private car, estate car, utility car or minibus;
   (b) "Motor Cycle" means any motor cycle, motor cycle and side-car or moped;
   (c) "Commercial Vehicle" means any motor vehicle or motor vehicle and attached trailer other than
      (i) a Private Car, or
      (ii) a Motor Cycle, or
      (iii) a steam driven vehicle
   which is insured under this Policy and is described in the current Certificate of Motor Insurance;
   (d) "trailer" means any trailer the property of the Insured or for which the Insured is responsible which is
      (i) attached to any Commercial Vehicle, or
      (ii) attached to or detached from the Insured Vehicle (and not attached to any other vehicle) and has been declared to the Company.
   The expression "trailer" does not include a disabled mechanically propelled vehicle.

2 "Minibus" means a vehicle with a seating capacity of not more than sixteen persons excluding the driver.

3 "driver" means any person who is driving the Insured Vehicle and is entitled to do so by the terms of the current Certificate of Motor Insurance.

4 "Insured Person" means
   (a) the Insured;
   (b) the driver;
   (c) at the request of the Insured
      (i) any principal, director or employee of the Insured;
      (ii) any person (other than the driver) who is travelling in or on or getting into or out of the Insured Vehicle or any attached trailer or attached disabled mechanically propelled vehicle;
      (iii) the owner of a vehicle on hire or loan or leased to the Insured;
      (iv) any member or committee member of the Insured's Sports or Social Club;
   (d) any person who, with the permission of the Insured, is using (but not driving) the Insured Vehicle for social, domestic and pleasure purposes provided that such use is permitted by the terms of the current Certificate of Motor Insurance;
   (e) the employer or partner of any person whose business use is permitted by the terms of the current Certificate of Motor Insurance.

5 "road" means a road as defined in the Road Traffic Act or Road Traffic or Motor Traffic law operative within the areas covered by this Policy.

6 "driving licence" means a licence to drive a vehicle of the same class as the Insured Vehicle.

7 "accessories" include
   (a) spare parts and
   (b) radios, cassette players and communications equipment fitted to the Insured Vehicle.

CLAUSE 1   LIABILITY TO THIRD PARTIES

The Company will indemnify the persons detailed in Sections **1**, **2** and **3** of this Clause in respect of legal liability for death of or injury to any person and damage to property.

Third Party Indemnity

1   The Insured Person will be indemnified when liability arises out of an accident caused by or in connection with the Insured Vehicle or the loading or unloading of the Insured Vehicle.

Third Party Contingency Cover

2   The Insured alone will be indemnified when liability arises out of an accident caused by or in connection with any motor vehicle (not the property of nor provided by the Insured) while being used in connection with the Insured's business or trade.

Provided always that
(a)   the Insured shall take all reasonable steps to ensure that there is in force in respect of such vehicle an insurance valid for such use;
(b)   if any claim covered by this Section **2** is also covered by any other insurance then notwithstanding **Condition No. 4** the Company shall not be liable to make any contribution to such claim.

Unauthorised Movement

3   The Insured or any principal, director or employee of the Insured will be indemnified when liability arises out of an accident caused by or in connection with the moving aside without the authority of the owner of any motor vehicle parked in such a position as to obstruct the legitimate passage or the loading or unloading of the Insured Vehicle. In these circumstances the obstructing vehicle shall not be regarded as property held in trust by or in the custody or control of the Insured.

Third Party Property Damage Limit

Provided always that in respect of
(i)   any Commercial Vehicle;
(ii)   any vehicle bearing a Trade Plate
payment for damage to property is limited to £1,000,000 in respect of any one occurrence or series of occurrences arising out of one event.

4   Following the death of any person entitled to indemnity, the Company will, in respect of the liability incurred, indemnify such person's legal personal representatives in the terms of this Clause.

Legal Costs

5   In respect of any event which may be the subject of indemnity under this Clause the Company will also pay
(a)   solicitor's fees for representation at any court of summary jurisdiction or at any coroner's inquest or fatal inquiry;
(b)   the costs of legal services arranged by the Company for the defence of the Insured and the driver against a charge of manslaughter or causing death by reckless driving (or an equivalent local charge in a country detailed in **Section 2 of Clause 5**);
(c)   all other costs and expenses incurred with the Company's written consent.

EXCEPTIONS TO CLAUSE 1

The Company shall not be liable

1   if, to the knowledge of the Insured Person, the person driving does not hold a driving licence unless such person has held and is not disqualified from holding or obtaining such a licence.

2   to indemnify any person other than the Insured if that person is entitled to indemnity under any other insurance.

3   for
   (a) damage to or loss of property belonging to or in the custody or control of the Insured Person;
   (b) damage to premises (or to the fixtures and fittings therein) which are not the property of the Insured but are occupied by the Insured under a leasing or rental arrangement if such damage is also covered by any other insurance;
   (c) damage to or loss of property in or on the Insured Vehicle;
   (d) damage to or loss of the Insured Vehicle.

4   in respect of death of or injury to any person arising out of and in the course of such person's employment by the Insured or by any person who is driving the Insured Vehicle.

5   in respect of death, injury or damage arising while a Commercial Vehicle or plant forming part of the Commercial Vehicle or attached thereto is working as a tool of trade except so far as is necessary to meet the requirements of any compulsory motor insurance legislation operative within the areas covered by this Policy.
This exception does not apply to goods carrying commercial vehicles, agricultural tractors, self-propelled agricultural machines or fork-lift trucks.

6   in connection with any Insured Vehicle bearing a Trade Plate, for death, injury or damage caused or arising beyond the limits of any road except when, during the course of a journey, it is temporarily garaged elsewhere than in or on any premises owned by or in the occupation of the Insured.

7   in respect of death, injury or damage caused or arising beyond the limits of any carriageway or thoroughfare in connection with
   (a) the bringing of the load to any Commercial Vehicle for loading thereon, or
   (b) the taking away of the load from any Commercial Vehicle after unloading therefrom
by any person other than the driver or attendant of such vehicle.

8   death, injury or damage caused by or attributable to the spraying or spreading of any chemical by any agricultural tractor or self-propelled agricultural or forestry machine insured under this Policy or any trailer attached to such tractor or machine.

9   under **Section 3**
   (a) if the obstructing vehicle is
      (i) moved by any person other than the Insured or a principal, director or employee of the Insured
      ii) owned, held under a hire purchase agreement, hired by or loaned or leased to the Insured
      (iii) driven by any person who does not hold a driving licence unless such person has held and is not disqualified from holding or obtaining such a licence.
   (b) in respect of damage to or loss of property in or on the obstructing vehicle.

EXCEPTIONS **1** and **9(a)(iii)** TO **CLAUSE 1** SHALL NOT APPLY WHEN THE INSURED VEHICLE IS DRIVEN UNDER THE TERMS OF **CLAUSE 7**.

CLAUSE 2 DAMAGE TO OR LOSS OF VEHICLE

1 The Company will indemnify the Insured against damage to or loss of the Insured Vehicle and accessories on the Insured Vehicle. This indemnity

    (a) shall not exceed the market value of the Insured Vehicle immediately before such damage or loss and in respect of any vehicle bearing a Trade Plate indemnity shall be limited to £25,000 or the market value of the Insured Vehicle immediately before such damage or loss, whichever is the less;

    (b) extends to include Private Car accessories in the Insured's private garage.

"New for Old"

2 If any Private Car is owned or held under a hire purchase agreement by the Insured and, having been purchased as new by the Insured, is within one year of the date of purchase

    (a) damaged to the extent that the cost of repair would exceed 50% of the manufacturer's recommended retail price plus taxes, or

    (b) lost by theft and not recovered

the Company will replace it with a new vehicle of the same make and model.

Provided that

    (i) the Insured requests it, and

    (ii) any other interested party known to the Company consents, and

    (iii) such replacement is available.

In such an event the Company shall become entitled to possession and ownership of the damaged or lost vehicle.

Under this Section **2** the Company will, in addition, indemnify the Insured against damage to or loss of any accessories on the Private Car or in the Insured's private garage.

Hire Purchase and Leasing Agreements

3 If to the knowledge of the Company the Insured Vehicle is the subject of a hire purchase or leasing agreement any payment for damage to or loss of the Insured Vehicle which is not made good by repair, reinstatement or replacement may, at the discretion of the Company, be made to the owner whose receipt shall be a full discharge of the Company's liability.

Repairs

4 Reasonable and necessary repairs may be authorised by the Insured without previously obtaining the consent of the Company provided that notification (in accordance with **Condition No. 2**) is given to the Company without delay and a detailed estimate of the cost of repairs is sent to the Company as soon as possible.

Recovery and re-delivery

5 In connection with any claim covered by this Clause the Company will pay the reasonable cost of removing the Insured Vehicle from the place where damage occurred to the premises of the nearest competent repairer and re-delivering the Insured Vehicle from such premises after repair.

EXCEPTIONS TO CLAUSE 2

The Company shall not be liable to pay for

1   wear and tear.

2   depreciation.

3   loss of use.

4   mechanical or electrical breakage, failure or breakdown.

5   damage to tyres caused by braking or by cuts, punctures or bursts.

6   damage to or loss of the Insured Vehicle caused directly by pressure waves from aircraft or other aerial devices travelling at sonic or supersonic speeds.

7   damage to or loss of any Insured Vehicle bearing a Trade Plate when such vehicle is beyond the limits of any road except when, during the course of a journey, it is temporarily garaged elsewhere than in or on any premises owned by or in the occupation of the Insured.

8   damage to or loss of the Insured Vehicle up to the maximum amount shown below in connection with any occurrence or series of occurrences arising out of one event while the Insured Vehicle is being driven by any person:

Young/Novice Drivers' Excess Foreign Licence Holders

(a)   aged under 21   £50

(b)   aged 21 to 24 (inclusive)   £25

(c)   aged 25 or over who has not held a full driving licence issued in Great Britain, Northern Ireland, the Isle of Man or the Channel Islands for the 12 months immediately preceding such damage   £25

This exception shall not apply

  (i)   in connection with any damage or loss by

    (A)   fire, lightning, self-ignition or explosion;

    (B)   theft or attempted theft;

 (ii)   when the Insured Vehicle is in the custody of a member of the motor trade for service or repair;

(iii)   in respect of a claim for breakage of glass in the windscreen or in the windows of the Insured Vehicle (or any scratching of bodywork resulting solely and directly from such breakage).

CLAUSE 3   PERSONAL EFFECTS

The Company will, at the request of the Insured, provide indemnity up to a maximum of £100 any one occurrence in respect of damage to or loss of personal effects while in or on the Insured Vehicle.

The owner's receipt shall be a full discharge of the Company's liability.

EXCEPTIONS TO CLAUSE 3

The Company shall not be liable in respect of damage to or loss of

1   money, stamps, tickets, documents or securities;

2   goods or samples carried in connection with any business or trade.

172

CLAUSE 4   MEDICAL EXPENSES

The Company will pay to the Insured medical expenses incurred by the driver or any other person travelling in or on any Insured Vehicle following injury caused by violent accidental external and visible means in direct connection with such Insured Vehicle.

The total liability of the Company under this Clause is limited to £150 in respect of each person injured.

CLAUSE 5   TERRITORIAL LIMITS AND FOREIGN TRAVEL

TERRITORIAL LIMITS This Policy applies in respect of accidents occurring in

1   Great Britain, Northern Ireland, the Republic of Ireland, the Isle of Man and the Channel Islands and during sea transit between ports in these areas including the processes of loading and unloading;

2   any other member country of the European Economic Community and any other country in respect of which the Commission of the European Economic Community is satisfied that arrangements have been made to meet the requirements of Article 7(2) of the European Economic Community Directive on insurance of civil liabilities arising from the use of motor vehicles (No.72/166/CEE) but only so far as necessary to comply with the compulsory motor insurance legislation of such countries.

FOREIGN TRAVEL During any period for which the Insured has requested and the Company has agreed to extend United Kingdom cover for use abroad (the Foreign Travel period) the following benefits apply in respect of the Insured Vehicle concerned:

3   This Policy applies to accidents occurring in
   (a)   any country declared to the Company by the Insured (the declared countries);
   (b)   course of transit (including the processes of loading and unloading) between ports in the declared countries provided the transit is by a recognised sea route the duration of which under normal conditions does not exceed 65 hours.

4   Provided that liability arises directly from damage or loss covered by this Policy, the Company will indemnity the Insured against

Customs Duty   (a)   liability for the enforced payment of customs duty in any declared country;

Other charges   (b)   the payment of General Average, Salvage and Sue and Labour charges arising from transportation by sea.

Under this Sub-section **4** the Company shall not be liable to pay more than the market value of the Insured Vehicle prevailing in the United Kingdom at the time of the incident giving rise to such payment.

Bail Bond   5   If as a direct result of an accident in Spain which is or may become the subject of indemnity under this Section (**FOREIGN TRAVEL**) the driver is detained or the Insured Vehicle is impounded by the competent authorities and a guarantee or monetary deposit is required for their release the Company will provide such guarantee or deposit not exceeding £1,000 in all.

Immediately the guarantee is released or the deposit becomes recoverable the Insured or the driver will comply with all necessary formalities and give the Company all information and assistance required to obtain the cancellation of the guarantee or the return of the deposit. If the guarantee or deposit is wholly or in part forfeited or taken for the payment of fines or costs in or as a result of any penal proceedings against the Insured or the driver, the Insured will repay such amount to the Company without delay.

CLAUSE 6   UNAUTHORISED USE

The Company will indemnify the Insured only in the terms of and subject to the limitations of **Clause 1** and **Clause 2** in the event of any accident occurring while the Insured Vehicle is being used or driven by any person without the knowledge or consent of the Insured for any purpose not permitted under this Policy.

Provided always that the Insured shall take all reasonable precautions to ensure that all persons who may use or drive an Insured Vehicle are made aware of the permitted Purposes of Use as defined in this Policy.

CLAUSE 7   UNLICENSED DRIVERS

The requirement of the Certificate of Motor Insurance that the driver must hold a driving licence or have held and not be disqualified from holding or obtaining such a licence shall not apply in circumstances where a licence to drive is not required by law.

Provided always that

1   the terms of the Certificate of Motor Insurance shall otherwise apply;

2   the person driving is of an age to hold a licence to drive the Insured Vehicle.

CLAUSE 8   TOWAGE

Clause 1 applies to any trailer or disabled merchanically propelled vehicle while attached to the Insured Vehicle.

EXCEPTIONS TO CLAUSE 8

The Company shall not be liable to make any payment

1   If any trailer or disabled mechanically propelled vehicle is being towed otherwise than in accordance with the law.

2   for damage to or loss of property being carried in or on any trailer or disabled mechanically propelled vehicle.

3   for damage to or loss of the towed trailer or disabled mechanically propelled vehicle.

CLAUSE 9   SERVICE AND REPAIR

This Policy will indemnify the Insured alone when the Insured Vehicle is in the custody of a member of the motor trade for service or repair.

CLAUSE 10   PRINCIPALS CLAUSE

Notwithstanding **General Exception 3** but subject otherwise to the terms, limitations, exceptions and conditions of this Policy the Company will indemnify the Insured under **Clause 1** in respect of liability assumed by the Insured under an agreement with any person (''the Principal'') for the execution of work or services, or in connection with access to any premises or road in the ownership or occupation of the Principal.

Provided always that the Insured shall have arranged with the Principal for the conduct and control of all claims for which the Company may be liable by virtue of this Clause to be vested in the Company.

EXCEPTIONS TO CLAUSE 10

The Company shall not be liable in respect of

1   death of or injury to any person in the employ of the Principal arising out of and in the course of such employment.

2   liability which attaches to the Principal under an agreement which would not have attached in the absence of such agreement.

3   injury to the Principal for any amount for which the Insured would not be liable in the absence of such agreement.

4   damage to property belonging to or held in trust by or in the custody or control of the Principal for any sum in excess of the amount required to indemnify the Principal.

5   liability arising otherwise than by reason of the negligence of the Insured or a person in the employ of the Insured.

CLAUSE 11   GENERAL EXCEPTIONS

The Company shall not be liable

1   for any claim while the vehicle in connection with which indemnity is provided under this Policy is, with the general consent of the Insured, being
     (a)   used for any purpose not permitted by the current Certificate of Motor Insurance;
     (b)   driven by any person not authorised by the current Certificate of Motor Insurance.
     This exception shall not apply to claims under **Clause 9**.

2   for any claim while the vehicle in connection with which indemnity is provided under this Policy is being driven
     (a)   by the Insured unless the Insured holds a driving licence or has held and is not disqualified from holding or obtaining such a licence;
     (b)   with the general consent of the Insured, by any person who the Insured knows does not hold a driving licence unless such person has held and is not disqualified from holding or obtaining such a licence.
     This exception shall not apply to claims under **Clause 7**.

3   for any liability accepted by agreement which would not have attached in the absence of such agreement.

4   for any consequence of war, invasion, act of foreign enemy, hostilities (whether war be declared or not), civil war, rebellion, revolution, insurrection or military or usurped power.

5   for any accident, injury, damage or loss (except under **Clause 1**) arising during or in consequence of
     (a)   earthquake occurring elsewhere than in
        (i)   Great Britain, Northern Ireland, the Isle of Man, the Channel Islands or the Republic of Ireland, or

175

    (ii) (during any Foreign Travel period as defined in **Clause 5**) any other member country of the European Economic Community;

  (b) riot or civil commotion occurring elsewhere than in

    (i) Great Britain, the Isle of Man, the Channel Islands or the Republic of Ireland, or

    (ii) (during any Foreign Travel period as defined in **Clause 5**) any other member country of the European Economic Community.

6 to indemnify the owner of a vehicle leased to the Insured where indemnity arises out of the negligence of such owner or the servants or agents of such owner.

7 for

  (a) damage to or loss or destruction of any property whatsoever or any loss or expense whatsoever resulting or arising therefrom or any consequential loss

  (b) any legal liability of whatsoever nature

directly or indirectly caused by or contributed to by or arising from

  (i) ionising radiation or contamination by radioactivity from any irradiated nuclear fuel or from any nuclear waste from the combustion of nuclear fuel

  (ii) the radioactive toxic explosive or other hazardous properties of any explosive nuclear assembly or nuclear component thereof.

CLAUSE 12   CONDITIONS

Premium   **1** Prior to the commencement of the Period of Insurance the Insured shall pay to the Company an agreed premium deposit. The Insured shall supply to the Company on request the necessary information required to calculate the actual premium in accordance with the rates agreed by the Insured and the Company. If the premium due differs from the deposit, the difference shall be adjusted as appropriate.

Accidents   **2** Details of any event which might result in a claim under this Policy and all subsequent developments must be reported to the Company as soon as possible. Notice of any prosecution, inquest or fatal inquiry and every letter, claim, writ or summons must be sent to the Company on receipt.

Claims Procedure   **3** Except with the written consent of the Company no person shall make any admission of liability, offer, repudiation or promise of payment on behalf of the Insured or any person claiming indemnity under this Policy.

The Company shall be entitled to take over and conduct in the name of the Insured or of any person entitled to indemnity under this Policy the defence or settlement of any claim or to prosecute any claim in the name of such person. The Company or a solicitor appointed by the Company shall have full discretion in the conduct of any proceedings and in the settlement of any claim and shall be given all such information and assistance as they may require.

Other Insurances   **4** If any other insurance covers the same damage, loss or liability the Company shall not be liable to pay more than its rateable proportion. Provided always that

  (a) nothing in this Condition shall impose on the Company any liability from which it would have been relieved by **Section 2(b)** of **Clause 1** or **Exceptions 2** and **3(b)** to **Clause 1**;

  (b) this Condition shall not apply when the Insured Vehicle

    (i) is the property of or on hire or loan or leased to a person in the employ of the insured, and

    (ii) has not been provided by the Insured, and

    (iii) is being used in connection with the business or trade purposes of the Insured.

176

Vehicle Maintenance	5	The Insured shall maintain the Insured Vehicle in efficient and roadworthy condition and take all reasonable steps to safeguard it from damage or loss.

Cancellation 6 (a) The Company may cancel this Policy by sending thirty days notice by registered letter to the Insured at the Insured's last known address and will, in that event, return to the Insured a proportionate part of the premium in respect of the unexpired term of this Policy.

(b) The Insured may cancel this Policy at any time, such cancellation being effective from the date of receipt by the Company of the appropriate Certificate(s) of Motor Insurance. If cancellation is during the first year of insurance any return premium will be calculated using the Company's current short period rates; otherwise a pro rata refund of premium will be allowed.

Arbitration 7 If any difference shall arise as to the amount to be paid under this Policy (liability being otherwise admitted) such difference shall be referred to an arbitrator to be appointed by the parties in accordance with current Statutory provisions. Where any difference is by this Condition to be referred to arbitration the making of an award shall be a condition precedent to any right of action against the Company.

Property Damage Claims 8 In connection with any one claim or series of claims arising out of any one event in respect of damage to property caused by or in connection with a Commercial Vehicle or any vehicle bearing a Trade Plate the Company may at any time pay to the Insured the amount of the indemnity provided by this Policy (after deduction of any sum already paid as compensation) or any less amount for which such claim(s) can be settled and from the date such payment is made the Company shall relinquish control of the negotiations and legal proceedings in connection with such claim(s). From the date of such payment the Company shall be under no further liability in connection with such claim(s) other than for costs and expenses incurred with the written consent of the Company prior to the date of such payment.

Joint Insured 9 If more than one Company or individual is named as the Insured in the Schedule of this Policy, the insurance granted shall apply jointly and individually to all such Companies and persons.

Observance of Terms 10 The observance and fulfilment of the terms of the Policy so far as they relate to anything to be done or complied with by the Insured Person shall be conditions precedent to any liability of the Company to make any payment under this Policy. Upon proof of breach of this Condition the Company shall be entitled to recover from the Insured Person all sums paid by the Company including those for which the Company would not have been liable but for the provisions of any compulsory motor insurance legislation operative within the areas covered by this Policy.

APPENDICES TO THIS MOTOR POLICY FORM — FL 862

Appendix 1 — Extent of Cover

DEFINITIONS (WHICH APPLY ONLY AS SPECIFIED IN THE SCHEDULE OF VEHICLES)

A COMPREHENSIVE
The full insurance as within written.

C THIRD PARTY ONLY
Clauses **2**, **3** and **4** are inoperative.
Otherwise as within written.

B THIRD PARTY, FIRE AND THEFT
Clause **2** is inoperative except for
damage or loss by
(a) fire, lightning, self-ignition or
explosion
(b) theft or attempted theft.
Clauses **3** and **4** are inoperative.
Otherwise as within written.

D THIRD PARTY ROAD RISKS ONLY
Clauses **1**, **8** and **10** are inoperative
when liability arises out of death, injury
or damage caused or arising beyond
the limits of any road.
Clauses **2**, **3**, **4** and **7** are inoperative.
Otherwise as within written.

Appendix 2 — Endorsements

AN ENDORSEMENT FROM THIS APPENDIX APPLIES ONLY IF IT IS

1   SPECIFIED IN THE SCHEDULE, OR

2   MADE EFFECTIVE BY A SEPARATE ENDORSEMENT ISSUED BY THE COMPANY

EXCEPT AS EXPRESSLY VARIED BY AN ENDORSEMENT THE POLICY REMAINS SUBJECT
TO THE TERMS, LIMITATIONS, EXCEPTIONS AND CONDITIONS CONTAINED WITHIN IT.

E, F, G, H, I and J EXCESSES — OWN DAMAGE

It is a condition of this Policy that the Insured shall pay or refund to the Company all claims
and expenses under **Clause 2** up to the agreed amount in connection with each and every
occurrence or series of occurrences arising out of one event.

Provided that
1   this condition shall not apply in connection with any damage or loss by
(a) fire, lighting, self-ignition or explosion,
(b) theft or attempted theft;
2   this condition shall not apply in respect of a claim for breakage of glass in the
windscreen or in the windows of the Insured Vehicle (or any scratching of bodywork
resulting solely and directly from such breakage);
3   in respect of Endorsements G, H, I and J: **Exception 8** to **Clause 2** is cancelled and of
no effect;
4   the agreed amount is additional to any other amount for which the Insured may be
responsible under this Policy.

The agreed amount shall be under

Endorsement E	£25	Endorsement H	£100
Endorsement F	£50	Endorsement I	£150
Endorsement G	£75	Endorsement J	£250

K AND L   MOTOR TRADE — VEHICLE VALUE LIMIT

In **Section 1(a)** of **Clause 2** the limit of the Company's liability in respect of any vehicle bearing a Trade Plate is increased to the agreed amount or the market value of the Insured Vehicle immediately before damage or loss, whichever is the less.

The agreed amount shall be under

Endorsement K   £50,000   Endorsement L   £75,000

P   ISLE OF MAN LAW

This Policy has been entered into in the Isle of Man and is subject to the laws of such Isle and in respect of occurrences in such Isle may (subject to any provision for arbitration contained in this Policy) be enforced by proceedings taken in the Courts of such Isle. In the event of arbitration under this Policy in respect of any occurrence in the Isle of Man such arbitration shall be held in such Isle.

Chapter 14

EUROPEAN AND NORTH AMERICAN LEGAL LIABILITIES

14.0   Comparative Liability Law

A comparison of the legal systems of European and North American countries will enable the risk manager to gauge potential liabilities for injury and damage to persons and property arising from activities overseas, apart from product liability discussed in Chapter 6. There will be no attempt here at an in-depth comparison of liability laws, which is a daunting task, but merely to contrast, broadly, the approaches to civil responsibility.

There is, as you would expect, a diversity of laws. Each country has its own legal system and in some instances several different laws co-exist within the same country. In the USA for example (see Chapter 6: 6.7), federal law and the laws of the individual states interact. In Canada and in Switzerland also, there are laws of the provinces or districts which co-exist with the state laws. The student will conclude that there is a constant element in the liability laws of Western countries whereby the person at fault must make reparation to his victim, and that diversity of laws is mainly in the rules that are laid down.

14.1   Classification of Laws into Families

In their book entitled *Major Legal Systems in the World Today* (Stevens & Sons) Authors Rene David and John E. C. Brierley elect to classify contemporary laws into families: the Romano-Germanic family, the Common Law family and the family of Socialist law. The Romano-Germanic family is of European origin and embraces the systems of both Latin and Germanic countries including those countries colonised by the "source" countries. It extends to Latin America, countries of the Near East, Japan and Indonesia. The Common Law family includes the law of England, the latter occupying a pre-eminent place within that family and upon which other common law systems have been modelled. English law is not, of course applicable to the United Kingdom as a whole because Scotland, for example, is not ruled by "English" law. The law of England was received by countries of the British Empire and with this expansion came changes and modifications in the course of adaption to particular countries. British settlers in the American colonies took their law with them with the result that the basis of American law is Common Law. In other instances outwith Europe the common law was only partially received, for instance in certain Muslim countries and in India.

The Family of Socialist Laws originated in the Union of Soviet Socialist Republics and the reception of laws by the Eastern European countries has resulted in a mix of the new laws and the pre-existing Romano-Germanic based systems of law. As a consequence, the laws of the socialist republics of Europe and Asia, whilst belonging to the Socialist family, are distinct from Soviet law.

14.2   The Concept of Tort in European and North American Countries

In countries which adopt the Common Law system, tort is identified in the context of Winfield's definition: "Tortious liability arises from the breach of a duty primarily fixed by the law (see Chapter 1, 1.2): such duty is towards persons generally and its breach is redressible by an action for unliquidated damages" or alternatively as: "a civil wrong, other than a breach of contract, which the law will redress by an award of damages". Traditionally, there have been laws of tort and laws of contract and these two spheres of law have been distinguished in nearly every country.

14.2.1   France

In French law which is based on Roman law, the law of tort is termed "la responsabilite civile delictuelle". "Responsabilite" is liability or the responsibility to answer for damage or injury. "Civile" is in contrast to "penale" and "delictuelle" contrasts with "contractuelle". Tort implies the existence of three elements: (a) fault, (b) damage and (c) a causal connection between the fault and the damage.

The French law of torts falls under three headings:

- Liability for damage caused by one's own fault;
- Liability for damage caused by another person (vicarious liability);
- Liability for damage caused by things.

14.2.1A   Damage Caused by One's Own Fault

The concept of tort is based on Article 1382 of the Code Civil: "Any act by which a person causes damage to another makes the person by whose fault the damage occurred liable to make reparation for such damage". This is the basic regulatory provision applicable to all citizens who are not bound by contract. France has a general law of tort based on the principles of Articles 1382 and 1383 and the duty of care is a general duty to the public at large and not to certain people or sections of the public. As regards fault, the criterion is behaviour which would not have been the behaviour of a reasonable man who is careful and mindful of others. The behaviour could be an act or an omission. French courts tend to give the plaintiff generous damages, including damages for non-pecuniary loss such as the death of a relative.

14.2.1B   Vicarious Liability

Article 1384 provides for three kinds of vicarious liability: liability of the parent; liability of teachers or artisans; liability of masters and employers. Only the latter category will be considered here. Liability of the master involves fault of the servant committed in the course of his employment and is based on the presumption of lack of control on the part of the master or that the master has been negligent in the selection of the servant. The question of what constitutes "in the course of employment" presents similar difficulties to that experienced in English law. Where the plaintiff knew that the servant was acting outwith the scope of his employment, there will be no problem, but where the plaintiff is not an accessory to the fact that the servant is acting outside his duties, the issue of vicarious liability may not be easy to decide.

14.2.1C   Liability for Damage Caused by Things

Article 1384: "One is responsible not only for the damage caused by one's own act, but also for that caused by the things which are in one's custody". The element of fault is not always necessary. The custodian of the thing is responsible for damage caused by the thing but he will not be liable where damage is caused by the act of the plaintiff, act of a third party or by a fortuitous event or vis major. The principle laid down in Article 1384 has been developed by judicial decisions and it governs the settlement of traffic accidents, where the law is based largely on fault. If there is a collision between two cars, say, and it is established that one of the drivers caused the accident through his negligence, responsibility will rest with him. There may be contributory fault in which case it will be determined on comparative liability. Where no sufficient evidence is available to point to one wrongdoer, each of the parties is considered responsible to the other and will have to compensate him. The law imposes liability for damage caused by the fall of a building which is a form of strict liability.

14.2.2   Belgium

Under Belgian law liability for injury or damage relates to the fault concept also, as laid down in Article 1382 of the Code Civil and is similar to that applicable in French law. In fact, Articles 1382 and 1383 of the Belgian Code Civil are identical with the French ones. Liability arises out of the breach of a general duty of care and it refers to the standard of conduct of a careful and prudent person. Foreseeability of damage is also a condition for liability, the criteria being one of reasonable foreseeability.

In addition to the fault concept, Belgian law, in common with most legal systems, imposes liability without fault, i.e. strict liability. Examples are:

   (i) liability for defective property;
  (ii) liability of the employer for injury caused to his employee;
 (iii) liability of the keeper of an animal; and
  (iv) liability of the owner of a building for the damage caused by its collapse.

Strict liabilities are also laid down in various statutes dealing with, inter alia, mining, toxic waste, ground water, nuclear reactors and transportation of natural gas.

The concept of strict liability for "created risk" is similar to that applicable in English law, i.e. those who benefit from dangerous activities have to bear the burden of the loss created by such activities.

14.2.3   West Germany

The West German Civil Code has no general provision for tort which is similar to that of Article 1382 of the French Code Civil. For personal liability the law lays down three general and three specific rules. The three general rules refer to:

   (i) violation of certain "Rechtsguter" or absolute rights, where the violation is unlawful and takes place deliberately or negligently. The German Civil Code art. 823 paragraph 1: "A person who, intentionally or negligently, unlawfully injures the life, body, health, freedom, property or any other right of another, is bound to compensate him for any damage arising therefrom".

(ii) culpable breach of a law or regulation designed for the protection of another, e.g. breach of a criminal statute protecting reputation, property, the infringement of a traffic regulation, etc. Article 823 para. 2: "A person who infringes a statutory provision intended for the protection of others incurs the same obligation. If, according to the purview of the statute, infringement is possible even without any fault on the part of the wrongdoer, the duty to make compensation arises only if some fault can be imputed to him".

(iii) damage caused by improper conduct and deliberately. Article 826: "A person who by improper conduct and intentionally causes damage to another is bound to compensate the other for the damage".

The three specific rules cover injury to credit, seduction of women, and the breach of a duty imposed by public office. "Injury to credit" is making an untrue statement which is likely to injure the credit of another, or to cause other damage to his business or prospects. Additional rules create liability not depending on the act of the tortfeasor himself, including liability for:

(i) act of the employee
(ii) act of person under care
(iii) damage done by animals
(iv) damage caused by structures.

In common with other systems, certain civil liabilities are regulated specifically by statutory provisions and these include the supply of gas and electricity, nuclear power, air and road transport and unfair trade competition.

Other countries of the Germanic legal family are Switzerland and Turkey.

14.2.4   Italian Law of Obligations

The Italian law of obligations includes liabilities arising out of "civilly illicit acts" which in this context excludes contractual obligations. Liability for "civilly illicit acts" or tort follows the lines of other systems described already and can be deduced from the following summary of the relevant Articles of the Italian Civil Code:

2043: Compensation for unlawful acts. Any fraudulent, malicious, or neligent act that causes an unjustified injury to another obliges the person who has committed the act to pay damages.

2049: Liability of masters and employers: Masters and employers are liable for the damage caused by unlawful act of their servants and employees in the exercise of the functions to which they are assigned.

2050: Liability arising from dangerous activities. Whoever causes injury to another in the performance of an activity dangerous by its nature or by reason of the instrumentalities employed, is liable for damages, unless he proves that he has taken all suitable measures to avoid the injury.

2051: Damage caused by things in custody. Everyone is liable for injuries caused by things in his custody, unless he proves that the injuries were the result of a fortuitous event.

2052: Damage caused by animals: liability attaches unless the person in charge can prove that the damage was the result of a fortuitous event.

2053: Collapse of buildings: Owner is liable for damage caused by its collapse, unless he proves that such damage was not caused by defective maintenance, or by a defect in construction.

2054: Circulation of vehicles (meaning the operation or movement of vehicles): The operator of a vehicle which is not guided by rails is liable for the damage caused to persons or to property by operation of the vehicle unless he proves that he did all that was possible in order to avoid the damage. Where two vehicles collide, it is presumed, until proof to the contrary is offered, that each operator contributed equally toward causing the damage suffered by each vehicle. The owner of the vehicle is liable "in solido" with the operator of the vehicle, unless he proves that the vehicle was being operated against his will.

2055: Liability "in solido" (or joint liability). If the act causing the damage can be attributed to more than one person, all are liable "in solido" for the damages. The person who has compensated for the damage can recover from each of the others in proportion to the degree of fault of each. This is the same provision as applies to joint tortfeasors in English law.

For liability to attach the alleged wrongdoer or actor must have the capacity to understand his action and intend it. Thus the person carrying out the act must not be in a state of unconsciousness nor lacking in the powers of discernment, provided he did not put himself in that psychological state through his own fault or intent, for example, in taking drugs.

There are many instances of strict liability, the most frequent being the responsibility of employers for the illicit acts of employees committed in the performance of their duties (Article 2049). Strict liability applies for damage caused by things or animals in the custody of the defendant (2051 and 2052), unless he can prove fortuitous circumstances, for example "forza maggiore", or act of a third party, or the exclusive fault of the plaintiff. Damage caused through the disrepair of buildings (2053), unless the defendant can show that the disrepair was not due to either a lack of maintenance or a defect in construction, will involve strict liability. Strict liability also applies to damage caused by dangerous activities, unless the defendant can show that he adopted all the suitable measures necessary to avoid the damage (2050). Finally, strict liability arises in damage caused by the circulation of motor vehicles (2054), unless the owner can show that the use of the vehicle was contrary to his will.

14.2.5   Liability in Socialist Countries

In European Socialist countries, as in other European systems, tortious liability is usually distinguished from contractual liability. Fault is the main basis of the Socialist laws of tort and therefore they do not seem to differ from the laws of Western European countries. The following brief summaries of the main dicta will give an indication of liabilities:

Hungarian Peoples Republic: Civil Code states: "The person who causes damage to another unlawfully is bound to compensate him. He is absolved from liability if he proves that he has acted as could generally be expected in the situation".

Czechoslovakian Socialist Republic: Civil Code states: "Every citizen is liable for the damage he has caused by breach of a duty provided by law. The citizen exonerates himself of any liability if he proves that he has not caused the damage by his fault".

Peoples Republic of Poland: Civil Code reads: "Whoever by his fault causes damage to another shall be liable to repair it".

Yugoslavia: In Yugoslavia the law of tortious liability is not general, but varies from state to state.

The Socialist laws impose a presumption of fault on the person carrying out the act who is liable for damage unless he can prove he was not at fault. In addition a stricter liability applies where activities or instruments (say, motor vehicles) create extra hazards for the citizens. An organisation can be liable for the fault of one of its members even where it is properly organised and no fault has been committed by anyone other than the tortfeasor.

14.2.6   Canada

In Canada legislation is the single most important source of law in both federal and provincial jurisdiction. The provincial legislatures are sovereign authorities except when subject to the powers of disallowance (rarely exercised). Jurisdiction in a large part of private law is vested in the Provincial Legislatures and, as in other federal systems, this leads to multiplicity of laws with attendant problems. Tort law follows closely the principles of the English law of torts and its most important function is its role in settling disputes arising out of automobile accidents.

14.2.6A   Automobile Liability

In the matter of automobile accidents considerable debate has taken place in recent years, because of dissatisfaction expressed about the way in which tort law deals with automobile accident liabilities. Moreover, the problem is taken together with the wider issue of reducing accidents on the highway and legislative measures have been taken to deal with drunk drivers, vehicle safety features, speed limits and, in some provinces the wearing of seat belts. Various highway traffic Acts articulate rules of the road and proof that a provision has been violated will be considered prima facie evidence of negligence. In addition to the negligent operator of a vehicle, the owner will, through legislation, be liable for damage or injury, unless the vehicle was used without the owner's consent in the possession of some person other than the owner or his chauffeur. When a pedestrian is involved in an accident and proves that he was struck by a motor vehicle on a highway, the onus rests with the operator or owner of the vehicle to satisfy the court that injury or loss did not arise through the latter's negligence or improper conduct. This shift in the onus of proof from the plaintiff does not apply in cases of collision between two vehicles or in actions brought by passengers. Compulsory motor insurance is general to all provinces except Ontario.

14.2.6B   General Tort Liability

In tort law, negligence is the most important basis of liability and the concept is in line with English law therefore a brief summary only will suffice here.

The elements for a cause of action in negligence correspond to requirements of English law (see Chapter 2: 2.4.1). The standard of care expected is that of the reasonable person: this being again an objective test. Defences in negligence are:

- Contributory negligence including the seat belt defence.
- Voluntary Assumption of Risk, in which the concept of Volenti Non Fit Injuria includes participating in sports actively and as a spectator and willing passengers in vehicles.

Strict liability in tort follows the principles of English law (see Chapter 3, 3.0).

14.2.6C   Workers' Compensation

By virtue of various Workers' Compensation Acts dating back to 1915 all provinces operate a "no fault" insurance system for workers' injuries but in lieu the statutes remove the employee's right to sue for damages in civil courts. This position is now being challenged following a decision by the Newfoundland Supreme Court in Piercey v General Bakeries Ltd., 1987, that the statutory denial of the right to sue is unconstitutional in accordance with the 1985 Charter of Rights. At the time of going to print, this matter looks likely to be taken to the Supreme Court of Canada and if the Newfoundland decision is upheld, it will make the employer's liability risk more onerous.

14.2.7   United States of America

The reader should refer to Chapter 6, 6.7 and recall that the USA legal system is comprised of both federal law and the rulings of the courts of fifty individual states. The problems for defendants in product liability suits are also common to liability litigation generally and by the mid 1980's a liability crisis had developed which seriously affects every area of American life. As a consequence the US Government decided in 1985 to set up a Tort Policy Working Group to investigate the causes. This development will be considered later, following a brief summary of liability in tort.

14.2.7A   Liability in Tort

The law of torts is still the source of most civil actions in the US with automobile accidents the primary cause. The American Law Institute's Restatement (Second) of Torts (see Chapter 6, 6.7.1) sets out the standard by which Negligence is determined (Section 282) and defines negligence as ". . . conduct which falls below the standard established by law for the protection of others against unreasonable risk of harm. It does not include conduct recklessly disregardful of an interest of others". A person is negligent if he has not complied with his duty of care and has not acted as "a reasonable and prudent man". Section 283 dealing with the standard of conduct of a "reasonable man" defines it thus: "Unless the actor is a child, the standard of conduct to which he must conform to avoid being negligent is that of a reasonable man under like circumstances".

The concept of "a reasonable man" is the same as that envisaged in English law. The duty of care must be owed to the plaintiff and there is no duty owed to the public at large. A lesser duty of care is owed to trespassers than that owed to invited guests or visitors. Voluntary assumption of risk is a possible defence and likewise contributory negligence. In some states any degree of negligence by the plaintiff can exclude all liability on the part of the tortfeasor, but in the main the comparative negligence rule applies.

Strict liability existed originally in respect of keeping dangerous animals, defamation and in instances of "res ipsa loquitur" (Chapter 2, 2.4.7) and later applied to products liability (Chapter 6, 6.7.1).

"No-Fault" law in respect of automobile accidents is applicable in a number of states.

14.2.7B   The Liability Crisis

Laws that make it too easy to sue and which encourage excessive settlements to be handed out are blamed for a state of affairs where insurers have been compelled to curtail cover or in some instances withdraw from the market altogether. Because a plaintiff in a civil action has the right to try his claim before a jury, the defendant, especially if it is a corporation, finds that the jury will give more credence to human aspects than to legal considerations. Moreover, damages awarded consist not only of actual loss but also intangible damage and on occasion, punitive damages. The attorney for the plaintiff is entitled to a contingency fee which often may amount to as much as 33% of the award.

During the period from 1962 to 1982 there were over 1,100 awards in excess of one million dollars. Of these, product claims numbered 285, medical malpractice claims accounted for 196, automobile accidents 125 and there were 124 claims for accidents at work (US Insurance Information Institute statistics). Medical malpractice liability has reached its own crisis (1987) and as a result 12% of American obstetricians have stopped delivering babies, doctors treating cancer use milder doses of chemotherapy and 38% of surgeons are avoiding high risk cases. Some of the more extreme examples of the workings of liability will demonstrate the problems facing businesses. A man who suffered a heart attack whilst trying to start a lawnmower sued the manufacturers and succeeded. A burglar, disturbed by the householder fell and injured himself whilst escaping through a roof. The burglar successfully sued the householder. A participant in a heavyweight lifting competition injured himself whilst lifting a piece of machinery and recovered damages against the organisers of the event.

It is contended that the tort system has, in effect, been replaced by what is virtually an unlimited no-fault system and that reform of the law is overdue.

14.2.7C   Tort Reform

The Tort Policy Working Group reported in 1986 and updated its original report in 1987. Four particular factors were identified as the chief causes of the expansion of liability risks in the United States and they are:

  (i) substantial increase in the size of jury awards, especially in medical malpractice and product liability claims

 (ii) erosion of fault as the basis of tort liability

(iii) high costs of litigation, including excessive contingency fees for attorneys

(iv) an undermining of the principle of proximate cause.

Among the reform measures recommended for both state and federal laws are:

(a) Return to a fault-based standard in liability law

(b) Eliminate joint and several liability in cases where tortfeasors have not acted in concert

(c) Limit contingency fees to reasonable amounts on a sliding scale

(d) Take account of certain collateral sources of compensation, in order to reduce awards

(e) Limit non-economic damages to a fair and reasonable maximum, for example $200,000

(f) Findings to be based on credible scientific and medical evidence

(g) Periodic payments of damages for future lost income or medical care, instead of a lump sum

(h) Encourage use of alternative dispute resolution mechanisms and thus reduce the number of court actions.

At the time of writing there has not been in evidence a uniform movement towards implementing the above measures but at least thirty-seven of the fifty states have taken on board some tort reform legislation. Examples are restrictions on punitive damages, attorneys fees and economic damages. The recommendations in respect of collateral sources of compensation and the elimination of joint and several liability have also been adopted by some states.

The law reform process is gaining momentum in the US and the Reader should endeavour to keep up-to-date on developments.

General Index

191